MW01283863

Berkshire Destinations

An Explorer's Guide to Waterfalls, Boulders, Vistas and Points of Interest of the Berkshire Hills and Western Massachusetts.

Jan & Christy Butler

z

Many outdoor activities by their very nature involve exposure to possible hazards and unknown or changing variables such as trail erosion, obstructions, variance of weather, etc. At the time of this writing, the authors have done their best to ensure that all the information contained in *Berkshire Destinations* is as accurate as possible. They cannot accept responsibility for any loss, injury, or inconvenience sustained by readers as a result of information or advice contained in the book. Hikers need to be respectful of private property and go no further should posted signs be encountered. Ownership or polices change with unexpected changes in access, fees or parking may result.

In cases where the information presented appears to be in error, or where material has become dated and needs updating, please contact the author at: www.berkshire-destinations.com

KDP ISBN:
ISBN: 9781790318414
Independently published

Photography & Illustrations by Christy Butler

Cover Photo:
Keystone Bridge. Becket- Middlefield: N42° 18' 19.90" W73° 0' 19.47"
Clark Art Museum. Williamstown: N42° 42' 33.37" W73° 12' 51.18
Titanic Boulder. Monroe State Forest: N42°42' 54.0" W72° 59' 28.2"
Sanderson Brook Falls. Chester State Forest: N42° 15' 20.78" W72° 56' 49.5"

Back Cover:
The Hopper. Mt Greylock Reservation: N42° 38' 39.09" W73° 11' 37.15"
Norman Rockwell Museum. Stockbridge: N42° 17' 17.77" W73° 20' 14.72"

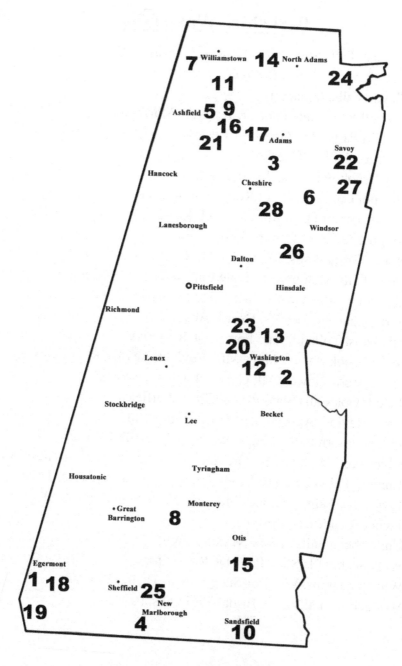

Berkshire Waterfalls

Berkshire Waterfalls

1. Bash Bish Falls State Park- DCR: (Mt. Washington)
2. Becket Ravine. (North Becket)
3. Bellevue Falls. (Adams)
4. Campbell Falls State Park-DCR: (New Marlborough)
5. Deer Hill Falls. Mt. Greylock Reservation-DCR: (Williamstown)
6. Dry Brook Falls. (Cheshire)
7. Haley Brook Falls. (Williamstown)
8. Konkapot Cascades River Road. (Monterey)
9. March Cataract Falls. Mt. Greylock Res-DCR: (Williamstown)
10. Marguerite Falls. (Sandisfield)
11. Money Brook Falls. Mt. Greylock Reservation-DCR
12. Navin Falls. October Mt. State Forest-DCR: (Washington)
13. No-Name Falls. October Mt. State Forest-DCR: (Washington)
14. North Adams Cascades. (North Adams)
15. Otis Falls. Tolland State Forest-DCR: (Otis)
16. Pecks Brook Shelter Falls. Mt. Greylock Res-DCR: (Adams)
17. Pecks Brook (lower) Mt. Greylock Glen: (Adams)
18. Race Brook Falls State Park-DCR: (Sheffield)
19. Sages Ravine. Appalachian Trail: (Egremont)
20. Schermerhorn Falls. October Mt. State Forest-DCR: (Lenoxdale)
21. Silver Fox Cascades. Mt Greylock Reservation-DCR: (Cheshire)
22. Tannery Falls & Parker Brook Falls. Savoy State Forest-DCR
23. Tory Cave Falls. October Mt. State Forest-DCR: (Lenox)
24. Twin Cascades. (Florida)
25. Umpachene Falls. (New Marlborough)
26. Wahconah Falls State Park-DCR: (Dalton)
27. Windsor Jambs. Windsor State Forest- DCR: (Windsor)
28. Woodchuck Falls a.k.a Bridal Veil Falls. (Cheshire)

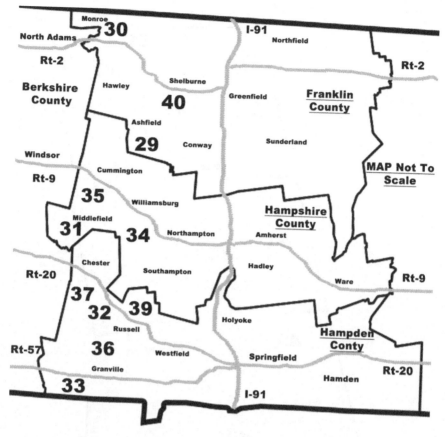

Massachusetts Western - Waterfalls

29. Chapel Brook Falls. Trustees of Reservations: (Ashfield)
30. Dunbar Brook. Monroe State Forest-DCR: (Monroe)
31. Glendale Falls. Trustees of Reservations: (Middlefield)
32. Goldmine Falls. Chester State Forest-DCR: (Chester)
33. Granville Falls. Granville State Forest-DCR: (Granville)
34. Manhan Falls. (Westhampton)
35. Oak Hill Cascades. (Chesterfield)
36. Pitcher Falls. Noble View Center - AMC: (Russell)
37. Rivulet Falls. Trustees of Reservation: (Cummington)
38. Sanderson Brook Falls. Chester State Forest-DCR: (Chester)
39. Shatterack Brook Falls. (Russell)
40. Sluice Brook Falls. Mahican-Mohawk Trail: (Shelburne)

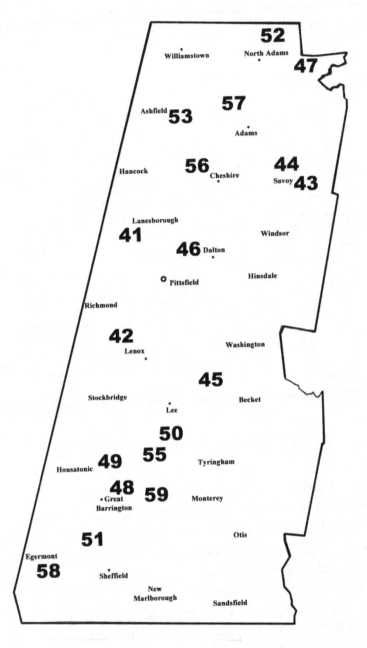

Berkshire Glacial Erratics - Boulders

<u>Berkshire Glacial Erratics – Boulders</u>

41. Balance Rock. Pittsfield State Forest-DCR: (Lanesborough)
42. Balance Rock. Kennedy Park (Lenox)
43. Balance Rock #1. Savoy Mountain State Forest-DCR: (Savoy)
44. Balance Rock #2. Savoy Mountain State Forest-DCR: (Savoy)
45. Basin Pond. Berkshire Natural Resource Council: (Lee)
46. Boulders, The. Berkshire Natural Resource Council: (Dalton)
47. Boundary Boulder. Florida State Forest (Florida)
48. East Rock. Town Forest (Great Barrington)
49. Flag Rock Boulder Field. (Housatonic)
50. Gorilla Profile Rock. (Tyringham)
51. Limekiln Farm Wildlife Sanctuary Boulder (Sheffield)
52. Natural Bridge State Park–Rock Profiles-DCR: (North Adams)
53. Northrup Trail Boulders. Mt Greylock-DCR: (Lanesborough)
54. Painted Rocks: Frogs Landing, Shark.
55. Rabbit Rock. Tyringham Cobble (Tyringham)
56. Reynolds Rock. Appalachian National Scenic Trail (Cheshire)
57. Thunderbolt Rock. Mt Greylock Glen-DCR: (Adams)
58. Turtle Rock. Mill Pond Dam-Route-41: (South Egremont)
59. Whale Rock. Thomas Palmer Brook. BNRC: (Great Barrington)

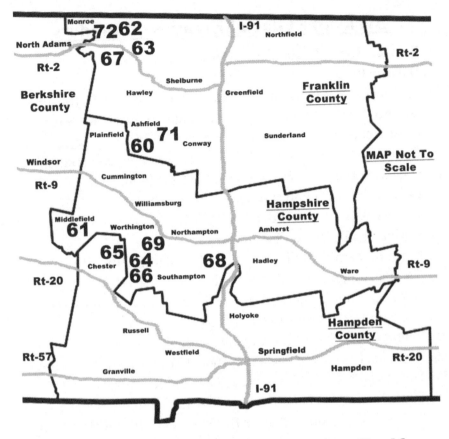

Western Massachusetts Glacial Erratics - Boulders

60. Balancing Rock. DAR State Forest-DCR: (Goshen)
61. Big Rock. (Middlefield)
62. Blue Dot Boulder. Monroe State Forest-DCR: (Monroe)
63. Elephant Head Arch-Deerfield River: (Zoar)
64. Fish Mouth Rock & Boulders. (Huntington)
65. Hiram's Tomb Boulder. (North Chester)
66. Leaning Rock. (Huntington-Knightville Dam)
67. Mohawk Rock. Mohawk Trail State Forest: (Savoy)
68. Mt. Tom Reservation Boulder & Moss Rock-DCR: (Holyoke)
69. Old Man-in-the-Rocks. Chesterfield Gorge: (West Chesterfield)
70. Painted Rocks: Fish, Flag, Fish Mouth, Rock, Bear Rock
71. The Pebble Bullitt Reservation. (Ashfield)
72. The Titanic. Monroe State Forest-DCR: (Monroe)

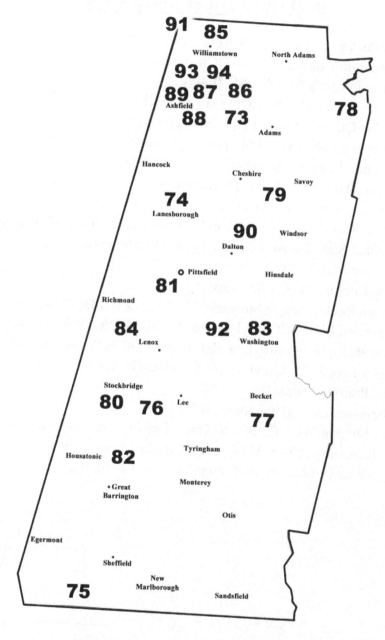

Berkshire Hikes and Vistas

Berkshire Hikes and Vistas

73. Adams Vista. Mt Greyock Reservation-DCR: (Adams)
74. Ashuwillticook Rail Trail – DCR: (Adams - Lanesborough)
75. Bartholomew's Cobble. (Sheffield)
76. Beartown State Forest CCC Ski Lodge: (Lee)
77. Becket Quarry. Becket Land Trust: (Becket)
78. Busby's Knob-Spruce Hill. Hoosac Range-BNRC: (North Adams)
79. Cheshire Cobble. Appalachian Trail: (Cheshire)
80. Laura's Tower- Ice Glen. (Stockbridge)
81. Mahanna Cobble BNRC: (Lenox)
82. Monument Mountain. Trustees of Reservations: (Great Barrington)
83. October State Forest. Fountain DCR: (Washington)
84. Parsons Marsh. BNRC: (Lenox)
85. Pine Cobble Vista. (Williamstown)
86. Raven Rocks. Ragged Mountain. Mt Greylock Res-DCR: (Adams)
87. Robinson Point. Mt Greylock Reservation-DCR: (Williamstown)
88. Rounds Rock. Mt Greylock Reservation-DCR: (Lanesborough)
89. Stony Ledge. Mt Greylock Reservation-DCR: (Williamstown)
90. The Prairie. (Dalton)
91. The Snow Hole. (Petersburg, N.Y)
92. Washington Mt. Lake Marsh Trail. October State Forest-DCR
93. Williamstown Vista: Mt. Greylock Reservation- DCR
94. Williams College Harris Cabin & Bernard Trail: (North Adams)

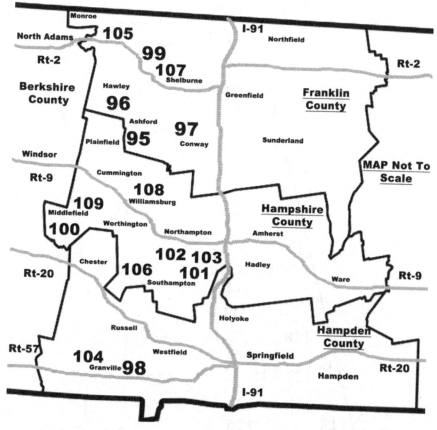

Western Massachusetts Hikes and Vistas

95. Chapel Ledge. Trustees of Reservations: (Ashfield)
96. Charcoal Kilns. Hawley State Forest-DCR (Hawley)
97. Conway Station Dam. South River: (Conway)
98. Drake Mountain – Granville Reservoir. (Granville)
99. High Ledges. Audubon Sanctuary: (Shelburne)
100. Keystone Bridges. (Becket-Middlefield-Chester)
101. Manhan Rail Trail. (Northampton-Easthampton)
102. Northampton- Haydenville Bikeway (Northampton)
103. Norwottuck Rail Trail. (Northampton-Hadley-Belchertown)
104. Phelon Memorial Forest. North Lane: (Granville)
105. Raycroft Look Out. Monroe State Forest-DCR: (Florida)
106. Stevens Property. Hilltown Land Trust: (Huntington)
107. Stone Fire Tower. Massaemett Mt: (Shelburne)
108. Williamsburg 1874 Dam Trail (Williamsburg)
109. WWII Aircraft Crash Memorial. Garnet Hill: (Peru)

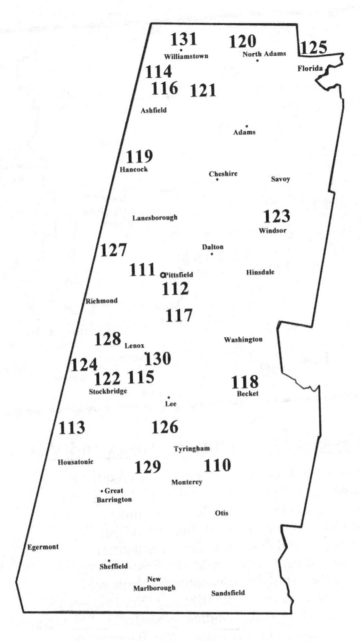

Berkshire Points of Interest

Berkshire Points of Interest

110. Ashintully Gardens. Trustees of Reservations: (Tyringham)
111. Berkshire Carousel. (Pittsfield)
112. Berkshire Museum. (Pittsfield)
113. Chesterwood. (Stockbridge)
114. Clark Art Institute. (Williamstown)
115. Edith Wharton's The Mount. (Lenox)
116. Field House. Trustees of Reservations: (Williamstown)
117. Herman Melville Homestead. (Pittsfield)
118. Jacobs Pillow. (Becket)
119. Jiminy Peak Mountain Resort. (Hancock)
120. Massachusetts MOCA. (North Adams)
121. Mt Greylock Veterans Memorial Tower. DCR: (Adams)
122. Naumkeag. Trustees of the Reservation: (Stockbridge)
123. Norman Rockwell. Rt-183: (Stockbridge)
124. Notchview Reservation. Trustees of Reservations5d : (Windsor)
125. Railroad History. Hoosac Tunnel, Washington Cut.
125a. Hoosac Tunnel - Alignment Towers.
125b. Rowe Alignment Tower.
125c. Whitcomb Hill Alignment Tower. (Florida)
125d. Spruce Hill Alignment Tower. (North Adams)
125e. West Mountain Alignment Tower. (North Adams)
126. Santarella a.k.a. The Gingerbread House. (Tyringham)
127. Shaker Village. (Hancock)
128. Tanglewood. (Lenox)
129. The Bidwell House. (Monterey)
130. Ventfort Hall. (Lenox)
131. Williams College Museum of Art. (Williamstown)

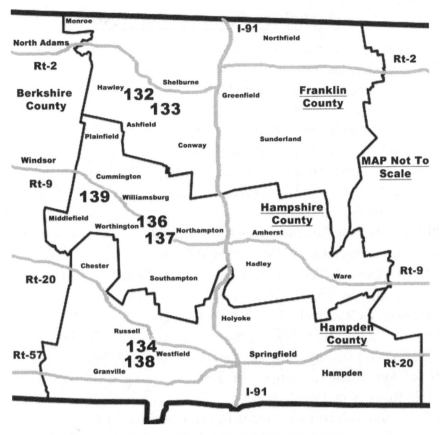

Western Massachusetts Points of Interest

132. Berkshire East Mountain Resort. (Charlemont)
133. Bridge of Flowers. (Shelburne Falls)
134. Grandmother's Garden. Chauncey Allen Park. (Westfield)
135. Mill River Historic Sites. (Plainfield)
136. Smith College Botanical Garden. (Northampton)
137. Smith College Museum of Art. (Northampton)
138. Stanley Park. (Westfield)
139. William Cullen Bryant Homestead. (Cummington)

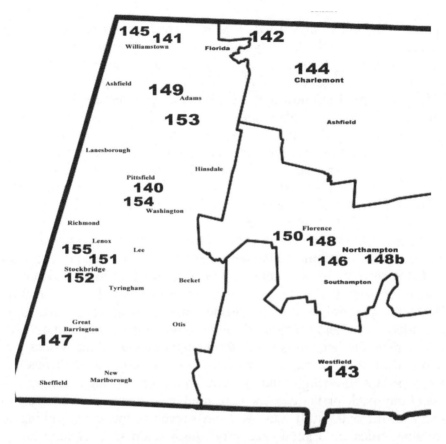

Berkshire & Western Massachusetts Statues

140. Civil War Soldier Park Square. (Pittsfield)
141. Civil War Soldier Williams College. Williamstown
142. Elk Whitcomb Summit. (Florida)
143. General William Shepard. Augustus Lukeman: (Westfield)
144. Hail to the Sunrise. (Charlamont)
145. Haystack Prayer Monument. Williamstown
146. Lanning Fountain - Smith College. (Northampton)
147. Newsboy. (Great Barrington)
148. Pregnant Women II. Lou Stubs: (Florence)
149. President McKinley. Augustus Lukeman: (Adams)
150. Sojourner Truth. (Florence)
151. Spirit of Life-Daniel Chester French. (Stockbridge)
152. Spitting Cat Dog Fight. (Stockbridge)
153. Strafford Hill Memorial 1927. (Cheshire)
154. WWI Memorial Veterans Park. Augustus Lukeman: (Pittsfield)
155. Young Faun with Heron. Naumkcag: (Stockbridge)

New England's *"urban wildernesses"* are four season destinations that require you to think safely and ecologically. Becoming completely lost or blundering through a mucky bog can be completely avoided. A compass and GPS devise are also great items to keep your adventure safe and happy, learn how to use them before you venture out. Ask and tell people what your plans are and familiarize yourself to the area through topographical maps, Google Earth and other search engine results. In addition, readers are reminded to stay alert in "urban" settings where matrixes of unmarked paths are constantly being created by "someone." This can add to overall confusion, especially with your first visit to a new location—another reason why GPS coordinates prove so invaluable.

Practice environmental etiquette; Carry in and Carry Out all your trash, no fires or camping allowed other than in designated areas. Plan and prepare for all your outings with good hiking boots and proper clothing, bring water, some energy or emergency foods, matches, flashlight and a first aid kit stashed into a fanny pack are good considerations. Being self-sufficient with proper preparation may have a little extra burden, but is worth so much more than all the wishes you had not left them in the car. Water, snacks, matches, a small first-aid kit, repellant, flash light and camera, whatever you might desire. A small day pack or fanny pack is a good investment allowing you to carry all the extra stuff. Jan & I have recently found that hiking or trekking poles are a good accessory to utilize on short or long hikes. Adjustable poles give extra stability up or downhill, they are extensions of your arms providing stability coming downhill and assist you by allowing a little extra exertion pushing you uphill. We love them.

The selection of titles or names for many of these boulders can vary. Boulderer's have more often than not, provided me with multiple, colorful and sometime humorous labels, often to the same boulder with many monikers usually relating to a particular boulder challenge or its various climbing routes. For my sanity, I have labeled many GPS coordinates numerically and usually with some sort of a name. Some names are created and attached in the moment; others are used with historical distinction or were positivity identified via the status quo of answers to questions.

Hikers today are increasingly using GPS-related programs and devices for navigation. Unlike roads and trails that can be altered, repositioned or destroyed, GPS coordinates are not subject to the whims of humans or the alteration of nature. Therefore, GPS latitude and longitude coordinates have validity that will remain unchanged.

Global Positioning System (GPS) coordinates presented in this book are given in *Degrees-Minutes-Seconds* using a map Datum-*WGS 84*. Which particular format utilized is not as important, but conversion to additional formats may need to be performed depending on the application or devise you use or prefer. Matching a device for various formats are often found under settings, simply set your preference to degree-decimals or degrees, minutes, seconds, your choice.

A dedicated hand-held GPS device is probably your best or most reliable GPS receiver; GPS devices such as automotive, camera or cell phones often do not have the sensitivity for deep forested, mountainous terrain or battery longevity. As a tool, GPS devices function differently for off-road than turn for turn with city street addresses. There will be no step by step turns for trails or bushwhacking terrain towards a destination. Off-road GPS definitely will show your present location to your destination only. Also, specialized topographical maps can be uploaded to dedicated GPS devices which will show the terrain off road and not a blank screen after the road ends. One can construct a route within mapping applications, but maps from kiosks or web sites will be your guide.

We encourage readers to utilize the GPS coordinates we have provided as a way of reconnoitering locations prior to making an actual visit. This can be done through mapping applications such as Google Earth, Google Maps or other topographical mapping applications and devices. In doing so, you will find that having an increased understanding of the type of terrain you'll be encountering can help in preparation for a hike, provide insight to time expectations, identify other points of interest nearby, and overall create a safer experience through awareness. There are some chapters with explicit GPS coordinates needed to safely find and arrive at the destination.

Google Earth or other applications are as good as your knowledge on how to use them. E.g. Google Earth has a "Historical History" a toolbar icon that is a clock symbol. The drop-down menu has a slider that changes the acquisition dates and imagery. Often by using this, a previous date or season will change the imagery from a forest canopy showing only the summertime heavily foliage to a date where the acquisition was during the fall or spring without any leaves allowing a clearer understanding or better visual rendition of the terrain.

In most of the photographs shown, a human presence has been included, this is done intentionally. A person standing within a photograph or next to a boulder provides you a sense scale and its dimension. Without one, there is no way to form conclusions or valid estimates about the rock's size dimensions.

One last and extremely important observation, in the spring into summer, a very good bug repellant or even a meshed head-net may be required. Also, think ticks! Body checks after a hike could save you from sickness by removing ticks before they embed into your skin. If any tick is found implanted, use a safe removal tool or procedure, watch the site, if it produces a rash or you start to feel ill with fever, body ache or flu like symptoms seek medical attention. Not every tick illness is Lyme's Disease. Ticks do harbor and spread many other illnesses that have similar flu like symptoms, body ache, chills or fever. When unsure always seek the advice of medical professionals.

Easy walking is for everyone. Gentle grades, smooth footing, short distances.

Easy side of Moderate walking, but with some uphill and downhill sections that will get the heart pumping!

Strenuous, but no problem for anyone who can walk for an hour and climb a few flights of stairs without needing to rest.

Strenuous due to length and/or terrain; this may be a test if you're not accustomed to 2–3-hour hikes.

Difficult. Steep, sustained climbs and descents, uneven footing, and sheer length make this a trail for those with complete confidence in their stamina and fitness.

There is also a risk of slipping and falling on your hike to a waterfall or swimming-hole etc. Always watch your footing, hiking after the leaves drop in the autumn. Fallen leaves can be extraordinarily slippery and they can mask other dangers on the ground e.g. holes or raised roots.

Of course, winter ice or snow can be slippery. A set of slip-on ice stabilizers or crampons are worth their extra weight during the winter months.

Happy Trails, Stay Safe and Enjoy.

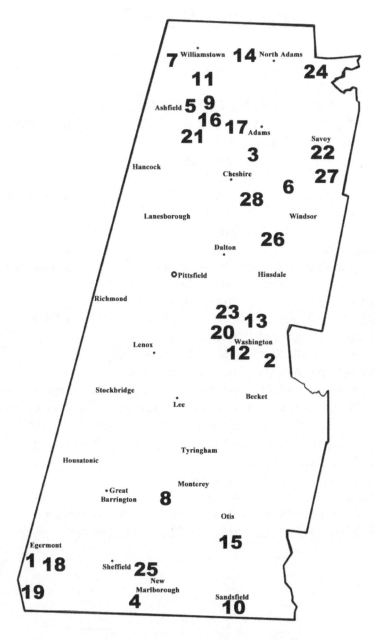

7 Williamstown **14** North Adams

24

11

Ashfield **5** **9**
16 **17** Adams

21

Savoy

22

3

Hancock

Cheshire

27

6

28

Lanesborough

Windsor

26

Dalton

○Pittsfield   Hinsdale

Richmond

23 **13**
20
Washington
12 **2**

Lenox

Stockbridge   Becket

Lee

Tyringham

Housatonic

• Great
Barrington   **8**

Monterey

Otis

15

Egermont

1 **18**
Sheffield **25**
19   New
Marlborough
4   Sandsfield
10

Berkshire Waterfalls

Berkshire Waterfalls

1. Bash Bish Falls State Park- DCR: (Mt. Washington)
2. Becket Ravine. (North Becket)
3. Bellevue Falls. (Adams)
4. Campbell Falls State Park-DCR: (New Marlborough)
5. Deer Hill Falls. Mt. Greylock Reservation-DCR: (Williamstown)
6. Dry Brook Falls. (Cheshire)
7. Haley Brook Falls. (Williamstown)
8. Konkapot Cascades River Road. (Monterey)
9. March Cataract Falls. Mt. Greylock Res-DCR: (Williamstown)
10. Marguerite Falls. (Sandisfield)
11. Money Brook Falls. Mt. Greylock Reservation-DCR
12. Navin Falls. October Mt. State Forest-DCR: (Washington)
13. No-Name Falls. October Mt. State Forest-DCR: (Washington)
14. North Adams Cascades. (North Adams)
15. Otis Falls. Tolland State Forest-DCR: (Otis)
16. Pecks Brook Shelter Falls. Mt. Greylock Res-DCR: (Adams)
17. Pecks Brook (lower) Mt. Greylock Glen: (Adams)
18. Race Brook Falls State Park-DCR: (Sheffield)
19. Sages Ravine. Appalachian Trail: (Egremont)
20. Schermerhorn Falls. October Mt. State Forest-DCR: (Lenoxdale)
21. Silver Fox Cascades. Mt Greylock Reservation-DCR: (Cheshire)
22. Tannery Falls & Parker Brook Falls. Savoy State Forest-DCR
23. Tory Cave Falls. October Mt. State Forest-DCR: (Lenox)
24. Twin Cascades. (Florida)
25. Umpachene Falls. (New Marlborough)
26. Wahconah Falls State Park-DCR: (Dalton)
27. Windsor Jambs. Windsor State Forest- DCR: (Windsor)
28. Woodchuck Falls a.k.a Bridal Veil Falls. (Cheshire)

1. Bash Bish Falls-Mt Washington

Bash Bish Falls-Mt. Washington, MA

Location: Mount Washington DCR (Berkshire County)
Parking GPS: N42° 6' 53.80" W73° 29' 29.77" (DCR, Massachusetts)
Parking GPS: N42° 7' 1.33" W73° 30' 27.39" (Taconic Park, New York)
Destination GPS: N42° 06' 56" W73° 29' 38"
Wow Factor: 9 **Accessibility:** 1.5 mile-RT, NY; 0.6 mile-RT, MA

Information: The legend of *Bash Bish Falls* centers on a beautiful Native American Indian maiden named "Bash Bish" who is jealously accused of adultery. The chief of the tribe deems that the "Great Spirit" will pass judgment. So, the Indian maiden was set adrift in her canoe. However, just prior to her careening over the brink of the thunderous falls, a shaft of sunlight, with a halo of birds, butterflies and canaries formed above her head. Later the tribe finds the shattered wreckage of the canoe in the pool below, but never her body. To this day, if you look closely to the falls, you'll see her silhouette outlined in the falling waters. In photographs, her innocence and simplicity is easily seen in the right side of the falls, her tall single feather juts above her head; with long hair that flows down over her shoulders covering her buxom torso.

Swimming is not authorized here, the Great Spirit has frowned upon twenty-five individual fatalities that swam, fell or jumped into its shallow pools here in past and recent years. With many accidents resulting in serious injury or death occurring, a speculative and contemporary lore on how Bash Bish Falls received its name; *Inquisitive tourists who venture close to the edge for a better view, slip into the gorge and go BASH!...BISH! Before striking bottom. The same goes for those who dive into the inviting pools beneath the falls and downstream, only to BASH or BISH into the many unseen rocks and ledges.*

A frozen Bash Bish Falls in mid-winter-Mt. Washington, MA

Even in February, Bash Bish Falls is very accessible. Usually plowed roads with paths beaten in the snow will precede you. Just watch for icy, slippery rocks, dress warm and utilize poles or stabilizers. During the summer months attendance to the falls does increase making Bash Bish Falls one of the most visited falls in Massachusetts. Another spectacular sight located directly above the falls is Bash Bish Gorge. With its sheer 190-foot cliffs, it's an impressive sight created by the glacial forces and thousands of years of erosion by Bash Bish stream. A sturdy cable fence has been in place to guard the and assist those scaling up the southern perimeter ridge. Crossing the stream in itself can be restrictive or hazardous during high water conditions both up and downstream.

Directions: Access from Great Barrington; travel Route-23 west, through South Egremont Village. Turn south onto Route-41(next to Mill Pond), then turn at the next immediate right onto Mt. Washington

Road. Travel straight for the next 1.8-miles, continue straight and climb the hill for another 2.6-miles and bear left onto East Street (basically stay on the main road) Another 3.2-miles you'll be at a Cross Road, (a small Chapel on your left.) Take a right, onto Cross Road, which becomes a twisty, downhill and brings you down to Wright Brook which Bash Bish Falls is on. Following along the brook for 1.5-miles to the Bash Bish Falls upper parking lot. The trail is maintained and is easy downhill, but more moderate too strenuous on returning back up-hill. Hiking boots or sneakers with treaded soles are strongly recommended over sandals. You can continue to drive down into New York for parking, and then follow the 0.75-mile trail back to the falls along the stream which is longer, but level. The falls are located near the border of Massachusetts and Copake, N.Y. and are managed by the Massachusetts Department of Conservation and Recreation.

2. Becket Ravine - North Becket

Becket Ravine – Becket, MA

Location: Brooker Hill Road, North Becket. (Berkshire County)
Parking GPS: N42° 19' 51.60" W73° 5' 15.20"
Destination GPS: N42°19' 51.24" W73° 5' 18.25" (View Point)
Wow Factor: 7 **Accessibility:** No marked paths, short walk 0.1mile-RT
Information: This location is just a stone throw from the center of North Becket. While many have called it "Becket Center Falls," it is correct and now better known as the "Becket Ravine." At one time the hub and center of activities for the Becket Township was in North Becket. Presently, the development in the geographic center of Becket is correctly referred to as Becket Center.

While parking is limited, the cascading falls are impressive, making the venture down to the cascading falls worth the effort. Swimming not applicable.

Directions: From the center of Becket Village on Route-8, take Brooker Hill Road uphill for 0.2-mile. A small pull off for one car is located on the right side of the Road between the guard rails. Over the embankment of hemlocks, you'll see Mill/Morgan Brook below and the Becket Ravine. While no postings about parking or access have been seen, some of the abutting land may be posted so be wary of trespassing.

3. Bellevue Falls - Adams

Bellevue Falls – Adams, MA

Location: Bellevue Cemetery. Adams (Berkshire County)
Parking GPS: N42° 36' 8.39" W73° 7' 31.67"
Destination GPS: N42°36' 6.00" W73° 7' 32.00"
Wow Factor: 6 **Accessibility:** Short foot path 0.1 mile-RT

Information: Bellevue Falls is a small, but popular local waterfall for sunning and as a swimming hole. However, swimming is at one's own risk, for no life guard is present. While not posted, swimming is not "authorized", but becomes a popular location on hot summer days. Jumping into the shallow pool from the rocky shore is also probably not recommended, for a cross and small shrine has been noticed here for a teenager who evidently perished.

Located on Dry Brook, the swimming hole can shrink up during a hot stretch of summer weather to a mere trickle of water. Presently, there are no parking issues for this area. Parking and access to the falls has been mainly allowed by the cemetery authority. I would suggest that to maintain this allowance, park without damaging or rutting up the grassy area and remove one's trash, keeping this area clean will assist in preventing closure or loss of access to this area. Several smaller wading pools are located up stream.

Directions: From the center of Adams at the junction Route-116 & Route-8, take Route-8 south for .8 of a mile, turn left onto Leonard Street (large old granite bldg. on corner) follow Leonard Street for .2

of a mile, bear left, just over a small bridge and turn right onto Bellevue Ave which will lead you into the Bellevue Cemetery. With entry into the cemetery bear right onto its rotary; take a right off the "circle" at the 1 o'clock position, keep to the right for less than 0.1-mile. You should see a worn grassy parking area, no graves here at this time. A path to the falls is off on the left, down a short unimproved steep path reaching the falls within 100-yards.

A serene location for a short stroll.

4. Campbell Falls - New Marlborough

Campbell Falls – New Marlborough, MA

Location: DCR New Marlborough (Berkshire County)
Parking GPS: N42° 2' 41.82" W73° 13' 53.04"
Destination GPS: N42° 2' 44.00" W73° 13' 59.00" (View Point)
Wow Factor: 8 **Accessibility:** Short steep downhill 0.4-mile RT

Information: A wonderful waterfall with a short 300-yard moderate hike. "Good things come in small "Parcels." The state land parcel for Campbell Falls State Park is only 3 acres and was primarily developed to protect this jewel of a waterfall. Located in New Marlborough, Massachusetts MA it is right on the border where Canaan and Norfolk, Connecticut abut. This waterfall may be a little tough to locate on the twisty rural roads. It is well worth the persistence to locate the parking area and trail head for the short 300-yard walk, down a moderately steep path, to its base. The Massachusetts and Connecticut boundary marker is located half-way down the trail to the falls.

Located on the Whiting River, the falls provides an impressive display as it funnels torrents of water in a two stage drop of 75-feet joining Ginger Creek a short distance away. The falls are managed by the Massachusetts Department of Conservation and Recreation. There are no parking or admission fees, no camping or fires permitted and swimming is not applicable.

Campbell's Falls is a 5 star and 4 season location. With spring run-off providing a thundering cascade, summer providing a cool location, fall is colorful and winter is surreal as the waterfall often appears frozen in time. However, there are no panoramic vistas here. While Connecticut does manage an abutting 100-acre state park, hiking trails are limited. The beauty of Campbell Falls is the solitude one discovers shortly after arriving at its base. Isolated from traffic and congestion, along with the constant "white noise" the abstraction of falling water creates an environment allowing one to slip into a meditative state called relaxation!

Directions: From the center of New Marlborough travel south on New Marlborough/Southfield Road 1.3-miles. At the fork, take a left onto Norfolk Road, travel 4.5-miles south. Right on the Massachusetts and Connecticut state line bear right onto Campbell Falls Road. Approximately 0.5-miles further is a dirt parking area. There is a steep dirt path from rear of parking area. It is moderately steep, but short. Leave the high heels in the car.

Campbell Falls – New Marlborough, MA

Swimming is not applicable and rocks can be slippery or icy during the winter months.

5. Deer Hill Falls - Mt. Greylock Reservation.

Deerhill Falls–Mt. Greylock Reservation, MA

Location: Mt. Greylock Reservation. Williamstown, (Berkshire County)
Parking GPS: N42° 37' 11.69" W73° 11' 57.09" (Campground Parking)
Parking GPS: N42° 37' 27.81"W73° 11' 26.12" (CCC Dynamite Trail)
Parking GPS: N42° 38' 11.02"W73°13' 7.78" (Roaring Brook Road)
Destination GPS: N42° 37' 52.00" W73° 11' 33.00" (Waterfall)
Wow Factor: 5 Accessibility: Steep strenuous trail 0.6-mile RT

Information: These falls flow best during the spring run-off or after long periods of a soaking rain. Even then, this waterfall is usually not the most impressive, nor is the base of the falls easily viewed or accessible due to downed tree and limbs that can degrade the visual experience. However, actually when the lighting and water flow are at optimum, a camera setting with a long-time exposure and a solid camera rest (tripod) can result with the creation of "Angle Hair" imagery. This technique can enhance this waterfall with its minimal water flow and create exceedingly beautiful photographs.

To reduce environmental impact, the Sperry Road campground entry is chained to prevent unauthorized vehicle traffic from entering. The Mt Greylock Campground is presently accessible only by hiking in from its Rockwell Road long term parking area, then following the Campground Trail for 1.2-miles to the Ranger Shack at the Campground entry. For day parking only, use the CCC Dynamite trailhead parking area at the junction of Sperry Road and Rockwell

Road and then hike down Sperry Road for 0.6 mile to access the Deer Hill Falls, March Cataract Falls, The Hopper Trail or out to the Stony Ledge vista.

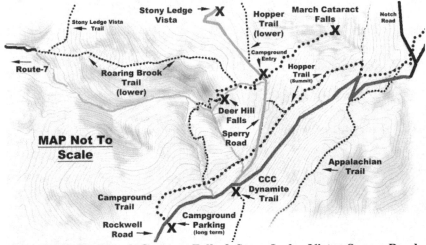

Deer Hill Falls, March Cataract Falls & Stony Ledge Vista. Sperry Road

Directions: From the Mt Greylock Visitor's Center and Lanesborough gate, drive north up the roadway; pass Rounds Rock, Jones's Nose and The Ash Fort. Just past the Ash Fort and 5.0-miles from the gate, the Long-Term Camping parking will be on your right. Continue up Rockwell Road and after an additional 0.6-miles, the CCC Dynamite Trail will be on your right. From here, walk down Sperry Road 0.6-mile to the campground entry, Stony Ledge is 1.1 miles past the ranger shack. Trailhead for March Cataract Falls is off on the right.

Deer Hill Falls: Beginning near the campground entry ranger shack, the falls are 0.3 mile downhill. Continuing from the Roaring Brook Group Shelter site, follow the Roaring Brook Trail west, down and beside its small stream. Immediately after crossing a small bridge, turn left, leaving the Roaring Brook Trail and continue to follow the stream, steeply downhill into this ravine. The Deer Hill Trail is a loop trail with strenuous steepness, worn and slippery switch-backs and multiple "Chocolate" topographical elevation lines. Most who reach the falls usually return the way they came.

Alternative access is to follow the lower Roaring Brook Trail uphill 1.6-miles to the Deer Hill spur trail. Parking is located on the Roaring Brook Road, 0.75-mile in from Route-7 in Williamstown. The Massachusetts D.O.T. Highway Garage is near the corner of Roaring Brook Road. The lower Stony Ledge Trail is also accessed from here. During the winter a private ski club is activate at the end of the road.

6. Dry Brook Falls - Cheshire

Dry Brook Falls (lower)-Cheshire, MA

Location: Sand Mill Hill Road. Cheshire (Berkshire County)
Parking GPS: N42° 33' 40" W73° 5' 40.6"
Destination GPS: N42° 33' 42.91" W73° 5' 41.72" (lower falls)
Destination GPS: N42° 33' 39.81" W73° 5' 39.33" (upper falls)
Wow Factor: 6 **Accessibility:** Roadside viewing, No trail 0.1-mile

Information: Both upper and lower Dry Brook waterfalls are within a private sanctuary with the owner allowing visitation. They are basically road side falls, yet driving past them is easy due to the recess of Dry Brook away from the road and natural coverage from evergreens and beech trees. Hence, these obscure falls are a treat to discover and enjoy. Parking will be your main consideration as to not block the neighborhood resident's drives or become an obstacle to the flow of local traffic on this narrow dirt road. No signs or paths lead to the falls. Hunting, camping or fires are not authorized.

Directions: From Cheshire, Route-116, follow Sandmill Road east for 1.8-mile. Prior to the large sweeping horseshoe corner, continue straight onto Windsor Road, a dirt road, continue east uphill for 0.3-mile, there are 2 small, dirt pull-offs, on the left for 1 or 2 cars.

7. Haley Brook Falls - Williamstown

Haley Brook Falls-Williamstown, MA

Location: Williamstown Rural Lands Management. (Berkshire County)
Parking GPS: N4° 42' 9.25" W732 ° 16' 13.62"
Destination GPS: N42° 42' 6.00" W73° 16' 24.00" (View Point)
Wow Factor: 6 Accessibility: Easy short walk, 0.4-mile RT
Contact: 671 Cold Spring Rd, Williamstown, MA 01267
(413) 458-2494   https://wrlf.org   ruraland@wrlf.org

Information: Haley Brook Falls is a small plunge, on a woodland stream. Swimming is not applicable and camping or fires not authorized. These falls are just perfect for a quick walk or for getting children outside into the woodlands.

Directions: Located on Williamstown Rural Lands Management (WRLM.) Travel south on Route-7/ Route-2 out of Williamstown, until you reach where Route-2 turns right towards New York State, travel .3 of a mile and turn left off onto Torry Woods Road. You will stay on Torry Woods Roads which will become Berlin Road for 2-miles. Continue on Berlin Road bearing left at the fork, the road will turn to dirt after the last house on the left, you'll see a small dirt parking area on the left. Follow the woodland trail from the parking area west for 150-yards, the trail is not well worn or marked. Turn left immediately after crossing a small bridge and head downhill towards Haley Brook. A very nice viewing platform has been built above the stream.

8. Konkapot Cascades - Monterey

Konkapot River Cascades – Monterey, MA

Location: River Street. Monterey (Berkshire County)
Directive GPS: N42°10'46.13" W73°12'47.14" (Monterey Center)
Parking GPS: N42° 10' 46.59" W73° 14' 59.28" (River Road)
Destination GPS: N42° 10' 47.66" W73° 14' 58.17"
Wow Factor: 6 **Accessibility:** Roadside, easy short walk, 0.1-mile RT

Information: While not the biggest or the longest, these roadside cascades usually have an ample supply of water all year long with easy access. Here the Konkapot River funnels down into a tight 75-yard channel that churns along as a spill-way emptying into a rather nice 30-to-40-foot pool. Apparently, the tell-tale rope-swing suggests this is a swimming-hole. Presently, I have not seen any posted signs about anything, nor is there a litter basket, so carry out what you bring in, maybe more. From the small 1 to 2 cars parking area, there are short paths leading down to the river edge and to the bottom of the chute. A slanted, smooth rocky ledge-shelving runs along the cascades and enters the water, beware slippery when wet or dry!

Directions: From the center of Monterey, travel west on Route-23 for 2.0-miles. River Street veers off on your left, down 0.2-mile on the left as the road curves left are a couple parking area.

9. March Cataract Falls - Mt Greylock

March Cataract Falls-Mt Greylock Reservation. Williamstown, MA

Location: Mt. Greylock Reservation. Williamstown, (Berkshire County)
Parking GPS: N42° 37' 11.69" W73° 11' 57.09" (Campground Parking)
Parking GPS: N42° 37' 27.81"W73° 11' 26.12" (CCC Dynamite Trail)
Destination GPS: N42° 38' 9.00" W73° 10' 45.00" (Waterfall)
Wow Factor: 7 Moderate 1.6-mile RT from Campground Entry.

Information: Located on Mt Greylock Reservation this waterfall is a very popular destination in the spring when the falls run best. Parking is at the CCC Dynamite trail parking area on Rockwell Road. Walk down Sperry Road 0.6 mile to the campground entry, bear right to the trailhead across from the Chimney Group site.

To reduce environmental impact, the Sperry Road campground entry is chained to prevent unauthorized vehicle traffic from entering. The Mt Greylock Campground is presently accessible only by hiking in from its Rockwell Road long term parking area, then following the Campground Trail for 1.2-miles to the Ranger Shack at the Campground entry. For day parking only, use the CCC Dynamite trailhead parking area at the junction of Sperry Road and Rockwell Road and then hike down Sperry Road for 0.6-mile to access the Deer Hill Falls, March Cataract Falls, The Hopper Trail or out to the Stony Ledge vista.

Directions: From the Mt Greylock Visitor's Center and Lanesborough gate, drive north up the roadway; pass Rounds Rock, Jones's Nose and

The Ash Fort. Just past the Ash Fort and 5.0-miles from the gate, the Long-Term Camping parking will be on your right. Continue up Rockwell Road and after an additional 0.6-mile-, the CCC Dynamite Trail will be on your right. From here, walk down Sperry Road 0.6-mile to the campground entry, Stony Ledge is 1.1-miles past the ranger shack. Trailhead for March Cataract Falls is off on the right.

10. Marguerite Falls - Sandisfield

Marguerite Falls-Route-8 Sandisfield, MA

Location: Sandisfield Route-8 (Berkshire County)
Destination GPS: N42° 2' 52.55" W73° 3' 33.50" (Route-8 Bridge)
Wow Factor: 6 **Accessibility:** Roadside, limited shoulder parking-access.

Information: Located 0.6-mile before the Massachusetts and Connecticut state line, the falls and stream flows beneath Route-8. Access requires scrambling down the bridge embankment and rock-hopping up the stream. During the summer "Gullywhumping" up this waterfall can be easy and very refreshing, caution slippery rocks.
Directions: From the junction of Route-8/Route-57 in Sandisfield, drive south on Route-8 for 3.6-miles. Parking just past the bridge provides a little wider area and better access on this busy route and speeding cars. Do not park on bridge.

11. **Money Brook Falls** - Mt Greylock Reservation

Money Brook Falls – Mt Greylock Reservation

Location: Williamstown, Mt Greylock Reservation. (Berkshire County)
Parking GPS: N42° 39' 51.75" W73° 9' 57.81" (Notch Road)
Destination GPS: N42° 39' 45.40" W73° 10' 2.80"
Wow Factor: 7 **Accessibility:** Moderate with steep return. 1.2 mile-RT

Information: Money Brook Falls is another popular waterfall located on the north end of Mt. Greylock Reservation. Lore has it that in earlier days the minting of counterfeit coins took place near the falls. The operation was disrupted, but not before the evidence was thrown and scattered down the brook---hence, *Money Brook Falls*. It is said you may occasionally find old coins among the cascading brook and further downstream. The falls, for some 100-feet, consist of a series of large blocks of cascades with no perceived trail to them. Bushwhacking through brush and up the streambe d is the only way to get closer.
Directions: From the bottom gate on Notch Road drive 2.4 miles up to a small parking area for 2-3 cars. (The pull-off is 0.3-miles above "Wilber's Clearing" were the Appalachian Trail crosses Notch Road.) From this corner parking area a short woodland spur trail descends 0.2-mile until it "T's"into the Money Brook Trail. Take a left and continue to descend south and down into the "Hopper." Continue for an additional 0.3-mile until reaching the bottom of the trail where a switchback turns sharply right and begins to follow the Money Brook

downstream west. Here, one exits off the trail and follows up along the stream embankment east 100-yards to the falls.

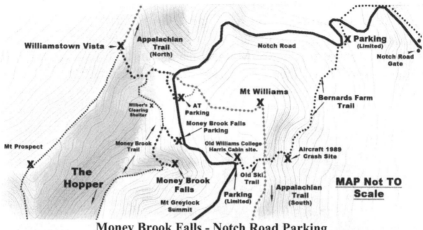

Money Brook Falls - Notch Road Parking

12. Navin's Falls- October Mt. State Forest

Navin's Falls-October Mountain State Forest, DCR. Washington, MA

Location: October Mountain State Forest. Washington (Berkshire County)
Parking GPS: N42° 21' 4.99" W73° 11' 45.60" (Navin Trail)
Old Farm House Cellar: N42° 21' 3.80" W73° 12' 12.40" (Navin Farm)
Cobble Stone Well: N42° 21' 3.97" W73° 12' 12.15" (Navin Farm)
Barn Foundation: N42° 21' 3.50" W73° 12' 14.30" (Navin Farm)
Destination GPS: N42° 20' 53.34" W73° 12' 11.39" (Navin's Falls)
Wow Factor: 8 Accessibility: Moderate with bushwhack. 1.8-mile RT

Information: It is generally accepted that in 1850 from his home "Arrowhead" Herman Melville wrote about the blaze of autumn foliage in an essay titled *October Mountain.* October Mountain State Forest is a 16,460-acre forest is located primarily in the town of Washington with adjoining acreage in Becket, Lee, and Lenox. It is the largest state forest in Massachusetts and is managed by the Massachusetts Department of Conservation and Recreation.

The Whitney's Estate "The Antlers" Circa 1898   Washington, MA

The Town of Washington was originally settled by a scattering of farmers; in 1894 an agent for William C. Whitney was purchasing land at $5.00-per acre and had amassed 24-farms with combined acreage of 14,000-acres. Ultimately, all the expenditure was to create William C. Whitney vision of a personal game preserve and summer home. The Whitney Estate grew rapidly with dozens of buildings; the center piece of construction was the "The Antlers" a two-half story cottage fitting for the gilded age with, running water (indoors) telephone with a fenced in 1000-acre parcel filled with exotic game Elk, Buffalo, Moose, and many species of deer. In 1974, evidence of the 10-foot fence could be seen nailed onto trees 10-feet up in the Washington Mountain Marsh area. In short, the Whitney Estate was the largest privately own piece of land in Massachusetts.

Easy come, easy go. The Whitney Estate was an economic boost for the Town of Washington. In its 10-years, the estate was a source of revenue and employed a multitude of men. Unfortunately, William Whitney died in 1904 from appendicitis. His heirs did not choose to maintain the property. Most of the building were razed or collapsed after a few New England winters. In 1929, "The Antlers" burnt with no loss of live.

N42°22'10.59" W73°11'34.62" Observation and Water Tower. Washington, MA

The last prominent structure to disappear was a tower located behind the stables. The ninety-foot observation and water tower stood until 1946 when it was torn down for safety concerns. Its location and footings were readily found near the intersection Lenox-Whitney Place Road and Lower Tower Road. Apparently recent logging activity has obliterated anything visible

At first, Navin's Falls were never part of the Whitney Estate. In fact, the Navin Farm was one of the few who did not sell and chose to continue farming. You could imagine this was probably not popular with Mr. Whitney, to the point, that the squeeze was placed upon him preventing access and expansion to his farming operations. Eventually, economics forced the sale of the farm and probably not at the same financial arrangement as the original offer. The farm's house and barn foundations, a cobblestone lined well and an impressive field stone dam that still holds water exists on the Navin Trail with the waterfall a short distance downstream from the dam. The impressive dam was built by Cobb Codding in the 1830's to power a sawmill.

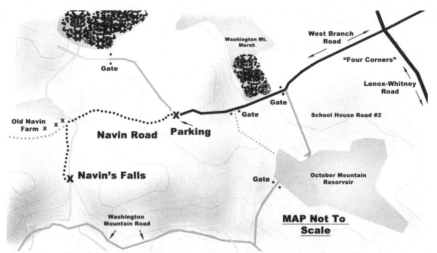

Navin's Falls in October State Forest-Washington, MA

Directions: Your first task is to locate what is known as 4-Corners in October Mountain State Forest. Most roads through-out the forest are graded dirt and gravel roads with no markings. Four corners is best approached off Washington Mountain Road turning onto West Branch Road (N42°21'57.19" W73° 8'36.82") and drive west for 2.2-miles. The other, is off Route-8 below North Becket, turning onto County Road (N42°18'52.76" W73° 5'40.02".) Follow County Road west for 0.9 mile, bearing right at the fork staying on County Road. Continue north for 3.75-miles, (the pavement ends ~ 2.0-miles) at the next fork, bear right, County Road becomes Lenox-Whitney Place Road with an additional 1.2-miles to 4-Corners.

Navin Trail: From 4-corners, head west on West Branch Road 0.5-mile, if the gate is open, stay straight for another 0.4 miles. At the top of the hill, where the road curves sharply to the right is the Navin Trail (road), park here. Walk the road west 0.8 miles until reaching the stream where the Navin Farm stood. Crossing the stream and 100-yards, the Navin Farm is to the north side of the road. On the left (south) is an old spruce grove, cross over the stone wall, walk south 100-yards. In essence, you are following the stream down to the falls, but give the stream a wide berth after you pass through the spruce grove for its can be marshy. From here its 0.2-mile to the falls, there is no marked trail, but the west side of the stream does conceal a heavily over grown road and is the better approach to the falls. It is somewhat easier to thrash through the sapling growth as the road will clear and will come down next to Navin's Falls in better fashion. The south brink of its small pool has the remnants of an old rudimentary stone dam which was evident subjected to many years of torrential waters.

13. No Name Falls - October Mt. State Forest

I have been enlightened to learn and perhaps provide a name for this waterfall.
In 1799, a William Congdon from Lenox purchased a substantial tract of land
within this area. Henry Congdon with Harriet (Sikes (Sykes) later in the 1860's
settled on some 200-acres and farmed within 0.25-miles from here.
Hence, *Congdon's Falls* seems a very appropriate choice for its title.

Location: October Mt. State Forest, Washington (Berkshire County)
Parking A GPS: N42° 23' 29.93" W73° 13' 36.25" (lowest parking)
Parking B GPS: N42° 23' 48.53" W73° 12' 31.16" (lower)
Parking C GPS: N42° 23' 30.40" W73° 12' 6.10" (upper/trailhead)
Destination GPS: N42° 24' 8.60" W73° 11' 58.90" (waterfall)
Wow Factor: 8 **Accessibility:** Moderate off-trail: 2.0-mile trail RT

Information: This obscure waterfall I have called "Curtin Falls" for
no better reason than one can walk behind this delightful and delicate
16-foot curtain of water. While it flows best during the spring run-off
or after heavy rains, it should not be thought of as seasonal. That said,
with the waterfall supplied only by a spring or woodland water table I
have seen a rather dismal flow in July and August, but not always.

Access to the parking locations B or C, are not for the BMW or
Mercedes. Entry into October Mt State Forest via New Lenox Road
begins as a residential and is paved, but after the first 0.5-mile
becomes a semi-maintained roadway with a 5-mph rock and puddle
route. However, it very passable for SUV and vehicles with clearance,
remember access to the Farnham Reservoir and its dam requires the
roadway to be passable for the water department.

There are no signs or blazed trails and for now this is probably the
only map to this gem of a waterfall. Travel by foot or mountain

bicycle needs to be accompanied with some faith in the usage of GPS coordinates, pre-reconnoitering using topographical maps or Goggle Earth is also recommended. Most of the access trails are old roads or foot paths with a small amount of bushwhacking to get to the lower base of the falls.

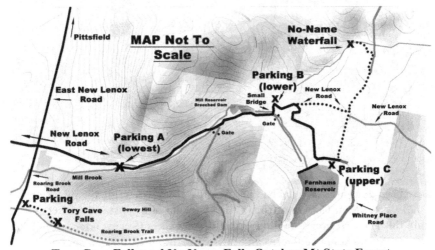

Tory Cave Falls and No-Name Falls-October Mt State Forest

Parking A (lowest) From Route-7 in Lenox, (GPS: N42° 23' 49.08" W73° 16' 10.66) turn onto, heading east onto New Lenox Road for 1.8-miles, just over the Housatonic River to the intersection of East New Lenox Road and New Lenox Road. Continue straight and east 0.5-mile until where the pavement ends. Shortly, on the right, is where you will park your vehicle if the road is too rough. Continue east on the road by foot for 1.1-mile to the **Parking area B (lower.)** From Parking B, the main dirt road becomes rougher; more up-hill, rutted and requires more attention to picking a line for the next 0.6-mile. The road will also become Whitney Place Road and continues until you reach to the Farnham's Reservoir Dam and the upper **Parking area C (upper.)**

To the falls from the lower Parking area B, continue up-hill east on New Lenox Road for 0.1 mile, at the first corner, bear left off the main dirt road (GPS: N42°23' 48.33" W73°12' 23.24".) Here, New Lenox Road become more of an ATV or 4x4 only trail. Remain on this road, east and up-hill 0.3-mile. Turn left, onto an unnamed old roadway heading north. (GPS: N42° 23' 45.90" W73° 12' 2.00".) Stay on this roadway for 0.4-mile until approaching the small marshy brook for this waterfall. On the left, (GPS: N42° 24' 5.30" W73° 11 '51.20") but prior to the brook, a matrix of small paths will enter into the woodlands.

While the paths meander, maintain a westerly direction, but basically look for and follow the brook for 0.1 mile. Your arrival from this approach will bring one to the brink of the falls, skirt down and around to its base. Access to the falls from parking area C is initially not as steep, heading north for the first 0.3 mile to where it will join the same GPS turn-off on New Lenox Road, continue north on the same unnamed road as if hiking from parking area B directions.

14. North Adams - Cascades

The Cascades - North Adams, MA

Location: Marion Avenue. North Adams (Berkshire County)
Parking GPS: N42° 41' 49.90" W73° 8' 11.90" (Brayton School)
Trail Head GPS: N42° 41' 38.50" W73° 8'7.70" (Marion Avenue)
Destination GPS: N42° 41' 7.50" W73° 7' 53.50" (Cascades)
Wow Factor: 8 Accessibility: Easy-Moderate 2.2-mile trail. RT

Information: The Cascades trailhead is at the end of Marion Avenue, which is off Route-2(State Road), just before Notch Road the north entry to Mt Greylock Reservation.

There is no legal parking at the Marion Avenue trailhead, legal public parking can be found at Brayton School area on Brayton Hill Terrace, 0.2-mile west on Route-2 from Marion Avenue on the left. During the summer parking here is easy, however when school is in session parking and school bus activity can make parking here busy.

From the easterly side of parking area, a path leads down into a woodland gully and stream, across Notch Road and straight 0.1-mile down Pershing Street turning right onto Marion Avenue heading south 0.1-mile for trailhead.

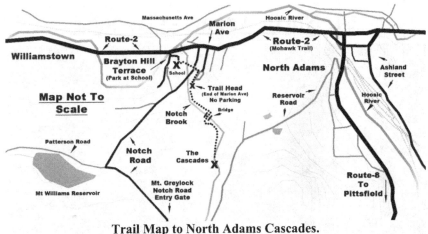

Trail Map to North Adams Cascades.

Continue south; move along the well-worn woodland path, you will be about half way there when you cross a wooden bridge that spans Reservoir Stream from the Notch Reservoir upstream.

Although located within a short distance of the downtown North Adams and surrounded by residential neighborhoods, the hike provides an unexpected remoteness of hemlock forest and is a refreshing hike to reach the Cascades.

Form the trailhead this area is an easy 0.6-mile trek. While the Cascades trail is basically an improved flat trail, the last 100-yards is the roughest and requires traversing slippery and steep hillside. Once there, you can view the falls from a distance or make your way over rock and log to enter the chasm where the falls creates a small pool. However, Warning - Danger, the rocks are slippery and during spring high water run-off, approaching the falls in this manner is very risky.

15. Otis Reservoir Falls - Tolland State Forest

Otis Reservoir Falls - Otis, MA

Location: Tolland State Forest. Otis (Berkshire County)
Parking GPS: N42° 9' 36.79" W73° 3' 27.64" (Roadside before Dam)
Destination GPS: N42° 9' 35.27" W73° 3' 32.69" (View Point)
Wow Factor: 8 **Accessibility:** No marked trail, short walk 0.2-mile RT

Information: Located within Tolland State Forest these falls are easy to access and provide a thunderous show when flowing. Their unique trait starts in early fall when the dam gates are opened to lower the reservoir's level for the winter, the falls start to roar, later in the spring the gates are closed to refill the reservoir and the falls stop. Somewhat backwards when compared to Mother Nature scheme of things when in the Fall streams are drier and in the Spring thaw water flow is rampant.

Directions: From the center of Otis, travel 3-miles south on Route-8, turn left onto Reservoir Road, travel 1.6-mile, and turn right onto Tolland Road. Another 0.8-mile brings you to the Otis Reservoir Dam. Park in small dirt pull-off before crossing the dam. A small path below the dam leads to the brink of the falls with another foot path to its base.

16. Pecks Brook Shelter Falls - Mt Greylock

Pecks Brook Shelter Falls- Mt Greylock Reservation

Location: Gould Trail, Mt Greylock Reservation (Berkshire County)
Parking GPS: N42° 37' 8.73" W73° 9' 1.66" (West Mountain Road)
Parking GPS: N42° 38' 1.26" W73° 10' 14.72" (Rockwell-Notch Road)
Destination GPS: N42° 37' 28.50" W73° 10' 0.20" (View Point)
Wow Factor: 8 **Accessibility:** Moderate-difficult 1.8 to 3.0 miles RT

Information: These falls in the early spring can surpass every other waterfall on the reservation. Access to the base of the falls has steep embankments and the trek in or out will require a good uphill chug.

Directions: From the top of Mt Greylock: Where Rockwell Road and Notch Road meet just below the summit, a small dirt parking area sits across from the end of Notch Road. Follow the "Gould " trail down for 1.8-mile RT, as you descend, you'll reach the "Pecks Brook Shelter" a trail spur and this is where the falls are just below the shelter's campsite.

Or one can drive from the center of Adams, from the William McKinley statue take Maple Street to its end, turn left onto West Road. Travel 0.5-mile and turn right on West Mountain Road. Drive up 1.0-mile to a dirt parking area located on a sharp bend of the road. From here the hike up to reach the shelter and the falls is 1.5-miles utilizing the Gould Trail to reach the Pecks Brook Shelter spur trail.

17. Pecks Brook Falls (lower) - Adams

Pecks Falls (lower) – Adams, MA

Location: Greylock Glen-Mt Greylock Reservation (Berkshire County)
Parking GPS: N42° 37' 26.74" W73° 8' 26.85"
Destination GPS: N42° 37' 23.54" W73° 8' 27.97" (View Point)
Wow Factor: 7 **Accessibility:** Roadside, short walk 0.1-mile RT

Information: Located within the Greylock Glen Land Trust with easy access makes this quick and simple get away spot. The low tiered waterfall is scenic and a natural swimming-wading pool. The pool is formed below the falls by a stone barrier; the stones may be used as stepping stone bridge to the other side. Access is easy most of the year and always a delight for each visit.

Directions: From the center of Adams at the William McKinley statue, take Maple Street west, to its end, turn left onto West Road. Travel 0.4-mile and turn right on Gould Road. From here follow Gould Road 0.5-mile to the top of the hill, turn left and follow the curve around to the right, as the road starts to go downhill, park on the right side of the road. Look for the trail sign and worn path to Pecks Falls, which is about 100-yards, down a steep embankment from the road.

18. Race Brook Falls - Sheffield

Race Brook Falls #3-Sheffield, MA

Location: Mt Washington State Forest-DCR. Sheffield (Berkshire County)
Parking GPS: N42° 5' 21.95" W73° 24' 40.25" (Route-41)
Destination GPS: N42° 5' 22.44" W73° 25' 18.76" (Race Brook #1)
Destination GPS: N42° 5' 22.48" W73° 25' 21.63" (Race Brook #2)
Destination GPS: N42° 5' 22.54" W73° 25' 23.28" (Race Brook #3)
Destination GPS: N42° 5' 22.70" W73° 25' 24.30" (Race Brook #4)
Destination GPS: N42° 5' 22.71" W73° 25' 26.05" (Race Brook #5)
Wow Factor: 8 **Accessibility:** Moderate to short Strenuous 2.5-mile RT

Information: Race Brook Falls are well worth the journey with five tiers of waterfalls. The upper most waterfall-#5 is a dynamic chute of water dropping sharply 35 to 40-feet, the next two lower falls-#4 & #3 consist of wider larger cataracts, cascading over blocks of ledge. Waterfall-#2 begins with a narrow flow of water, descends a sloped rocky surface as it fans open into a small pool below. The lowest waterfall-#1 while the lowest and easiest to view, has large boulders and cliff making access difficult, requires rock hopping and esthetically not the best of the bunch (In my opinion.)

Directions: From Great Barrington, MA travel Route-23 west, through S. Egremont village. Turn south onto Route-41 (next to Mill Pond) Travel south on Route-41 for 5.5-miles, on your right a paved

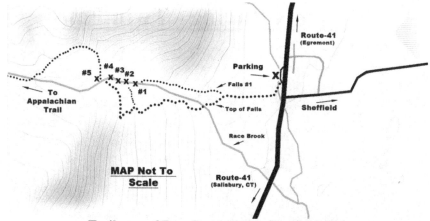

Trail map of Race Brook Falls – Sheffield, MA

pull off parking area for several cars. Just pass the information kiosk the trailhead begins with crossing a small brook, then through a field and shortly into the woodlands. Within the forest at 0.2-mile the trail will split. Bearing to the right, the trail will deliver one to the base of the lowest falls-#1. Bearing left, then crossing Race Brook and continuing uphill will eventually bring one to the upper most falls-#5. As one ascends there are small unmarked foot paths which branch off for falls-#2, #3 and the brink of falls #1. If planning to ascend or descend the terrain next to the waterfall good boots along with hiking poles are recommended, the slopes are very steep and slippery.

Race Brook Falls #2-Sheffield, MA

19. Sage's Ravine - Twin Falls

Twin Falls-Sage's Ravine from "Inspiration Point"-Sheffield MA/Connecticut

Location: Under Mountain Road/Route-41 (Ma/CT Border)
Parking GPS: N42° 2' 58.29" W73° 25' 33.74" (Route-41 shoulder)
Destination GPS: N42° 3' 0.27" W73° 25' 33.95" (Falls-Bridge #0)
Destination GPS: N42 03 00.0 W73 25 58.0 (Falls-Cascade #1)
Destination GPS: N 42° 2' 58.90" W73° 26' 0.20" (Falls-Cascade #2)
Destination GPS: N42° 2' 59.78" W73° 26' 4.52" (Inspiration Point Vista)
Wow Factor: 9 **Accessibility:** Moderate to Strenuous 1.4-mile RT

Information: Sage's Ravine Brook is a pristine tract of land with an impressive Berkshire terrain ruggedness. (The lower segment actually lies within Joyceville, Connecticut.} From the trailhead (no signs), on Route-41, a woodland path meanders along the southern side of the brook through Hemlocks and Mountain Laurel. As the rocky ravine walls ascend rapidly, the well-trodden path becomes a non-trodden path. Safety is a paramount concern, the utilization in a 3-points of contact while scrambling over craggy and steep embankment, inherit some associated risk in this bushwhack. A slip or fall back here will result in a difficult extraction. Twin Falls are located 0.6-mile up from the trailhead and best seen from "Inspiration Point." Here the vista is level with Twin Falls and is slightly below on the southern side of the brook and ravine. Even a venture attempting to get closer or lower down to these falls might create a serious problem in trying to get back up and out. In addition, there are no connecting paths from the lower segment of Sage's Ravine that will lead up to the upper segment of Sage's Ravine and the Appalachian Trail. Each year someone tries and requires assistance to be removed from the ravine. There are a couple of smaller falls and cascades on the lower portions of the brook that are still fabulous to experience during high water flow. Another waterfall often not seen, flows directly under the Route-41 bridge, access to under the bridge is difficult with no formal pathway and having steep embankments.

Sages Ravine-lower Falls-Cascades: #2 (left)   #1(right)

Sage's Ravine (lower)-Sheffield, Massachusetts-Connecticut border.

Directions: From Great Barrington, travel west on Route-23 for 3.8-miles. Passing through South Egremont, turn left onto Route-41, travel south for 8.0-miles to the Sheffield, Mass-Joyceville, Conn border. Just after going over the border and passing over the bridge that Sage's Ravine Brook flows under, parking will be on the right slanted embankment/shoulder with room for only a couple of vehicles. Ravine Ridge Road will be across the street, slightly south. In addition, this parking may not be viable during winter months due to the snow berm from plowing. Be cautious as you exit the vehicle for high-speed traffic traveling south on Route-41.

Sage's Ravine Brook-Waterfall under Route-41 Bridge. Joyceville, CT

20. Schermerhorn Gorge Falls

Schermerhorn Falls - The Gorge Trail - Lenox, MA

Location: Woodland Road. October State Forest. Lenox (Berkshire County)
Parking GPS: N42° 21' 25.78" W73°14' 12.65" (Woodland Road)
Destination GPS: N42° 21' 24.57" W73° 14' 7.52" (Falls)
Destination GPS: N42° 21' 42.67" W73° 13' 24.78" (Felton Pond)
Wow Factor: 5 **Accessibility:** Moderate marked trail, 1.5-mile RT

Information: These small falls lie at the bottom of the *Schermerhorn Gorge Trail* and are fed by Felton Pond, 0.8-mile above. The trail and stream run parallel to Schermerhorn Road, a steep, but popular entry from Lenoxdale that eventually will lead to 4-Corners via Lower Tower Road. The Gorge Trail is short, steep and requires a reasonable amount of heft to ascend this bluff that rises from the Housatonic River Valley below. Park off the Woodland Road just pass where the stream passes beneath the road and the Gorge Trail begins. From here, hike 0.1 mile up the trail to where the falls are located. In addition, continuing up the Gorge Trail will bring you to Felton Pond, which is where the defunct Boy Scout Camp Eagle was located.

Directions: From the intersection of Route-7/ Route-20 and Route 183 in Lenox, head southeast down Walker Street for 1.5-mile into Lenoxdale. From the center, turn right over the bridge onto Mill Street, head south on Mill Street for 0.6-mile. Turn left onto East Street and immediately turn left onto Woodland Road. Travel 1.75-mile heading northeast and past the DCR-October State Forest Campground. The pavement will end, at the intersection where Woods Pond is directly ahead, turn right, head east skirting Woods Pond on your left. In 0.5-mile, Schermerhorn Road will turn steeply uphill on your right. Continue straight for 0.3-mile and park just after the stream's bridge on the left.

21. Silver Fox Cascades - Mt Greylock Reservation

Silver Fox Cascades-Cheshire, MA

Location: Bassett Brook. Mt. Greylock Reservation (Berkshire County)
Parking GPS: N42° 36' 38.01" W73° 9' 22.87" (Cheshire Harbor Trail)
Destination GPS: N42° 36' 40" W73° 10' 19" (North Bassett Brook Falls)
Destination GPS: N42° 36' 12" W73° 10' 14" (Silver Fox Cascades)
Parking GPS: N42° 35' 47.65" W73° 8' 43.26" (Fred Mason Road)
Destination GPS: N42° 35' 55.09" W73° 8' 59.34" (Lower Bassett Brook)
Wow Factor: 7 **Accessibility:** Moderate loop trail 4.0 miles RT.

Information: On the east side of the Mt Greylock Reservation in the foothills of Saddle-Ball Mountain, Bassett Brook is formed by a trio of tributaries, amongst them a few waterfalls and cascades can be found. Located on the *South Branch of Bassett Brook*, Silver Fox Cascades is the most captivating and attractive of all the sites mention here. As always, it seems to be a hit or miss and luck of the draw, along with good wet weather for water flow at these cascades or waterfalls to be at optimum. For the loop trail, access is best starting up the *Cheshire Harbor Trail* from its parking area and traveling in a counter-clock-wise manner. This approach is better for its gradual rate of ascent and the return descending down the Silver Fox Trail which is the steepest portion of the loop hike.

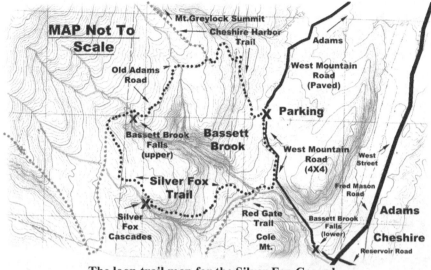

The loop trail map for the Silver Fox Cascades

Start up the Cheshire Harbor Trail, for 0.8 mile, until the first junction, the CHT continues north to the summit, turn left here onto the Old Adams Road heading southwest for 0.7 mile. At a stream crossing that may have a wooden snowmobile bridge, downhill is a small fall referred to as *Waterfall on the North Branch of Bassett Brook.* Not the most exciting, but runs well in the spring only.

Waterfall on the North Branch of Bassett Brook. Cheshire, MA

Continue pass the bridge for 0.2-mile, on the left, the junction of Silver Fox Trail begins to slowly descend and 0.6-mile east towards the top of the ravine, the cascades can be found. The slope descends steeply and quickly for the next 0.8-mile until towards the bottom where *The Red Gate Trail* junctions. Within the next 0.1-mile east, cross the stream (bridge) and connect with the West Mountain Road a dirt road on the other side of Bassett Brook. From here, turning left, back to the Cheshire Harbor Trail parking is 0.4-mile north.

Turning south for 0.5-mile until where the Bassett Brook passes beneath power lines is a configuration of boulders and the stream cascades, if they are running well, they will roar. Parking off Fred Mason Road and entry to these lower falls is much easier, 0.3-mile in from the Fire District Gate-Do not block! Again, not amazing, but fun.

Bassett Brook Lower Cascades and Boulders. Adams, MA

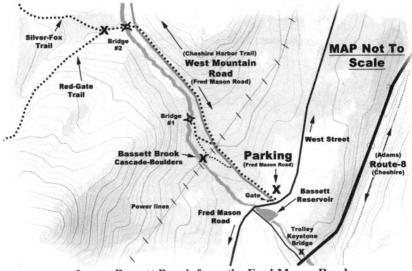

Lower Bassett Brook from the Fred Mason Road.

Bassett Brook Lower Cascades and Boulders. Adams, MA

Below the Bassett Brook Reservoir, 50-yards downstream from the dam spillway, is a small waterfall along with the old Cheshire Harbor Keystone Trolley Bridge further downstream, but before Route-8.

Old Trolley Keystone Bridge on Bassett Brook. From postcard, circa 1911.
(GPS: N42° 35' 38.83" W73° 8' 39.15")

22. Tannery Falls - Savoy State Forest

Tannery Falls on Ross Brook-Savoy State Forest. Savoy, MA

Location: Ross Brook. Savoy State Forest (Berkshire County)
Parking GPS: N42° 37' 19.72" W73° 0' 18.29" (Tannery Falls Parking)
Parking GPS: N42° 36' 55.39" W72° 59' 59.66" (Black Brook Road end)
Parking GPS: N42° 37' 25.16" W73° 2' 0.75" (New State Road end)
Destination GPS: N42° 37' 25.21" W73° 0' 12.57" (Parker Brook Falls)
Destination GPS: N42° 37' 26.74" W73° 0' 12.32" (Tannery Falls)
Wow Factor: 9 **Accessibility:** Moderate maintained trail. 0.6-mile-RT
Trail map; https://www.mass.gov/lists/dcr-trail-maps

Information: Tannery Falls is often mentioned as one the tallest waterfalls in Massachusetts. However, I am not sure what criteria are used to determine these comments. It certainly exceeds a vertical drop of 100 feet plus and is one of the tallest among DCR properties, (Bash Bish Falls itself has an 80 feet free fall into its pool below.) As a contender for the title of Massachusetts "tallest" or "longest" waterfall, Bear Rock Falls in Mt. Washington State Forest definitely is one tall and long impressive waterfall! During the spring run-off or from other periods of prolonged rain fall, the noted sections of upper, middle and lower of Bear Rock Falls becomes one uninterrupted cascade of water. In addition, another waterfall that can become a gusher is the left side of Twin Cascades in Florida, MA, but I digress.

Parker Brook Falls - Savoy State Forest - DCR. Savoy, MA

The good news is that if you visit Tannery Falls, you will also get to visit Parker Brook Falls only 100-yards away! You must descend to the bottom of the stairs and look back up-stream to view Parker Brook Falls, while Tannery Falls is over on Ross Brook, only 75-yards north. For Tannery Falls, the wet, smooth mossy rocks are very slippery with several falls requiring EMT's and medevac have occurred here in recent years. Yet, people persist to climb up the falls from the bottom. The stairs have been recently refurbished and rebuilt, use them.

Parker Brook Falls is fed from above by marshy Tannery Pond which warms the waters before the waterfall. Tannery Falls is fed by a woodland brook; Ross Brook has much cooler waters. It is mentioned that one can stand at the confluence of Ross Brook and Parker Brook with a foot in each and will able to feel the temperature difference. It's a good distraction for kids so as not to have them climb the falls looking for slippery rocks.

Directions: Off Route-116 near center of Savoy, turn north onto Center Rd (near Fire Station.) In 3.0-miles you will "T" into Adams Road, turn left, travel 0.2-mile and turn right onto New State Rd. After 1.3-miles Tannery Rd will be on you right. Tannery road is a dirt road which in the spring is muddy or is often washed out. If Tannery Road is not passable from the New State Road end, it is 1.8-miles hike to the Tannery Falls parking lot from here. However, from the top of the hill from the Black Brook Road end, it is only 0.5-mile to the Tannery Falls parking area, a much closer location to hike from if muddy or snowy conditions result in closure to Tannery Road.

23. Tory Cave Falls-Lenox

Tory Cave Falls – October Mountain State Forest. Lenoxdale, MA

Location: Roaring Brook-October State Forest DCR (Berkshire County)
Destination GPS: N42° 23' 49.08" W73° 16' 10.66 (Route-7 Turn Lenox)
Parking GPS: N42° 23' 16.08" W73° 14' 16.17" (Roaring Brook Road)
Destination GPS: N42° 23' 10.80" W73° 14' 3.50" (Tory Cave-Waterfall)
Wow Factor: 4 **Accessibility:** Easy short walk 0.5-mile RT

Information: By all accounts, *Tory Cave* is a historic and physical curiosity. It seems that *Tory Cave* obtained its name due to the fact that a Gideon Smith was a British loyalist who hid in this cave for several weeks during the Revolutionary War. Reportedly the cave did have ample room for Gideon for a stay. However, at the turn of the 20th century, an earthquake destroyed the natural cave structure trimming its depth down to just a few feet of over-hang. . In 2013, the deluge of rain from Hurricane Irene flooded Roaring Brook, which in turn eroded any remaining cave remnants. There is a small 4-foot waterfall above the cave location, along with a wide and deep fissure in the rocky stream bed this keeps a small pool suitable for wading or trout fishing. You cannot see the falls-pool from the trail, just past the trail for Dewy Hill (off on the left) and just as the path starts to go uphill, a foot path on the right goes down to the stream for access.

Location of Tory Cave and Falls. Lenox, MA

Directions: From Route-7 in Lenox, (GPS:) turn onto, heading east on New Lenox Road for 1.8-miles, just over the Housatonic River to the intersection of East New Lenox Road and New Lenox Road, turn right onto Roaring Brook Road. Heading south for 0.4-mile, at the small bridge is where Roaring Brook flows beneath the road. Parking and trailhead is just before the bridge and heads east up stream along the brook.

Tory Cave Falls – October Mountain State Forest. Lenoxdale, MA

24. Twin Cascades – Florida

Twin Cascades - (right side) Florida, MA

Location: River Road. Town of Florida (Berkshire County)
Parking GPS: N42° 40' 28.02" W72° 59' 44.32" (River Road)
Destination GPS: N42° 40' 36.12" W73° 0' 11.12" (Twin Cascades)
Destination GPS: N42° 40' 33.32" W73° 0' 7.65" (lower falls)
Wow Factor: 7 Accessibility: Moderate-unmarked foot-path 0.8 mile-RT

Information: With Twin Cascades you get two waterfalls for the price of one. At the base of the falls, you can look right to view a (3) tiered waterfall fed by Cascade Brook and then just look left for another equally magnificent waterfall cascading down its lofty hillside. They are both located 0.3-mile behind the eastern portal of the Hoosac Tunnel. Originally this was a water supply reservoir to operate steam boilers for pneumatic air compressors and drill equipment utilized in the construction of the legendary tunnel. There are remnants of the dam and piping still in place. The dam is now filled with rocks and silt. In addition, there is a smaller waterfall below the trail which is seen half way as you walk up from the tunnel portal.

The railroad tracks are posted and prohibit entry into the tunnel or tresspassing on the railroad tracks in general. There are frequent frieght trains through the tunnel in both directions. Massachusetts State and local police will enforce the no tresspassing. Trail access to the falls, is located to the right and behind the Hoosac Tunnel portal. Move quickly to become *Out of sight, is out of mind.*

At the beginning, quickly leave the railroad tracks behind skirting to the right of the eastern portal where a stream, old dam and sluiceway retaining wall. Crossing over the old dam you'll pick up a foot path on its other side, it will follow high and above on the left side of the Cascade Brook leading to the falls in 0.3-mile. Final access to falls is slippery rock and scaling the old upper dam.

Twin Cascades are not maintained by any organization, the trails are narrow and good hiking boots are recommended. There are no markings, stairs, or ladders to assist hikers. Swimming is not applicable. While the falls have no posting, access from the Hoosac Tunnel portal is posted. Other "Bushwhacking" access points will encounter very steep 50° to 65° slopes or greater with slippery moss-covered rocks or loose humus soil, not environmentally recommended.

Twin Cascades – (left side) Florida, MA

Directions: From the top of Whitcomb Summit, Florida, MA take Route-2 east for 0.5-mile, turn left down onto Monroe Road/Whitcomb Hill Road, quickly take your 1st right and follow Whitcomb Hill Road steeply downhill (1.9-miles) to where it "T's" into River Road. Turn Left onto River Road and drive 0.8-mile, park before the railroad crossing on the Deerfield River Catch and Release area on the right. Staying well away from the railroad tracks and staying next to the old retaining wall of the old sluiceway near the tunnel portal. Note: In the summer, there is often a large growth of stinging nettle by this sluiceway until you clamor over the end wall and follow the trail up to the falls. Upon return, use caution again around this active rail line as you exit from the woodlands.

25. Umpachene Falls - New Marlborough

Umpachene Falls - New Marlborough, MA

Location: Umpachene Falls Road, New Marlborough (Berkshire County)
Parking GPS: N42° 5' 42.07" W73° 16' 15.75"
Destination GPS: N42° 5' 37.47" W73° 16' 17.26" (View Point)
Wow Factor: 8 **Accessibility:** Roadside, level walk, 100-yards to falls.

Information: Operated by the Town of New Marlborough the park provides a swimming and picnic area for its residents, although short visits to the falls are permitted for non-residents. Umpachene Falls is easy to access and readily flows year-around.

Directions: From the Mill River section of New Marlborough, head south and turn right onto Mill River Rd, travel south 1.4-miles and take the 1st left onto a dirt Umpachene Falls Road, down a slight hill and over a small 1-lane bridge. Off-season, you will often find a cabled gate at the park's entry. If the gate is open enter the dirt parking lot which is just inside the park. From here walk south across the lawn to the river where the falls are located.

As of this writing the small bridge has been closed to vehicle traffic. Park in front of the temporary cement barriers for the short walk across the bridge into the park then back to the rear to find the waterfalls.

26. Wahconah Falls - Dalton

Wahconah Falls (lower) - Dalton, MA

Location: Wahconah Falls Road. DCR. Dalton (Berkshire County)
Parking GPS: N42° 29' 21.70"N W73° 6' 54.15"
Destination GPS: N42° 29' 16.28" W73° 6' 54.19" (Lower Falls)
Destination GPS: N42° 29' 14.08" W73° 6' 50.85" (Upper Falls)
Destination GPS: N42° 29' 13.30" W73° 6' 46.87" (Mill Foundation)
Destination GPS: N42° 29' 11.47" W73° 6' 44.93" (Soap Stone Mine)
Destination GPS: N42°29' 18.30" W73° 6'36.07" (Dam)
Wow Factor: 8 **Accessibility:** Short walk to main falls 0.1-mile.

Information: Situated on 48 wooded acres the park is operated by the Department of Conservation and Recreation. Wahconah Falls is one of the most popular and dynamic waterfalls in Berkshire County, while at the same time being one of the easiest to access. The Main block of falls is ~40-feet-tall and can often be seen with an impressive display of careening and churning water or it may dwindle down to a dribble of water. Some of this variation is the result by the Windsor Reservoir Dam located approximately 0.5-mile upstream, although there are no daily water releases. FYI: The main lower waterfall is actually in Windsor, while the upper waterfall is in Hinsdale and the parking lot is in situated in Dalton.

While no marked trail is provided, many will access the brink of the falls by back-tracking on the entry path some 50-feet to where the rocky cobble gives way to sloped woodland. Just before the actual brink, a higher rocky outcrop is noted as "Lover's Leap" this where the grieving Princess Wahconah jumped? Waterfalls are beautiful, but dangerous. Jumping and swimming here have seen accidents with some turning deadly. The lower pool is posted with *"No Swimming"* signs.

Continuing up stream there are many small pools and rocks; within 100 yards you will encounter another small impressive double tiered waterfall. You may have noticed that the embankment and landscape has been disrupted by hand-dug sluiceways diverting the water to turn waterwheels for a gristmill or lumber-mill. Above the second waterfall is another large, hand-built fieldstone foundation which was an old talc mill. All being a reminder how early inhabitants and their resolve to obtain power from the water with gravity. In addition, where the stream turns 90° north, on the opposite-side, is an old hand dug soap-stone mine.

Booth-Bardin Saw Mill Site-Wahconah Falls-(upper stream) Dalton, MA

There are many, many legends and lore written about the naming of Wahconah Falls. All center upon the extremely lovely Princess Wahconah of the Pequot tribe. Nessacus, a young brave from the Wampanoag tribe, happens to fend off a bear saving Wahconah's life while she is bathing at the pool. Both become infatuated with each other. Unfortunately, a conflict arises as the princess is already betrothed to an older brave from the Mohawk tribe. Tashmu the Pequot's Tribe medicine man devises a plan to have Wahconah set adrift in a canoe upstream allowing the "Great Spirit" to decide which brave would be her suitor according to which side of a rock the canoe flows by.

As it would happen, Tashmu also has his allegiance to the Mohawk brave and instructs the older brave to deepen the channel causing a swifter and deeper current to insure diverting the canoe in the Mohawk's direction.

The day arrives, Wahconah is set adrift upstream, and as the canoe approaches the deciding rock it appears to be swiftly heading towards the Mohawk side. Then…unexpectedly, the canoe makes a decisive turn and ends up drifting over to Nessacus. Tashmu perplexed, has to agree that the Great Spirit has spoken. Later, Tashmu investigates, he finds that Wahconah had fashioned a rudder from a stick, for she knew what side of the rock she wanted the canoe to flow pass.

But wait, there is more! Other versions offer that Nessacus dies while dueling the other brave… or… falls to his death in a contest of bravery leaping across the falls from *Lover Leap*..or.. is called to battle and does not return. In any event, distraught with grief, the Princess Wahconah jumps from *Lovers Leap* falling to her death and that is why we call them Wahconah Falls.

Wahconah Falls Stream Trail Map.

Directions: From the junction of Route-8 & Route-9 in Dalton, travel north on Route-9 for 2.3-miles. Turn right onto Wahconah Falls Road, travel 0.5-mile, through a small mobile home park, the road turns to dirt and travels over a small hill to the falls paved parking lot. During off-season or during winter months, the road may not be passable or not fully plowed. Hiking from where the plow creates a snow berm, caution in parking, for it is often considered a snow-plow turn around. In addition, the gates to the parking area can be closed to vehicle access.

27. Windsor Jambs - Windsor

Windsor Jambs - Windsor, MA

Location: School House Road. DCR Windsor (Berkshire County)
Parking GPS: N42° 31' 23.91" W72° 59' 33.54" (Windsor Jambs)
Wow Factor: 7 **Accessibility:** Roadside, short walk 0.1 mile

Information: Windsor State Forest is operated by the Department of Conservation and Recreation, and for many years been a location with swimming, camping, hiking and the "Jambs" for recreation. For the past several years with Boston's budget cuts, all swimming and camping facilities have ceased operations. Although, access to the Jambs is still allowed. The waterfalls alone are not spectacular, but the gorge is impressive with sheer 50 to 80-feet stone vertical walls and 30-feet-in-width. The Jambs gorge runs south ~ 0.2-mile, for safety, fencing runs along the edge of this gorge to prevent accidental falls. The upper end of the gorge has the best views and limited access to the stream before the fence starts.

Directions: Accessible by River Road that runs between Route-9 from West Cummington or from Route-116 in Savoy. Driving from either end, it is 3.0-miles to where the DCR parks swimming area and campground are located. From River Rd, turn up onto Lower Road and follow straight through a hemlock forest across Windigo Road (0.4-mile) from River Road. Another 0.3-mile to the next intersection, bear right onto School House Road, in 0.1-mile you will see the parking area gate for the Jambs. The gate is seasonally open May to October.

28. Woodchuck Falls - Cheshire

Woodchuck Falls a.k.a Bridalveil Falls - Cheshire, MA

Location: Fish & Wild Life Management. (Berkshire County)
Parking GPS: N42° 33' 26.33" W73° 7' 28.70" (Windsor Road)
Destination GPS: N42° 32' 55.00" W73° 7' 23.00" (Waterfall)
Wow Factor: 7 **Accessibility:** Unmarked trail ~ 2.0-mile RT

Information: For unnamed waterfalls, a status quo approach is by attaching to geographical landmarks such as Woodchuck Hill from where this stream originates, hence Woodchuck Falls. Previous ascertainment among neighbors, town assessors and longtime residents couldn't remember any moniker other than "The Falls." Massachusetts Wildlife Management had no name for these falls, an old map had the brook penciled in as *"Prince Falls"* but that did not work, for who, why or how did they derived to the name was unsettling. Originally between friends, we called it *"Horse Head Falls"* for such a skull was found slightly above them, but that was not right either. At low water flow *"Bridalveil Falls"* does fit the nature of this waterfall nicely, but during higher volumes it may not. In addition, the name is a cliché that several waterfalls already have in New England and the northeast.

Directions: In Cheshire, from the traffic light junction of Route-8 and Church Street, head east down through Cheshire center for 0.5-mile. Church Street quickly changes into Main Street, go pass the Ashuwillticook Rail Trail and shortly after crossing a small bridge, turn right onto East Main Street. .

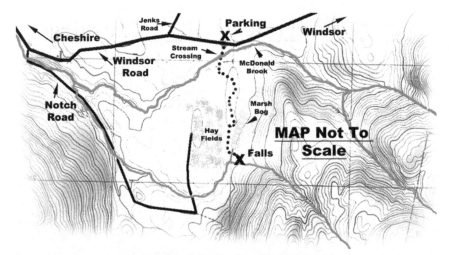

Woodchuck Falls Trail – Cheshire, MA

In 0.2-mile, East Main Street become Windsor Road; continue uphill for an additional 1.5-mile. You will go uphill, pass the turn for Notch Road (on your right), level out and then go uphill again, at the top of the 2nd hill Jenks Road will be on your left. Continue downhill, at the sump or bottom of this hill is where the entry into the Massachusetts Fish & Game Wildlife Management Area. If you start to go uphill again you missed it. No sign, no markings. Park well off on either side of the road. The farm gate is no longer intact; a steel cable is strung across between trees. There is evidence of other people using this access.

From Windsor Road, an old over grown woodland road starts downhill, shortly you will come to McDonald Brook, there is no permanent bridge here and you need to cross the brook going in and out. Usually, it is not that bad. Once on the other side, do not take the first old road on your left, go straight 100-yards and follow the other old road, uphill, slightly eroded. Continue on this road as it heads east and winds around heading south for 0.3-mile. At this point **do not enter the private hay field;** Do bushwhack through the woodlands staying parallel to the field for 0.1-mile until reaching another woodland road with a wooden plank over the bog stream. Cross the stream and follow the road 0.1-mile until you reach the falls.

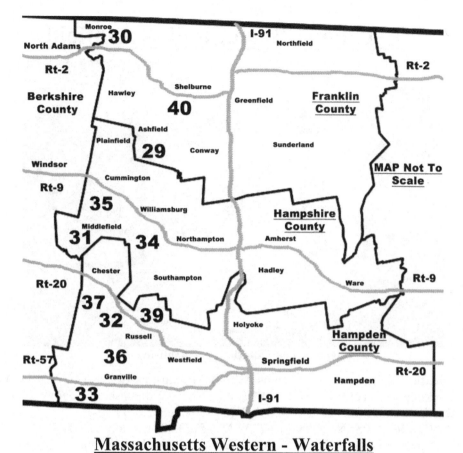

Massachusetts Western - Waterfalls

29. Chapel Brook Falls. Trustee of the Reservations: (Ashfield)
30. Dunbar Brook. Monroe State Forest-DCR: (Monroe)
31. Glendale Falls. Trustees of Reservations: (Middlefield)
32. Goldmine Falls. Chester State Forest-DCR: (Chester)
33. Granville Falls. Granville State Forest-DCR: (Granville)
34. Manhan Falls. (Westhampton)
35. Oak Hill Cascades. (Chesterfield)
36. Pitcher Falls. Noble View Center - AMC: (Russell)
37. Rivulet Falls. Trustees of Reservation: (Cummington)
38. Sanderson Brook Falls. Chester State Forest-DCR: (Chester)
39. Shatterack Brook Falls. (Russell)
40. Sluice Brook Falls. Mahican-Mohawk Trail: (Shelburne)

29. Chapel Brook Falls - Ashfield

Chapel Brook Falls (lower) – Ashfield, MA

Location: Trustee of Reservations Ashfield (Hampshire County)
Parking GPS: N42° 28' 57.22" W72° 45' 36.86" (Williamsburg Road)
Destination GPS: N42° 28' 56.84" W72° 45' 35.66" (Top Falls)
Destination GPS: N42° 28' 57.42" W72° 45' 33.89" (Middle Falls)
Destination GPS: N42° 28' 58.00" W72° 45' 32.60" (Lower Falls)
Wow Factor: 9 **Accessibility:** Easy short Trail 0.2-mile RT

Information: Located in southeast Ashfield, Chapel Falls Reservation borders upon The DAR-DCR State Forest in Goshen and Conway State Forest to its east. The original endowment and 173 acres were by Mrs. Henry T. Curtiss in 1964 in memory of her husband. Two main sections lie within close proximity to each other. The Chapel Brook Falls consist of 3-waterfalls 10, 15 and 25-feet-high, just downstream from the parking area and readily accessible on an easy foot path. The lowest waterfall is probably the most dynamic with good waterfall with a wading pool below.

Above the falls is Pony Mountain a.k.a. Chapel Ledge, its trail ascends to the 1,420-foot summit vista, half-way up you will pass its popular 100-foot sheer cliff which attracts experienced rock climbers and beginners as well. A complete venture to both locations comes complete with a good dose of serenity with minimal effort and time.

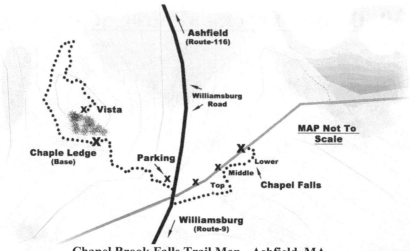

Chapel Brook Falls Trail Map.- Ashfield, MA

From Ashfield center, travel east on Route-116 into South Ashfield for 1.5-mile, at the sharp bend/fork in Route-116, bear right taking Williamsburg Road south for 2.2-miles. You'll notice Trustees of Reservation sign for Chapel Brook, park here or across the road where a small lane is located.

From Williamsburg center, off Route-9, follow Ashfield Road, north (becomes Williamsburg Road), for 6.7-miles until the parking area on your left.

Chapel Brook Falls (middle) - Ashfield, MA

30. Dunbar Brook - Monroe State Forest

Dunbar Brook Falls - Monroe, MA

Location: Raycroft Road. Monroe State Forest (Franklin County)
Parking GPS: N42° 43' 12.84" W72° 59' 30.19" (Tilda-Main Road Entry)
Parking GPS: N42° 43' 09.88" W72° 59' 31.62" (Parking Area)
Destination GPS: N42° 43' 10.48" W72° 59' 30.64" (Lower Falls)
Wow Factor: 6 **Accessibility:** No Trail-Rock Hopping. 0.2 mile-RT

Information: I favor this approach and locale at the top of the Dunbar Brook Trail for its large area of rock for sun basking along with a couple of cascading waterfalls and pools to savour on sunny summer days. The Dunbar Brook Trail does descend an additional 2.5-miles to River Road in Florida. You can continue downstream and undoubtedly discover more cascades or pools as you descend. I have not exerted myself choosing to stay put enjoying the brook as it splashes around, down and over the rocks or boulders to a small waterfall at its base.

Directions: From North Adams at Hairpin turn on Route-2, head east for 2.5-miles. When you come to Tilda Hill Road (Fire Station on the corner), turn left and proceed north for 4.1-miles. Turn right at the sign for the DCR Monroe State Forest onto unpaved, unmarked Raycroft Road, head downhill for 100-feet and cross over the Dunbar Brook bridge to a dirt parking or park immediately to your left near the Kiosk and walk over. The falls are adjacent to the parking area with large rocky surfaces giving access to them or for sunning oneself.

31. Glendale Falls - Middlefield

Glendale Falls - Middlefield, MA

Location: Trustees of Reservation. Middlefield (Hampshire County)
Parking GPS: N42° 20' 59.30" W72° 58' 0.90" (Clark-Wright Road)
Destination GPS: N42° 21' 1.99" W72° 57' 59.91" (Old Mill Foundation)
Destination GPS: N42° 21' 2.93" W72° 57' 55.64" (Bottom of Falls)
Wow Factor: 8 **Accessibility:** Short moderate trail 0.5-mile-RT

Information: This cascading waterfall is noted for having an overwhelming water-flow during the spring thaw, but later being reduced to a mere trickle during the summer months. The center piece to this 60-acre Trustees of Reservation property, is the 160-foot cascading waterfall, along with its pool and some old grist mill ruins. Descending on a short 0.1-mile improved trail to its pool below makes access to the falls is relatively easy. Returning back uphill while short, will require some effort. An old field stone foundation can be found across the stream at the top of the falls just inside the tree line.

Directions: From Peru center, follow Route-143 east for 3.8-miles. Turn right onto River Road in West Worthington, follow this road for 5.5-miles and turn right onto Clark-Wright Road. Go uphill for 0.4-mile, just before a small bridge on your right; you will notice a Trustees of Reservation sign at the opening of a parking lot with room for several cars. A trail to the waterfall's bottom starts behind the kiosk, the kiosk also has additional information or directions.

32. Goldmine Falls - Chester

Goldmine Falls (lower) 100 yards upstream from Route-20. Chester, MA

Location: Route-20 Chester-Blandford State Forest (Hampden County)
Parking GPS: N42° 14' 51.77" W72° 55' 27.70" (Route-20 parking)
Destination GPS: N42° 14' 48.30" W72° 55' 30.41" (Lower Falls)
Destination GPS: N42° 14' 47.20" W72° 55' 30.30" (Upper Falls)
Wow Factor: 8 **Accessibility:** Easy side of moderate 0.1 mile.

Information: This waterfall is rather hidden, has no maintained trail, yet is surprisingly easier to find and access than one would think. Located on Goldmine Brook, approximately 300-feet upstream from a cement bridge-culvert where it crosses beneath Route-20. You will need to bushwhack up through the woodlands on the eastern side of the brook; you might find a worn foot-path just prior to the guardrail, although leaves and debris may cover this. An upper waterfall is located just above the lower falls, both are very nice.

Directions: From Chester, junction of Middlefield Road/Main Street and Route-20, drive east on Route-20. After 2.5-miles you will go pass the parking area for Sanderson Brook Falls on the right, continue east on Route-20 for an additional 1.5-miles. Just as Route-20 starts to straighten you'll be looking for a large cement bridge/culvert with large boulders uphill. You will find an unimproved parking pull-off on the Westfield River side in a short distance. Bushwhack up the forested hill following the Goldmine Brook up on the left side; it is easier to get above the lower falls to the upper falls with a flanking maneuver on the left side.

Goldmine Falls (upper) - Chester, MA

Despite the name Goldmine Falls, I find no reference to any actual gold mining attempt or operation in the area. There has been emery, soap stone or mica mines. Perhaps an optimistic prospector panning the gold expecting a favorable outcome, but died broke. I can say that in October when the foliage is lit by a setting sun, the forest does become an exquisite shimmering expanse of golden woodlands.

A wider view of the upper Goldmine Falls.

33. Granville Falls - DCR

Granville Falls - Hubbard Brook-Granville, MA

Location: West Hartland Road, Granville State Forest (Hampden County)
Parking GPS: N42° 3' 49.79" W72° 57' 56.76" (Parking Near Bridge)
Destination GPS: N42° 3' 31.10" W72° 57' 51.20" (Emerald Rock)
Destination GPS: N42° 3' 20.80" W72°57' 45.20"(Grandville Falls-Pool)
Wow Factor: 7 **Accessibility:** Easy short walk to falls only. 1.4-mile RT

Information: On a sunny spring, summer or fall day, a hike down the northern side of Hubbard Brook, is ripe with cascades and is an easy hike any time of the year. From the bridge, the first 0.5-mile is paved road; it leads down to a now defunct camping and picnic area. From where the pavement ends the main trail is obvious, within 0.2-mile, a smaller side path (unmarked) returns over towards the Hubbard Brook where it narrows down and creates a small waterfall with an excellent pool. (It is posted *No Diving or Jumping from the cliffs*.) Otherwise, the trail continues down near the brook revealing many other cascades with smaller pools and sunny rocks.

> Cascades A GPS: N42° 3' 13.30" W72° 57' 38.10"
> Cascades B GPS: N42° 2' 59.80" W72° 57' 15.80"
> Cascades C GPS: N42° 2' 59.00" W72° 57' 14.20"

Other items we found is a large boulder covered completely in an emerald-colored moss, hence *Emerald Rock*. Directly on the trail below the falls some is a large rusting heat-exchanger-boiler. Since streams and waterfalls were utilized for power, it might have been a boiler in the modernization of an earlier sawmill or tannery. (Idk)

Cascades on Hubbard Brook - Granville State Park, MA

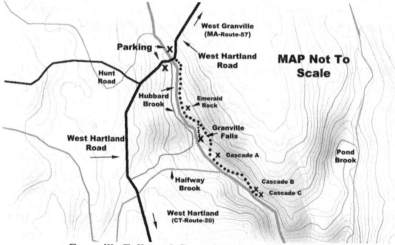

Granville Falls and Cascades along Hubbard Brook.

Directions: From the junction of Route-8 (South Main Street) and Route-57 (Tolland Road) in Sandisfield, head east on Route-57 for 6.5 miles towards West Granville. On your right, (you may see the sign for Granville State Forest), turn onto West Hartland Road and head south for 1.0 mile. When you come to the bridge over Hubbard Brook Park either end, but follow the paved road down on the north side of the bridge. Where the pavement ends, the trail leads inland away, but parallel to the brook. Seek a worn foot-path that will lead to falls or can bypass the falls continuing down additional 0.6 mile to Cascade C.

34. Manhan Falls -Westhampton

Manhan Falls – Perry Hill Road Extension – Westhampton, MA

Location: Perry Hill Road Extension, Westhampton (Hampshire County)
Parking GPS: N42° 19' 6.70" W72° 46' 17.24" (Parking Near Bridge)
Destination GPS: N42° 19' 8.45" W72° 46' 18.58" (Manhan Falls)
Wow Factor: 6 **Accessibility:** Roadside

Information: Small roadside falls, private dwellings border upon Manhan River, but no postings noted. Park away from the dwelling across the small bridge and access up-stream from that western side to the falls. A short over grown road parallels the river's western border.

The Manhan River begins near the towns of Huntington, flowing southeast through Westhampton and Southampton. The river continues southeast, then turns northeasterly and flows through the middle of Easthampton merging with the Connecticut River at the "Oxbow."

Directions: From the junction of Route-9/Route-10/ Route-66 in the center of Northampton, follow Route-66 west for 5.8-miles for Easthampton Road, or 7.2-miles turning right onto Southampton Road. Turn onto Southampton Road, head northerly for 1.2-miles, crossing over Stage Road; continue northerly for 0.4-mile until junction with North Road, cross directly over North Road onto Perry Hill Road.

Go north for 0.4-mile turn left onto Perry Hill Road Extension, a gravel side road which begins passing as a narrow lane through a busy sand & stone processing facility. Drive 0.3-mile to the small bridge that crosses the Manhan River. The falls are up-stream. Crossing the bridge and following the gravel road 0.1-mile up to Kings Highway – Easthampton Road.

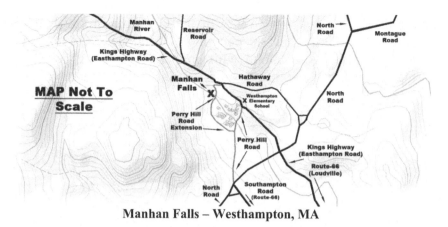

Manhan Falls – Westhampton, MA

35. Oak Hill Falls - Chesterfield

Oak Hill Cascades (lower) – Chesterfield, MA

Location: Fish & Game Management. Chesterfield (Hampshire County)
Parking GPS: N42° 25' 5.65" W72° 50' 59.86" (Willcut Road)
Destination GPS: N42° 25' 11.50" W72° 51' 41.10" (Cascade upper)
Destination GPS: N42° 25' 12.20" W72° 51' 44.90" (Cascade lower)
Wow Factor: 7 **Accessibility:** Moderate to Strenuous-no trail 2.0-mile RT

Information: Oak Hill Wildlife Management Area in Chesterfield recently acquired parcels of land extending its boundaries now to include Oak Hill Brook Cascades. These cascades empty into the Westfield River and are the most dynamic from its river embankment and uphill for the last ~150-yards of the Oak Hill Brook. Did I say steep? The downhill slope steepens more at its base, it is not a cliff, although trekking poles along with good boots will be helpful and during winter month's some sort of crampons would be a good option.

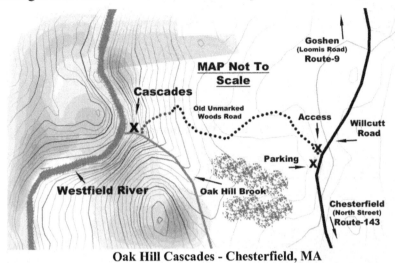

Oak Hill Cascades - Chesterfield, MA

Directions: From the center of Chesterfield (First Congregational Church on the corner) take North Street heading north for 0.9-miles to the intersection of Smith Road, Damon Pond Road and Willcutt Road. Continue across onto Willcutt Road, heading north for 1.0-mile. Shortly after the pavement ends, on the left, a small dirt pull-off parking area for 3-4 cars will be found. From the parking area directly west, there is wetland and boggy woodlands; it is not a good way to go.

The best access point at this time is 100-yards further north on Willcutt Road where the boundary for the Wildlife Management area is also located. On the left is an old road, slightly over-gown with a few downed trees, if followed westerly for ~0.6-mile, it will provide the best access inland until it reaches the brink of a steep embankment that descends to the Westfield River. Once here, you need to descend, but you also need to sweep over southerly across the slope to reach the breath of the cascades. Leaving the trail and bushwhacking across the slope be mindful of safety and environment impact of your actions. In addition, relatively remember where this road is located for the return trek. As mentioned, this is a relatively new and undeveloped area for the public to visit with little if any trail markings or development.

Returning from the river's edge and following uphill along the cascades, the rocks are slippery, along with steep terrain and with no developed or maintained trail. It can become strenuous for many; you will need good shoes and there will be exertion for young and old alike. Sooner or later, you will need to bear uphill away from the stream and cascades, heading closer to the top your path needs to head northeasterly, seeking the road you followed in.

36. Pitcher Falls - Russell

Pitcher Falls (Big) – AMC Noble View Center. Russell, MA

Location: AMC 635 South Quarter Road. Russell, (Hampden County)
Parking GPS: N42° 8' 20.55" W72° 52' 1.88" (Main Gate Kiosk)
Parking GPS: N42° 8' 5.96" W72° 51' 41.32" (Visitor's Parking Lot)
Destination GPS: N42° 7' 46.20" W72° 52' 15.10" (Pitcher Falls-Little)
Destination GPS: N42° 7' 42.78" W72° 52' 14.43" (Pitcher Falls-Big)
Wow Factor: 7 **Accessibility:** Easy side of Moderate Trails

Information: The trek to Pitcher Brook Falls is well-marked with many signs at trail junctions making it very pleasurable to hike at the Appalachian Mountain Club's, Noble View Outdoor Center. For an outdoor enthusiast, the 358-acres consists of well-maintained trails through reforested farm fields, woodlands, stone walls, cellar holes and streams is perfect for all levels of hikers. If the main gate is closed or if one has concerns of being locked-in after dark, one can park at the main gate and hike from there. Otherwise, drive 0.5-mile on the gravel road and park at the visitor's parking lot. There is a suggested donation fee for visitors.

The *Pitcher Brook Trail* starts from the lower southeast corner of the visitor's parking lot (Post #4.) The trail meanders slightly and crosses other trail junctions (Posts #14, 15, 16) just stay straight on the red-blazed trail. In 0.4 mile from the visitor's parking lot, you will reach Post #17 where the *Border Trail* from the main gate will junction with the Pitcher Brook Trail. From this junction, continue west on the Pitcher Brook trail, you will reach Little Pitcher Brook Falls in 0.1-mile. Both falls have large pools at their bases, but require scrambling down embankments which causes damage to various mosses, lichen and plants.

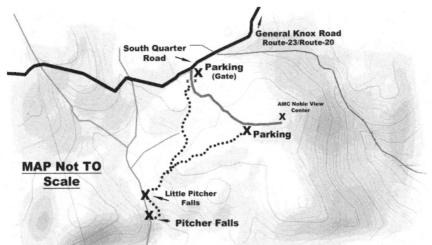

Trail to Pitcher Falls - AMC Noble View Center - Russell, MA

Main gate: From the main gate kiosk, hike up the road 0.1 mile, on the right, the *Border Trail* (Post #2) is blazed with yellow markings. Follow the trail 0.5 mile until it junctions the Pitcher Brook Trail (Post #17). This is the same location as if you came from the other visitor's parking area. Either entry is essentially the same distance to Post #17. Turn right, onto the red blazed Pitcher Brook Falls Trail. Continue west on the Pitcher Brook trail, you will reach *Little Pitcher Brook* Falls in 0.1 mile. Another 0.1 mile downstream is Pitcher Brook Falls.

Directions: From the junction of Route-202/10 with Route-20 in Westfield, travel west on Route 20 (Franklin Street) towards Russell for 5.75-miles, turning left onto Route-23 (Blandford Road.) Continue uphill and west on Route-23 for 1.6-mile, turning left onto General Knox Road. Head south for 1.3-mile, turning right onto South Quarter Road. Heading west for 1.2-mile, the entry main gate to Noble View Center is on your left.

37. Rivulet Road Falls - Cummington

Roaring Brook Falls - Old Rivulet Road-Cummington, MA

Location: Old Rivulet Road. Cummington (Hampshire County)
Parking GPS: N42° 28' 31.07" W72° 55' 21.20" (Old Rivulet Road)
Destination GPS: N42° 28' 26.20" W72° 55' 19.90" (Roaring Brook)
Destination GPS: N42° 28' 27.93" W72° 55' 23.24" (Rivulet Brook)
Wow Factor: 6 **Accessibility:** Old Rivulet Road-abandon. 0.2-mile RT

Information: Off of Route-9 in Cummington, Rivulet Road is an old paved road that has been abandon for some time now. Of interest here are two brooks that flow downhill from the William Cullen Bryant Homestead above. Both Roaring Brook and Rivulet Brook flow into the Westfield River with each having cascades or small waterfalls. Above, at his homestead, *The Rivulet Trail* winds through old growth forest and follows the Rivulet Brook, but there is no direct trail down to this location which is the bottom most point to the Trustees of the Reservations property.

The abandon road has weathered badly, with culverts eroded, large piles of dirt and rubble placed to restrict entry or passage by 4x4's or ATV, along with the moss and bramble, it can be slippery and aggravating as well. As you enter, within 150-feet you will encounter the washed-out culvert of Rivulet Brook, the cascades and small waterfall(s) can be seen upstream. (Rivulet Brook is noted to be the inspiration for Bryant's poem *The Rivulet*.) The Roaring Brook Falls is reached 300-feet further in by skirting around dirt piles before reaching a dilapidated cement bridge span. Roaring Brook Falls can run with vigor and judging by the bridge span it has taken its toll upon it. Noticed in my initial visit, there was a large and deep pool built up behind the bridge. Although, the plug of debris must have become unplugged for no pool has not existed lately.

The Rivulet Brook-Old Rivulet Road - Cummington, MA

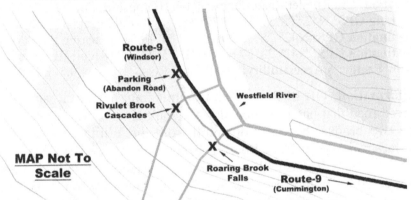

Trail Map of Old Rivulet Road - Cummington, MA

Directions: In Cummington, at the junction where Route-112 and Route-9, follow Route-9 west for 1.25-miles. On the left there is an old street sign where the woodlands meet the open field. Set-back 100-feet the old Rivulet runs parallel to Route-9. Just 0.1-mile prior on the left, is an old rest area where additional parking can be found.

38. Sanderson Brook Falls - Chester

Sanderson Brook Falls – Chester, MA

Location: Chester-Blandford State Forest, DCR (Hampden County)
Parking GPS: N42° 15' 20.78" W72° 56' 49.48" (Sanderson Brook Road)
Turn off trail to falls: N42° 14' 46.10" W72° 57' 22.60"
Destination GPS: N42° 14' 42.50" W72° 57' 25.70" (View Point)
Wow Factor: 8 **Accessibility:** Easy 2.2-mile RT

Bridge A: N42° 15' 15.92" W72° 56' 53.75"
Bridge B: N42° 14' 59.00" W72° 57' 11.76"
Bridge C: N42° 14' 54.98" W72° 57' 13.55"

Information: Located in Chester-Blandford State Forest, the hike to these particular falls is pleasant and impressive. From the parking area, head south on the gravel service road (Sanderson Brook Road.) Pass by the gate and cross the 1st bridge. The road is level and easy to follow as you walk beside the babbling Sanderson Brook; you will cross over 2 more steel grated bridges. After crossing the 3rd bridge the road will go uphill, continue ~0.2-mile until on the right, a narrow foot path will descend to the brook and to the base of the falls. The top block of the falls has a distinctive up-kick that at times is rather impressive jettisoning up and out 10 to 15-feet from the base of the falls. The rest of the falls cascades down and can be approached by hiking up rocks with care for they can be very slippery.

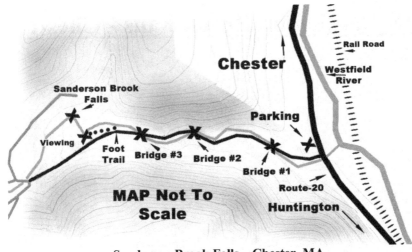

Sanderson Brook Falls – Chester, MA

Directions: In Huntington: at Route-20 junction with Route-112, head west on Route-20 for 4.2-miles. The DCR parking area for Sanderson Brook will be on your left.

From Main Street Chester center: drive east on Route-20 for 2.5-miles. On the right, across from a lumber yard, is the entry to a gravel parking area denoted by a DCR sign. From the parking area hike up the gated gravel road, your 1.0-mile from the falls.

39. Shatterack Brook Falls - Russell

Shatterack Falls #1.   Russell, MA

Location: Fish & Game Management. Russell (Hampden County)
Parking GPS: N42° 11' 57.53" W72° 50' 9.33" (Russell Road)

Destination GPS: N42° 10' 54.7" W72° 50' 31.96" (#1)
Destination GPS: N42° 11' 9.70" W72° 50' 24.17" (#2)
Destination GPS: N42° 11' 10.71" W72° 50' 22.41" (#3)
Destination GPS: N42° 11' 13.00" W72° 50' 19.80" (#4)
Destination GPS: N42° 11' 21.65" W72° 50' 14.81" (#5)
Wow Factor: 6 Accessibility: Moderate to difficult. No trail markings.

Information: Shatterarck Falls are on Shatterack Brook, which flows down Shatterack Mountain, there are 5-small waterfalls and cascades with #1 at the bottom being the favorite. Recently acquired by Massachusetts Wildlife Management the property is rugged and not developed, having no facilities, trail maintenance or markings. Shatterack Brook and a woodland road originate from Russell Road descending downwards towards the Westfield River and rail-tracks 1.25-mile below. Russell Road thoroughfare is seasonal and has limited unimproved parking areas at the top. The 5-waterfalls are strung along the lower half of the brook and will require off-trail bushwhacking; the road follows the brook meandering along usually within ear shot of its babble. Listening for the waterfall locations by their increased din within the woodland tranquility for there are no signs. Approaching the brook, you may encounter slippery rocks and unsure footings. Good footwear along with trekking poles will assist your stability and safety.

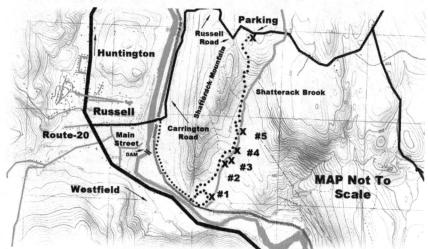

Shatterack Brook Falls - Russell, MA

Directions: From Route-20 in Russell: turn onto Main Street and travel 0.5-miles across the bridge over the Westfield River and railroad tracks. Bearing left onto Carrington Road, north for 1.4-miles, crossing into Montgomery, Russell Road will junction at a 45° angle on your right. Turn and travel uphill for 1.4 mile and just over the top and after a sharp left and right chicane, an unmarked dirt 4x4 road on your right with an unimproved parking area only. In addition, this access road is seasonal, being barricaded closed during the winter and re-opened in the spring by the town. Hiking from the top down, means hiking back up, however it is the safest approach.

From under the Main Street, Westfield River Bridge, following the railroad tracks East 0.7-mile to the first dirt road for the upper falls #2 to #5, an additional 0.1-mile down the tracks to the second dirt path in and away from the R&R tracks within 0.1-mile will bring you to the Shatterack #1 the main waterfall. Access from here does create a parking situation or safety concern, there is no sanctioned parking or trail, heed all postings, tread quickly and away from tracks for Amtrak and freight trains are active here on a daily basis.

#5 (left)   Shatterack Brook Falls. Russell, MA   #2 (Right)

40. Sluice Brook Falls - Shelburne

Sluice Brook Falls - (upper) - Deerfield River. Shelburne, MA

Parking GPS: N42° 35' 37.04" W72° 43' 34.30" (Route-2 Trailhead)
Parking GPS: N42° 35' 24.69" W72° 43' 8.56" (Wilcox Hollow Road)
Parking GPS: N42° 33' 26.07" W72° 40' 41.17" (Bardwells Ferry Road)
Destination GPS: N42° 34' 42.92" W72° 42' 27.36" (Falls-lower)
Destination GPS: N42° 34' 44.00" W72° 42' 25.43" (Falls-upper)
Wow Factor: 7 **Accessibility:** Moderate to difficult, poorly marked.

Information: A historic and unique 5-mile section of the Mahican-Mohawk Recreation Trail follows along the Deerfield River from the Shelburne State Forest-Wilcox Hollow to Bardwells Ferry Bridge. In 2005, this was an uninterrupted trail 5-mile trail, but things have changed. The corridor of this historic Native American path now has a portion of private property closed thereby preventing the 1.1-mile access from Wilcox Hollow to Sluice Brook Falls. Access to the Sluice Brook Falls, now requires one to start from the Bardwell Ferry and hike 2.5 miles to reach the falls and return the same way.

Route-2 Trailhead: In Shelburne, just 0.2-mile east of the Massachusetts State Police station is large dirt parking area and trailhead for the Mahican-Mohawk trail. I prefer go an additional 0.4-mile on Route-2 east and turn right onto Wilcox Hollow, a gravel road down to the Deerfield River. Heading east from Wilcox Hollow, it is approximately 1.1-miles to where property owners presently have posted the trail's end. This section was the closest and fastest way to reach the Sluice Brook Falls, a few large glacial erratics and the

Deerfield River still makes this section a nice exploration. Although the ups and downs along the steep embankments makes the hike more tedious than one might imagine.

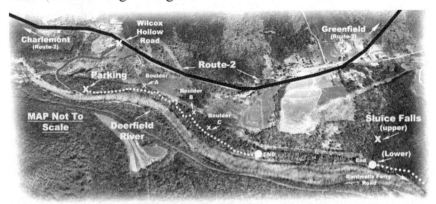

Mahican - Mohawk Trail, Deerfield River from Wilcox Hollow.

Erratic A GPS: N42° 35' 12.49" W72° 43' 9.26" (WOW-4)
Erratic B GPS: N42° 35' 2.30" W72° 42' 58.80" (WOW-6) ("Pug Rock")
Erratic C GPS: N42° 34' 57.70" W72° 42' 57.70" (WOW-5)

Mahican-Mohawk Trail -"Pug Rock"- Deerfield River. Shelburne, MA

Bardwell's Ferry Road to Sluice Brook Falls: From the R&R crossing, follow the railroad access road north for about 0.2-mile. Before the railroad trestle that spans across the Deerfield River, a well-trodden trail will be found that follows the river upstream. The trail shortly passes what appears to be an old bridge abutment and within 0.5-mile you will reach Dragon Brook. The brook can be problematic in crossing, no trail bridge has been installed and if the water flow is heavy, it will be difficult to cross with wading, not the best option and do not forget the return trip. Reaching Sluice Brook Falls, the lower falls is very dynamic, yet access is limited to steep embankment and the river. You will literally need to canoe or wade into the river. That said, occasionally the river will be low enough exposing a rocky shoal providing dry access. The upper segment is more accessible, with Sluice Brook descending and banking a 90° turn at its base, as it flows down to the lower falls eventually emptying into the Deerfield River.

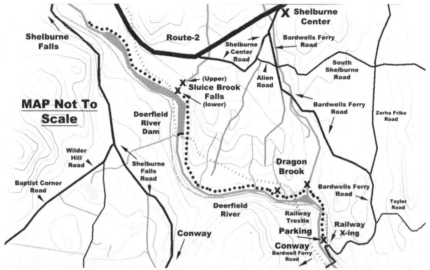

Sluice Brooks Falls west on Mahican-Mohawk Trail from Bardwell Ferry Road

Sluice Brook Falls-(lower)-Deerfield River. Shelburne, MA

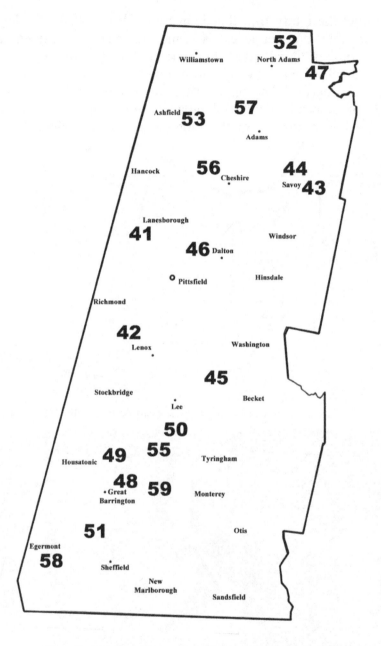

Berkshire Glacial Erratic - Boulders

Berkshire Glacial Erratics – Boulders

41. Balance Rock. Pittsfield State Forest-DCR: (Lanesborough)
42. Balance Rock. Kennedy Park (Lenox)
43. Balance Rock #1. Savoy Mountain State Forest-DCR: (Savoy)
44. Balance Rock #2. Savoy Mountain State Forest-DCR: (Savoy)
45. Basin Pond. Berkshire Natural Resource Council: (Lee)
46. Boulders The. Berkshire Natural Resource Council: (Dalton)
47. Boundary Boulder. Florida State Forest (Florida)
48. East Rock. Town Forest (Great Barrington)
49. Flag Rock Boulder Field. (Housatonic)
50. Gorilla Profile Rock. (Tyringham)
51. Limekiln Farm Wildlife Sanctuary Boulder (Sheffield)
52. Natural Bridge State Park–Rock Profiles-DCR: (North Adams)
53. Northrup Trail Boulders. Mt Greylock-DCR: (Lanesborough)
54. Painted Rocks: Frogs Landing, Shark.
55. Rabbit Rock. Tyringham Cobble (Tyringham)
56. Reynolds Rock. Appalachian National Scenic Trail (Cheshire)
57. Thunderbolt Rock. Mt Greylock Glen-DCR: (Adams)
58. Turtle Rock. Mill Pond Dam-Route-41: (South Egremont)
59. Whale Rock. Thomas Palmer Brook. BNRC: (Great Barrington)

41. Balance Rock - Laneborough

Balance Rock-Pittsfield State Forest - Lanesborough, MA

Location: Lanesborough (Berkshire County)
Parking #1 GPS: N42° 30' 32.0" W73° 16' 23.5" (*Interior parking area.*)
Parking #2 GPS: N42° 30' 29.9" W73° 15' 53.1" (*Entrance Gate.*)
Destination GPS: N42° 30' 32.0" W73° 16' 23.5" (*Balance Rock*)
Destination GPS: N42° 30' 33.0" W73° 16' 29.4" (*Cross Rock*)
Destination GPS: N42° 30' 33.6" W73° 16' 26.3" (*Whale Rock*)
Destination GPS: N42° 30' 39.0" W73° 16' 24.80" (*Split Rock*)
Contact Information: Department of Conservation & Recreation. Western Regional Headquarters. 740 South Street. Pittsfield, MA 01202
(413) 442-8928 www.mass.gov/dcr/western.htm
Trail map; https://www.mass.gov/lists/dcr-trail-maps

Information: *Balance Rock* is truly amazing, a 165-ton limestone boulder measuring 25-feet by 15-feet by 10-feet that rests three feet off the ground on top of another rock. The illusion of this boulder's precarious balance is simply striking—and yet Balance Rock has withstood centuries of pesky humans trying their best to topple it. Simply put, it's a world class glacial erratic which attracts scores of visitors from around the world.

Whale Rock is a small rock formation resembling the head of an Orca Whale with its head just rising up and breeching the surface.

Twin Rocks are just adjacent to Whale Rock, a set of two slabs up ended and buried upright allowing a person to walk between them

Cross Rock is a medium-sized boulder featuring a large cross over its face where two intersecting fractures have created an X pattern.

Split Rock Another iconic rock from the past. Originally, a large tree grew from its crack. Which will last longer, the tree or the rock? The rock was found, but no tree other than blow-downs and brush.

Old photographs show all these boulders out in the wide open, with nary a tree in sight for miles. Times have changed, natural growth and plantings of CCC's Spruce tree plantations in the 1930's, has all these boulders lying fully enveloped by the woodlands.

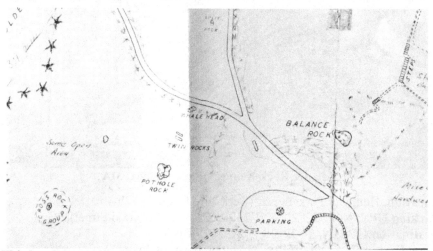

This hand drawn "Indiana Jones" style map from 1964 shows some additional named erratics just past the western end of the parking area.

Directions: From Pittsfield (junction of Route-7 North/Route-20 West), drive north on Route-7 for ~2.5 miles. When you come to a traffic light at the outlet of Pontoosuc Lake, turn left onto Hancock Road and go west for 1.4-miles. Then turn right onto Pecks Road and head north for 1.4-miles to reach the park entrance, on your left. Proceed west on Balance Rock Road for 0.5-mile to the interior parking area.

Off season and during the winter, the park road will be gated. You can park near the gate, but do not block it. You can also park across the street in a unimproved pull-off and walk up the access road, a distance of ~0.5-mile.

42. Balance Rock - Lenox

Balance Rock-Kennedy Park - Lenox, MA

Location: Kennedy Park-Lenox (Berkshire County)
Parking GPS: N42° 22' 20.8" W73°17' 22.4" (Cliffwood Street)
Destination GPS: N42° 22' 36.7" W73°17' 36.6"
Wow Factor: 7 **Accessibility**: Moderate 0.4-mile hike
Additional Info: Trail map at: www.townoflenox.com

Description: The Kennedy Park Balance Rock is a potato-shaped, 6-foot-long boulder balanced on top of a second, cradle-shaped, 8-foot-long boulder. Their combined height totals 7 feet. The rock next to Balance Rock also deserves a quick look. Its smooth, contoured surface suggests that waters from retreating glaciers once swept over the hillside at this location.

History: Kennedy Park, originally known as Aspinwall Park, was renamed Kennedy Park in 1973 after John Drummond Kennedy (1897–1975), a longtime resident of Lenox, and the main driving force behind the park's acquisition. The Park consists of 180-acres of land, with 7 main trails. The property is maintained by the Town of Lenox.

Not far from the main park entrance off of Route-7A is the site of the former, 400-room Hotel Aspinwall, which was built in 1902 by General Thomas Hubbard, and tragically burned down in 1931.

Directions: From Lenox (junction of Route-7A & Route-183), drive north on Route-7A (Main Street) for 0.2-mile. Turn left onto

Cliffwood Street and, after heading north for 1.0-mile, turn right into a small parking area for Kennedy Park just before the junction with Reservoir Road and Under Mountain Road.

From the kiosk, follow the main path north for 0.05-mile. Then turn left onto the Turkey Trail and head west. After several hundred feet, the trail crosses over a tiny brook. Turn right and begin following the Brook Trail, which soon becomes the Slippery Rock Trail. After a hundred feet from the trail sign, turn left and follow the Glade Trail uphill, proceeding northwest. (This path is less worn, so look carefully to ensure that you don't inadvertently pass by it). In less than 0.05-mile, you will reach the Balance Rock Trail (which, on the Kennedy Park kiosk map is identified as the Upper Slippery Rock Trail). Turn left, following a wide path that soon U-turns and heads uphill through a small rocky gully. In over 0.1-mile you will reach the higher Balance Rock Trail. Turn left here to reach Balance Rock, only 0.05-mile away sitting on the crest of the ridge over-looking Parsons Marsh through the trees.

43. Balance Rock #1 - Savoy

Savoy Balance Rock #1 – Tannery Road – Savoy

Location: Tannery Road. Savoy State Forest-DCR (Berkshire County)
Parking GPS: N42° 37' 25.10" W73° 2' 0.40" (Tannery Road)
Parking GPS: N42° 37' 17.70" W73° 1' 11.30" (Tannery Road Spur)
Parking GPS: N42° 36' 55.39" W72° 59' 59.66" (Black Brook Road-Winter)
Destination GPS: N42° 37' 13.23" W73° 0' 56.59"
Wow Factor: 7 **Accessibility** Road 0.9-mile trek from New State Road.
Trail map; https://www.mass.gov/lists/dcr-trail-maps

Description: Savoy Balance Rock #1 is a 250-ton boulder of granite gneiss that measures 10 x 15 x 18 feet in size. Both ends of the boulder are off the ground, and the rock is pitched at nearly a 45-degree angle, giving it the appearance of instability. Due to its remote location, you will likely have the rock all to yourself when you visit. The forest's most heavily visited attraction is not this boulder, but rather 80-foot-high Tannery Falls located down the road.

History: Created in 1918 Savoy Mountain State Forest when over 1,000-acres of abandoned farmland was purchased by the State. In the 1930s, the Civilian Conservation Corps (CCC) reforested much of the land with spruce plantations, as well as replacing dams at several of the ponds. Savoy Mountain State Forest has now grown to 10,200-acres of land and over 60-miles of trails, with four ponds and seven distinctive hills. Borden Mountain (earlier called Savoy Mountain) is the forest's highest point at 2,576-feet above sea level.

Directions: From Savoy (junction of MA 8A south & Route-116), go east on Route-8A/ Route-116 (Main Road) for 0.5 mile. Turn left onto Center Road and proceed north for 2.9-miles to Savoy Center. At a "T", turn left onto Adams Road and go west for 0.2-mile. When you come to a fork, turn right onto New State Road and proceed northeast for 1.4-miles to Tannery Road, on your right. Park off to the side of the road (often you will need 4-wheel drive, if you do continue in your vehicle). Walk (or drive) east for 0.7-mile. At the point where Tannery Road veers left and begins heading north, continue straight ahead on a dead-end spur road for another 0.2-mile to the boulder.
Black Brook Road Entry: Go pass the *Hail to the Sunrise* statue 4.0-miles west on Route-2, on your left and before the bridge, Black Brook Road steeply ascends for the first mile. Continue southwesterly for additional 1.5-mile, turn right onto Tannery Road. During winter, park at the top of the hill, in the summer drive down 0.7-mile to the parking lot.

44. Balance Rock #2 - Savoy

Savoy Balance Rock #2 – North Pond Loop - Savoy

Location: Savoy State Forest (Berkshire County)
Parking GPS: N42° 38' 49.8" W73° 02' 54.8"
Destination GPS: N42° 38' 49.4" W73° 03' 09.4"
Wow Factor: 6 **Accessibility**: Trail 0.5-mile RT
Additional Info: Savoy Mountain State Forest Campground, 260 Central Shaft Road, Florida, MA 01247; (413) 663-8469 https://www.mass.gov/ Trail map; https://www.mass.gov/lists/dcr-trail-maps

Information: Savoy Balanced Rock #2 is a 10-foot-high glacial boulder balanced on a mound of bare, inclined bedrock. The boulder is frequently visited due to its close proximity to the Savoy Mountain State Forest Campground and North Pond and South Pond.

Directions: From North Adams (junction of Route-2 & Route-8 North), head east on Route-2 for 4.4-miles. When you come to Central Shaft Road, turn right and proceed south for 2.1-miles at a fork, bear right, continuing south on Central Shaft Road for another 1.8-miles. Then turn right into the Savoy Mountain State Forest Campground.

From Savoy (junction of Route-8A south & Route-116), go east on Route-8A/ Route-116 (Main Road) for 0.5-mile. Turn left onto Center Road and proceed north for 2.9-miles to Savoy Center. At a "T", turn left onto Adams Road and go west for 0.2-mile. At a fork, bear right onto New State Road and proceed northeast for 1.5-miles. When you come to the next junction, turn left onto Burnett Road and go west for 0.5 mile. Then bear right and continue north on North Florida Road/Central Shaft Road for another 1.3 miles to the campground entrance, on your left.

Park in the main parking area and walk 0.1 mile to the trailhead for the North Pond Loop and the South Pond Loop.   Follow the trail downhill for 0.1 mile. At the bottom, faced with three different trails to choose from, take the middle "North Loop Trail" straight ahead for 0.1 mile, gradually heading uphill. You will come to the perched rock, on your left, identified by a sign that reads "Balance Rock."

45. Basin Pond Boulders - Lee

"Dog Head Rock" Erratic #1 on the Trail - Basin Pond. Lee, MA

Location: Basin Pond Trail-BNRC, Lee (Berkshire County)
Parking GPS: N42° 17' 45.37" W73° 9' 40.68" (Becket Road)
Wow Factor: 5-7 **Accessibility:** Moderate marked trail. 3.0-mile RT

History: The history of Basin Pond begins as manufacturing mill owners in East Lee were rapidly expanding and required an increased need for a constant water supply for power. In 1873, an earthen dam was built creating *Mud Pond* for that purpose, in April, 1886 that dam collapsed destroying many homes, 25-mills and several people. As history repeats itself, in 1965, a second dam was constructed on Greenwater Brook by real-estate developers to establish a resort community *Lee Colony on the Lake,* thus creating *Lake Lee.* In March of 1968, this 25-foot earthen dam broke with millions of gallons of water, causing millions of dollars in damage, along with the loss of two deaths. Since then, no more dams and *Lee Lake* has reverted to marshland, now called Basin Pond.

In 1992, Robert Thieriot purchased the property and bequeathed it to Berkshire Natural Resource Council, Basin Pond providing a diverse environment for diverse flora and fauna. With 3.0-miles of moderate hiking and with a loop trail, it is perfect place for an afternoon of exploration. There are large boulders on and off the trail, woodland brooks, and a spur trail down to a platform which allows views of the dam's remnants or Basin Pond itself.

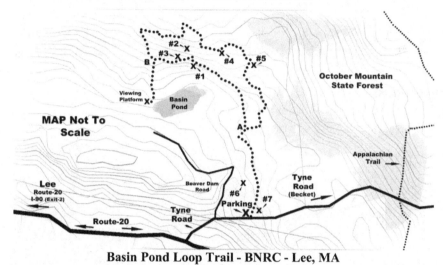

Basin Pond Loop Trail - BNRC - Lee, MA

Boulder #1 GPS: N42° 18' 14.80" W73° 9' 56.30" (Dog Head)
Boulder #2 GPS: N42° 18' 15.60" W73° 9' 58.20" (Off lower Trail)
Boulder #3 GPS: N42° 18' 15.10" W73° 9' 58.70" (Off lower Trail)
Boulder #4 GPS: N42° 18' 17.40" W73° 9' 51.90" (On upper Trail)
Boulder #5 GPS: N42° 18' 13.90" W73° 9' 41.50" (On upper Trail)
Boulder #6 GPS: N42° 17' 50.10" W73° 9' 41.40" (Off Trail)
Boulder #7 GPS: N42° 17' 45.20" W73° 9' 39.40" (Parking Lot)

Information: The trail heads north from the parking lot, in 0.4-miles you will come upon the 1st decision whether travel the upper loop (counter-clockwise) or the lower loop (clockwise)? We choose the lower loop which in 0.4-mile brought us to boulder #1 *"Dog Head Rock"* situated on the trail along with a couple other large boulders #2 and #3, both adjacent to the trail nearby.

Within 0.1-mile, another decision, Basin Pond spur trail or upper loop, we did both and returned by the upper loop trail, where you'll return back to the 1st trail junction and returning to the parking area. We found just east of the parking area another large boulder #7.

Off Trail Erratic #2 - Basin Pond. Lee, MA

Directions: From I-90 Exit-10 turning left onto Route-20 east for 4.0-miles. Turn left on Becket Road; drive uphill for 0.3-miles north, the trailhead and parking area is on the left with room for 8-10 vehicles.

Off Trail Erratic #3 - Basin Pond. Lee, MA

46. The Boulders - Dalton

At The Boulders – Dalton, MA

Location: Pittsfield - Dalton (Berkshire County)
Parking GPS: N42° 28' 54.17" W73° 10' 41.65" (*Gulf Road- East End)*
Parking GPS: N42° 28' 12.10" W73° 11' 48.60" (*Government Gate A*)
Destination GPS: N42° 28' 52.9" W73° 11' 55.8" (*The Boulders*)
Contact: B.N.R.C. 20 Bank Row, Pittsfield, MA 01201
www.bnrc.org   (413) 499- 0596   landkeepers@bnrc.org

Description: The Boulders consist of a series of massive boulders atop a 1,375-foot-high mountain pinnacle. This 645-acre area of diverse forests is heavily favored by mountain bikers, hikers or x-country skiing due to its abundance of abandoned roads and wide paths. The original Boulders Reserve was formed initially when Mass Wildlife bought a conservation restriction and affirmative right to public access in 2004. Crane continued to own and manage the property until 2015 when the Crane Company donated The Boulders plus 50-acres of adjacent, non-conserved land to be overseen by Berkshire Natural Resources Council. Mass Wildlife purchased a CR over the unrestricted land in 2016 and BNRC has begun upgrades to the trails and signage.

Directions: *Government Mill Gate A* -- From Coltsville (junction of MA 8 North & MA 9/MA 8 East), drive east on MA 9/MA 8 East (Dalton Avenue) for 0.4-mile. At the 2nd set of lights, turn left into a paved parking area just after Hubbard Avenue (which enters on your right) and across from the Government Mill (also on your right). The trail begins from the west end of the parking area and initially follows an old grassy road. Follow the blue-blazed trail north for ~0.3 mile.

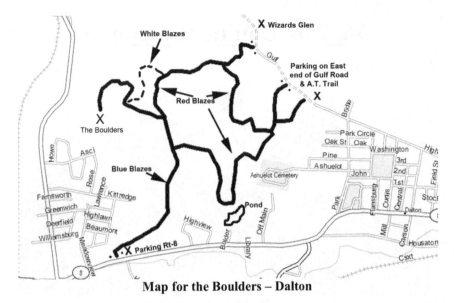

Map for the Boulders – Dalton

As a general rule of thumb for the blue trail; always bear left at major trail junctions. Within the next 0.4-mile, the red-blazed, central loop trail enters on you right and, once again, further north. Continue left and in 0.2-mile, a smaller, less used, white-blazed trail enters on your right. Continue left as the main trail begins a steeper, but short, moderate ascent. In another ~0.5-mile, you will reach The Boulders, which are located on the southern slope of the summit. The Blue Trail is a moderate ~2.8-miles round trip from the Coltsville entry.

Gulf Road-Eastern End Approach: From Coltsville (junction of Route- 8 North & Route-9/Route-8 East), drive east on Route-9/Route-8 East (Dalton Avenue) for 1.5-miles. Turn left onto Park Avenue and proceed north for 0.5-mile. When you come to Gulf Road, turn left and proceed west for 0.1-mile. Park in the area used by the Appalachian National Scenic Trail which passes through here with hikers traveling north and south.

Gulf Road is a heavily traveled, three-season dirt road with its east end in Dalton, and its west end in Lanesborough. Both ends are blocked by cement barriers after the first winter's snowfall. Parking on the west end is not encouraged due to residential property.

The main entry point begins off the south side of the Gulf Road parking lot. After entry find the red-blazed central circular trail and then navigate the red-blazed central loop trail either clockwise or counter-clockwise over to the blue-blazed trail. Either way, turn right onto the blue blaze trail and up to the Boulders. The kiosks have map and other information, no motorized vehicles.

47. Boundary Boulder - Florida

Boundary boulder – Florida, ma

Location: Florida State Forest (Berkshire County)
Parking GPS: N42° 41' 48.14" W73° 3' 45.82" (Small pull-off, Route-2)
Destination GPS: N42° 42' 27.40" W73° 3' 33.70" (Boundary Boulder)
Wow Factor: 8 **Accessibility**: Rugged, unmarked trail. 2.0-mile RT

Information: Description: Boundary Boulder is a 20-foot-high glacial erratic boulder that rests virtually on the Florida State Forest western borderline. There are no other rocks in sight, making this an unique stand-alone boulder. Our naming of the boulder is derived for its proximity to boundary marker of Clarksburg and North Adams just 75-feet north and that of Florida State Forest.

Directions: From North Adams (junction of Route-2 & Route-8 North), head east on Route-2 for ~3.9-miles (or 1.0-mile up from the famous hairpin turn). Turn left onto a small dirt access road that ends in 50-feet at a small parking area. Follow a well-defined, rutted, old logging road north for 0.8-mile. The road is basically level, brushy and can have large muddy puddles. Essentially you should be walking north and skirting along the border of the Florida State Forest. The boulder will be to your left along the side of the trail.

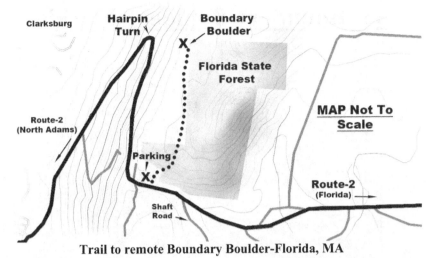

Trail to remote Boundary Boulder-Florida, MA

Every spring from the ice and wind, Boundary Boulder needs to be re-aligned with the North Adams, Clarksburg and Florida boundary marker which can be found 0.1 mile north of the boulder. (lol) GPS: N42° 42' 35.55" W73° 3' 34.06"

200-feet west behind Boundary Boulder: N42° 42' 30.03" W73° 3' 37.99"

48. East Rock - Great Barrington

East Rock – Great Barrington

Location: Town Forest of Great Barrington. (Berkshire County)
Parking GPS: N42° 11' 27" W73° 21' 10" (Quarry Street)
Destination GPS: N42°11' 26.3" W73° 20' 52.4"
Wow Factor: 8 **Accessibility**: Moderate uphill trail. 1.0-mile RT

Information: East Rock, also known as Prospect Rock, is located near the summit of 1,490-foot-high East Rock Mountain, hence the boulder's name. East Rock consists of two large boulders: a lower, 7-foot-high, 8-foot-long boulder, and an upper, 6-foot-high, 10-foot-long boulder, partially overhanging the lower one.

    Directions: From Great Barrington (junction of Route-7 & Route-23 East/Route-183 East), drive west on Route-7/Route-23 for 0.4-mile. Before crossing over the Housatonic River, turn left onto East Street and head south for 0.3-mile. When you come to Quarry Road, turn left and drive south for 0.3-mile. Look for an obvious pull-off on your left. Only a small unmark foot path through the roadside brush may be seen. Once into the woodlands an old road (now a trail) head uphill. Although the road splits initially, both sections rejoin later. The road to the right is our selection and after 0.2-mile takes you past the base of some very impressive rocky bluffs. You will reach East Rock in 0.5-mile from the start.

49. Flag Rock Boulder Field - Housatonic

Hole-in-the-Wall **(FLGR-8.) In Flag Rock Boulder Field – Housatonic MA**

Location: Trustees of Reservations. Housatonic (Berkshire County)
Parking GPS: N42°14'10.6" W73°20'52.2"
Degree of Difficulty: Access trail is moderate, with increased difficulty encountered once you leave trail to explore boulders on very steep slope with no signs or markings.
Accessibility: *To first boulder field -- 1.1- mile hike; to second boulder field – 1.3- mile hike; to Flag Rock Vista– 1.7- mile hike; 3.8 miles RT*
Destination GPS:
FLGR-0 -- N42°14' 54.1" W73°21' 06.4" (*Hanging Rock*)
FLGR-1 -- N42°14' 55.6" W73°21' 07.9"
FLGR-2 -- N42°14' 56.3" W73°21' 06.8"
FLGR-3 -- N42°14' 56.7" W73°21' 07.3"
FLGR-4 -- N42°14' 58.2" W73°21' 07.9"
FLGR-5 -- N42°14' 58.4" W73°21' 09.1"
FLGR-6 -- N42°14' 59.6" W73°21' 09.3"
FLGR-7 -- N42°15' 09.1" W73°21' 12.7" (*The Mall*)
FLGR-8 -- N42°15' 11.7" W73°21' 13.1" (*Hole-In-The-Wall*)
FLGR-9 -- N42°15' 10.7" W73°21' 13.2"
FLGR-10 -- N42°15' 09.2" W73°21' 15.6" (*Balance Rock*)
FLGR-11 -- N42°14' 56.7" W73°21' 05.3" (*Slant Rock*)
FLGR-12 -- N42°14' 55.3" W73°21' 06.5" (*Perched Rock*)
FLGR-13 -- N42° 14' 53.8" W73°21' 05.9" (*Over-Hang Rock*)
Flag Rock Vista -- N42°15' 17.2" W73°21' 17.6"
Type of formation: Large Talus Boulders, Balanced and Perched rocks.
Wow Factor: *FLGR-7, FLGR-8*--10; Other rocks -- 6–9

The Mall (FLGR-7) (side view.) In Flag Rock Boulder Field– Housatonic MA

Description: Huge boulders lie scattered along the western flank of Monument Mountain with Indian or small shelter caves being abundantly found among the bounder field jumble. The largest of these rocks is *FLGR-7*, which we have titled *"The Mall"* because its length is reminiscent of a strip mall. Of interest, is *FLGR-8 "Hole-in-the-Wall"* where a segment of the rock has shifted away from the cliff facing creating a pseudo archway allowing one to pass through. *Flag Rock* itself is not a boulder, but rather a high rocky bluff overlooking the town of Housatonic complete with a flag-pole and American Flag. Just a few hundred feet south of the vista, following the ridge line, is *FLGR-10 "Balance Rock."* This 8-foot roundish boulder is held uniquely in position atop two much smaller rocks. It must be noted that access for many of these boulders will require caution while walking and maneuvering upon slippery or mossy covered rock, steep terrain, and unstable talus slopes.

Directions: From north of Great Barrington (junction of Route-7 & Route-183), drive north on Route-183 (Old Stockbridge Road) for 1.1 miles, heading towards Housatonic. Go 200-feet past Ramsdell Road (a dirt road) on your right, and pull off onto the road shoulder. Parking at this time is unmarked, as is the trail-head.

A very faint opening and path can be found in the roadside tree line. Walk through the opening and Trustees of Reservations sign will come into view, confirming that you are at the right spot. In 2021, an updated trail map for Monument Mountain labels this as Willow's Trail which leads to Flag Rock Vista through the boulder field. In addition, approximately 0.5-mile up the trail, at a fork, the *Willow's Trail* will bare left to Flag Rock and to the right a newly blazed *Cross-Over Trail* heads east connecting on the backside of Monument Mountain with the *Mohican Monument Trail*. (See Chapter #82.)

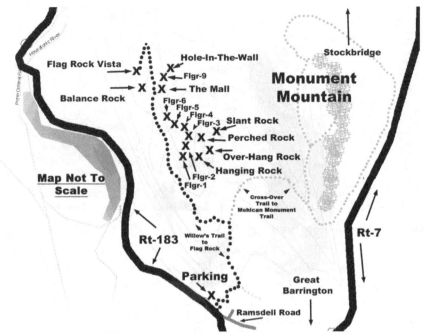

Map of Flag Rock Boulder Field – Housatonic, MA

Turn left (north) and follow the trail—an old back-woods road with few markings—for 0.2-mile. At an intersection, go left and continue north for another 0.3-mile. When you come to a fork, bear left and proceed uphill on a steeper, but still a moderate grade. At 1.1-miles from the start, you will reach a field of large boulders on your right that extends over the next 0.1–0.2-mile (FLGR-0 to 6, FLGR-11 to13).

Continuing north on the trail for 0.2-mile, you'll reach another field of large boulders located on the trail. If you wish to hike up to Flag Rock Vista, continue following the road north for another 0.3-mile. Then follow a spur trail on your left that will switch-back and proceed uphill, south down the ridge for 0.1-mile. (Below - Balance Rock)

50. Gorilla Rock - Tyringham

Gorilla Profile Rock – Tyringham, MA

Location: Tyringham (Berkshire County)
Parking GPS: N42° 15' 36.1" W73° 13' 21.6"
Destination GPS: N42° 15' 33.92" W73° 13' 22.53"
Wow Factor: 4 **Accessibility**: Roadside, situated in pasture.

Information: Description: Gorilla Rock is an 8-foot-high boulder located in a cow pasture. Under the right lighting conditions, the rock bears an uncanny resemblance to the profiled face of a gorilla. The pasture is enclosed by a barbwire fence and access is limited being private property. A telephoto lens or binoculars will assist for a closer viewing.

Directions: From I-90 (Mass Turnpike), get off at Exit-10 for Lee, turn left onto Route-20 east and proceed under the overpass, immediately after, turn right onto Route-102. Shortly, at the next set of lights, turn left onto Tyringham Road and continue south for ~2.7-miles (or 0.2-mile past Breakneck Road). Look for the boulder set back from the road about 200 feet on your right.

51. Lime Kiln Farm Boulder-Sheffield

Limekiln Farm Wildlife Sanctuary Boulder – Sheffield, MA

Location: Sheffield (Berkshire County)
Parking GPS: N42° 4' 57.90" W73° 21' 46.20"
Destination GPS: N42° 5' 6.57" W73° 22' 3.50" (Lime Kiln)
Destination GPS: N42°04' 55.9" W73°22' 11.0" (Glacial Erratic)
Wow Factor: 6 **Accessibility**: Easy 1.6-mile hike RT to Erratic.
Pleasant Valley Wildlife Sanctuary Silver Street. Sheffield, MA
413-637-0320 berkshires@massaudubon.org

Description: The Limekiln Farm Wildlife Sanctuary Boulder is an 8-foot-high by 12-foot-long glacial erratic perched on a dome of rock overlooking a large field. A bench for quiet meditation has been placed near the boulder at the edge of the field.

History: The 250-acre Limekiln Farm Wildlife Sanctuary encompasses the lands of a former farm and 50-foot-tall cement limekiln. In 1990, the property was deeded to Mass Audubon by Edna Sheinhart (with lifetime tenancy in the dwelling). It is presently managed by the Pleasant Valley Wildlife Sanctuary.

Sheinhart called her property the "Mount Everett Sanctuary," but Mass Audubon changed the name to Limekiln Farm Wildlife Sanctuary to avoid confusion with the nearby, state-owned Mount Everett Reservation.

The park was overseen for years by Marguerite D. Darkow and Dorothy Garfein, whose cremated ashes, along with Edna Sheinhart's, are next to the memorial plaque at the junction of the Lime Kiln Loop Trail and Quarry Trail.

Directions: From Great Barrington (junction of Route-7 & Route-23 West/Route-41 South), drive south on Route-7 for 7.0-miles When you come to Silver Street turn right and proceed southwest for 1.1-miles. Then turn right into the entrance for the sanctuary.

Limekiln Farm Wildlife Sanctuary Boulder – Sheffield, MA

From the parking area, head west for ~0.1-mile. When you come to the blue-blazed Lime Kiln Loop Trail, go straight (left), heading northwest for less than 0.3-mile. Along the way you will pass by a quarry to your left. When you come to a junction at an open field, turn left onto the Quarry Trail, immediately passing by a small boulder on your left with a memorial plaque on it. Follow the Quarry Trail south for less than 0.2-mile, passing between two large quarries. Turn right onto the Boulder Spur trail that leads northwest to the erratic within 150-feet.

On the way out, continue following the Lime Kiln Loop Trail clockwise from its junction with the Quarry Trail. In over 0.05-mile, you will come to the 50-foot-high cement kiln that operated from 1909 to 1912. The kiln is in remarkably good condition, with many cement foundation ruins scattered about, suggesting that this was once a very active place during its brief period of operation.

52. Natural Bridge State Park - North Adams

White Marble Dam-Natural Bridge State Park - DCR. North Adams, MA

Location: McAuley Rd. North Adams (Berkshire County)
Parking GPS: N42° 42' 30.47" W73° 5' 29.43" (Parking Visitor's Center)
Parking GPS: N42° 42' 30.47" W73° 5' 29.43" (Closed gate parking)
Destination GPS: N42° 42' 28.00" W73° 5' 34.00" (Natural Bridge)
Wow Factor: 8 **Accessibility:** Easy short walks, stairs and paths.

Information: A visit to the 48-acres of the Natural Bridge State Park a.k.a Hudson's Chasm, is a multifaceted experience of geological wonders and historical intrigue. First, it has natural bridge or arch consisting of white marble, a dam made of white marble, the only one constructed as such in North America. This was made possible for the site was an operational marble quarry from 1810 to 1947. The water from the dam flowed via a penstock pipe to power the Hoosac Marble Mill. Historically, Nathaniel Hawthorne recorded his visit here in 1838; being one of the several locations documented during his visits within the Berkshire County and later published in *An American Notebook*. Multitudes of visitors over the years have inscribed their monikers and names into the soft limestone marble. While interesting, this practice is not encouraged today. In addition, the remaining mill layout and industrial remnants become clearly understandable by knowledgeable park interpreters who during the summer are on hand to explain the human-related activities and natural forces for this natural wonder.

A DCR Park Interpreter provides insight at the Natural Bridge State Park.

Dog (Left)   (Right) Imp

GPS: N42° 42' 26.34" W73° 5' 32.44" Find one profile, you found both. Best
seen from the base of the above erratic and looking across the quarry towards
the upper rock rim of the north wall.   A line of trees continues to grow and may
eventually obscure these two unique profiles.

"Gargoyle - Cat" View Point GPS: N42° 42' 25.82" W73° 5' 33.81"

Located above Hudson Brook just below the outlet on the southern end of the chasm. Walk half-way down the "cat-walk" looking up, until you align just so to view.

53. Northrup Trail Boulders-Mt Greylock

Split Rock on the Northrup Trail, Mt. Greylock - Lanesborough, MA

Location: Rockwell Road. Mt. Greylock Reservation (Berkshire County)
Parking GPS: N42° 36' 5.70" W73° 12' 1.40" (Jones Nose)
Parking GPS: N42° 35' 36.10" W73°11' 50.11" (Rounds Rock)
Destination GPS: N42° 35' 23.07" W73° 12' 10.66" (Northrup Spur Trail)
Destination GPS: N42° 35' 46.60" W73° 12' 21.90" (Split Rock)

Information: On the Northrup Trail just about half-way between Jones Nose and Rounds Rock pass through a boulder field. One large split-rock sits on the trail with a few more scattered above the trail in the woodlands.

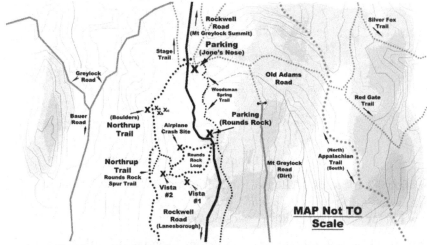

Northrup Trail Boulder Field – Mt Greylock Reservation.

Directions: Access is quickest by parking at Jones Nose and heading south on the Northrup Trail towards Rounds Rock. The Jones Nose parking area is 3.7 miles up from Lanesborough Gate. The Northrup Trail begins off the Rockwell Rock; it is 0.6 miles to the Split-Rock. You can create a longer 2.5-mile loop trail heading south 0.7 mile on the Woodsman Spring Trail south to and across Rounds Rock, down the connecting spur to the Northrup Trail and head north for 1.0 mile back to Jones Nose parking area. (See Rounds Rock-Chapter 88.)

Northrup Trail Boulder Field.

54. Painted Rocks of the Berkshires

"Shark Rock" Lenox Road. Richmond, MA

Location: Shark Rock on Lenox Road. Richmond (Berkshire County)
Destination GPS: N42° 21' 20.66" W73° 20' 13.93"
Wow Factor: 7 **Accessibility:** Roadside viewing.

Shark Rock is a 3-foot-high, 7-foot-long, roadside boulder painted to resemble the head of an enormous shark, complete with red and white razor-sharp teeth, a white eye, and snout. Reportedly, the original painting took place back in the late 1940's or early 1950's, although it is not clear if it was portrayed as a shark at that time. However, by the late 1960's it definitely had been repainted as "Sharky" and has become an iconic roadside staple with occasional community paintings occurring to maintain its robust grin over the years.

Directions: From the center of Lenox (junction of Route-183 & Route-7A North), drive west on Route-183 (West Street) for 1.5-miles towards Tanglewood. Just pass the main entry of Tanglewood, at the fork, Route-183 veers left, one needs to bear right onto Richmond Mountain Road (going west and uphill) which becomes Lenox Road. After 1.5-miles and at the top of the hill, on your left is Olivia's Overlook and trailheads for Yokem Ridge. Continue 0.3-mile, around the sweeping corner, past the junction with Lenox Branch Road (which enters on your left); continue straight ahead on Lenox Road for another 0.1-mile, *Shark Rock* is to your right.

"Frogs Landing" 1974 (top) - 2008 (bottom) Lenoxdale, MA

Location: In the Housatonic River. Lenoxdale (Berkshire County)
Parking GPS: N42° 20' 45.61" W73° 14' 41.71" (View Point)
Destination GPS: N42° 20 '49.01" W73° 14' 41.92" (Frog's Landing)
Type of Formation: Painted Rock **Wow Factor**: 7
Accessibility: Distant view from roadside or river embankment.

Information: The 25-ton, toad-shaped rock at Frog's Landing has a history dating back to well over a century ago to 1898! A Lenox resident named Peter Joseph Tyer (1864–1942) had the boulder painted to look like a frog by Amos Washburn, an area housepainter and artist. The upper half was done in a bright green; the bottom half, yellow, and the white-colored eyes and mouth were outlined in black

Tyer printed up and distributed 10,000 postcard images of the frog, and for a long time the boulder was a featured attraction in the village, particularly for passengers traveling along the New York, New Haven & Hartford Railroad line which passed by next to the rock.

When the old dam was rebuilt, the frog was moved from its original position on the west edge of the Housatonic River to a concrete pad situated within the river itself. Unfortunately, the move out into the river created a barrier making access a problem for its occasional painting and upkeep. Volunteers to tend to the Frog are needed.

Directions: From southeast of Lenox (junction of Route-20 & Route-7), drive north on Route-7/Route-20 for 0.3-mile. Turn right onto Walker Street, and head southeast for 1.5-miles. When you come to the Mill Street Bridge in the hamlet of Lenox Dale, turn left onto Crystal Street (which parallels the Housatonic River), and head north for 0.7-mile. Valley Street is on your right and will cross over a small metal bridge that spans the Housatonic River. Crossing the bridge, bear left proceed north with the Housatonic River to your left and industrial corporations on the right. After 0.1-mile, the roadway will cross over a sluiceway/channel. Park off to the side of the road just before crossing this channel. Look upriver to see the painted frog rock roughly 50-feet below the dam.

Frog Rock – Lee, MA

Location: Lee (Berkshire County)
Destination GPS: N42° 19' 6.89" W73° 14' 36.49"
Type of Formation: Painted Rock **Wow Factor**: 5
Accessibility: Roadside.

Directions: From Interstate I-90, get off at Exit-10 for Lee and proceed north on Route-20 (Housatonic Street/Main Street) 1.1-miles. Turn right onto Center Street, drive east for 0.3-mile, and bear left onto Columbia Street, following the Housatonic River (on your left) north for 0.5-mile. Frog Rock is to your right, atop a small outcrop of rock. I think the caretaker has passed or moved away for the frog is fading and is in need of fresh paint. Volunteers to tend to the Frog are needed. This is a busy roadway making parking problematic. A good place being across the street and, well off the roadway at the end of the guard rail.

55. Rabbit Rock - Tyringham Cobble

Rabbit Rock - Trustees of the Reservations - Tyringham, MA

Location: Jerusalem Road. Tyringham (Berkshire County)
Parking GPS: N42° 14' 35.60" W73° 12' 20.08"
Destination GPS: N42° 14' 29.3" W73° 12' 32.4"
Wow Factor: 7 **Accessibility:** Easy side of moderate maintained trail.

Information: Originally known as "Cobble Hill" Tyringham Cobble encompasses 206 acres of land, and is managed by the Trustees of Reservations. In 2008, a section of the 2,175-mile-long Appalachian National Scenic Trail (AT) was re-routed over the summit ledges of the cobble, thus increasing its familiarity to out-of-state hikers.

What's somewhat unusual about Tyringham Cobble is that the oldest rocks are found on top—not on the bottom as you would expect. Geologists conjecture that the cobble was dislodged from a nearby hill and flipped over during what can only be described as a violent or cataclysmic event.

The rock formation was officially mentioned as Rabbit Rock by Russell Dunn & Barbara Delaney in their book of history hikes, *Trails with Tales: History Hikes through the Capital Region, Saratoga, Berkshires, Catskills, and Hudson Valley*, published in 2006.

Directions: From I-90 (Mass Turnpike), get off at Exit-10 for Lee and proceed south on Route-102 for 0.05-mile. Turn left onto Tyringham Road/Main Street and head south for 4.2-miles. When you come to

Jerusalem Road, turn right and go southwest for 0.2 mile to the parking area, on your right.

From the parking area, walk northwest. When you come to the blue-blazed loop-trail, turn left and head south for 0.2 mile to reach Rabbit Rock, on the right side of the trail.

56. Reynold's Rock-Appalachian Trail-Cheshire

Reynold's Rock - Appalachian Trail-Cheshire, MA

Location: Outlook Avenue. Cheshire (Berkshire County)
Parking-Destination GPS: N42° 34' 32.90" W73° 9' 51.40" (Outlook Ave)
Wow Factor: 8 **Accessibility**: 150-foot walk. **Degree of Difficulty**: Easy

Directions: From the center of Cheshire (junction of Route-8 & West Mountain Road), head west up West Mountain Road for 0.3-mile and turn right onto Outlook Avenue. Proceed north for 1.0-mile and park off to the side of the road where the Appalachian Trail crosses over. Reynolds Rock is a massive, 40-foot-high, and clearly visible from the road. Upon inspection, an obvious route to the top of the rock which is flat and will provide an excellent view of the area.

Caution still needs to be used as rocks can be slippery and strong gusty winds can occur.

57. Thunderbolt Rock-Mt Greylock Reservation

Thunderbolt Rock – Mt Greylock Reservation – The Glen. Adams, MA

Location: The Glen-Mt Greylock Reservation, Adams (Berkshire County)
Parking GPS: N42° 37' 39.20" W73° 8' 15.30" (Thiel Road Barricade)
Trail Turn GPS: N42° 37' 47.50" W73° 8' 14.80" (Cut-Off Thiel Road.)
Destination GPS: N42° 37' 55.70" W73° 8' 16.80" (Thunderbolt Rock)
Wow Factor: 7 **Accessibility:** Unmarked snowmobile trail, 0.6-mile RT

Information: Thunderbolt Rock is the largest stand-alone boulder found in the Glen, if not all of Mt. Greylock Reservation. Access is from the Thiel Road barrier by following a snowmobile trail or walk 200-yards west on Thiel Road and finding the snowmobile trail cut-off on your right or continuing down Thiel Road until the pavement ends (N42° 37' 55.14" W73° 8' 19.25") and cutting down into the woodlands just below that location. The trail is not well marked at this time.

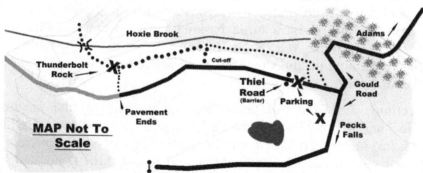

Thunderbolt Rock via the Thiel Road - Hoxie Brook Snowmobile Trail

Directions: From the President McKinley Statue on Park Street in Adams, follow Maple Street west 0.4-miles; turn left onto West Road for 0.4-mile turning right onto Gould Road, drive uphill pass the apple orchard for 0.3-mile, turn right at the fork onto Thiel Road, park near the barrier. (Gould Road turns left towards Pecks Falls.)

58. Turtle Rock - South Egremont

Turtle Rock basks just below the Mill Pond Dam - South Egremont, MA

Location: Mill Pond-Route-41, South Egremont (Berkshire County)
Parking GPS: N42° 9' 30.28" W73° 25' 17.71" (State Road/Route-41)
Destination GPS: N42° 9' 31.74" W73° 25' 17.14" (Turtle Rock)
Wow Factor: 8 **Accessibility:** Roadside.

Information: This large and definitely unique rock profile is really easy to locate and view. Originally my tip spoke as if the rock was on Mill Pond where Route-41 turns off Route-23 and heads south, searched and researched to no avail. Fortunately, our paths crossed again and we were able to straighten out that the rock formation is just pass and downstream from the bridge from Mill Pond. The large rock certainly appears to be a turtle basking itself on the shoreline and munching on some vegetation. It appears by the many different highway warning postings that this is an active turtle crossing, please brake for turtles.

Directions: Just south of Great Barrington center at the junction Route-7 and Route-23 follow Route-23 (Egremont Road) west for 4.0-miles. Just after you pass through the small village of South Egremont, turn left onto Route-41 (Under Mountain Road), Mill Pond will be seen on the right. Park on the left side on the shoulder and walk back to where the Mill Pond stream passes beneath a cement bridge to view the turtle.

This is a busy roadway, watch for traffic as you exit/enter your car or while walking to the bridge and while viewing Turtle Rock.

59. Whale Rock - Great Barrington

Whale Rock - Berkshire Natural Resource Council - Great Barrington, MA

Location: Route-23 Thomas-Palmer Brook Reserve (Berkshire County)
Parking GPS: N42° 11' 44.30" W73° 20' 12.80" (State Road/Route-23)
Turn GPS: N42° 12' 7.70" W73° 19' 42.40" (Off-trail turn)
Destination GPS: N42° 12' 10.56" W73° 19' 30.36" (Whale Rock)
Wow Factor: 8 **Accessibility:** Moderate w/bushwhack. 2.0-mile RT

Information: Recently acquired in 2015, the Thomas and Palmer Brook Reserve host 219-acres of wetland, woodland forest and the ridgeline of Three Mile Hill. The ridgeline is unique, having a long 200-foot rock spine which is being called *Whale Rock* for it resembles the back of a submerged whale and it definitely does, albeit a long one.

Presently, the reserve is under development for trails, although a parking lot and footbridge are already installed. There are old logging and woodland roads that we followed, bearing left at all junctions, until bushwhacking uphill off on our right 0.15-mile to *Whale Rock*. There were colored ribbons tied to branches and I have assumed this is where an access trail might be placed to the rock.

Direction: Just north of downtown Great Barrington, at the traffic light junction of Route-7 and Route-23, drive east of on Route-23 (State Road) for 0.75-mile. The Thomas-Palmer Brook Reserve parking area will be on your left. For access to Whale Rock, cross the foot bridge and bear right rear towards the woodlands. (Going left will bring you into the wetlands.) Towards the back right corner, an old woodland road heads east, walk in 0.15-mile, a small brook will be crossed; bear left uphill, in 0.25-mile at the next road junction, bear left and continue northerly. Travel 0.15-mile, you are below and parallel to the ridgeline and at this time a 0.15-mile bushwhack uphill and off the road is needed to reach Whale Rock. I have no doubt that a blazed trail will be in place before long.

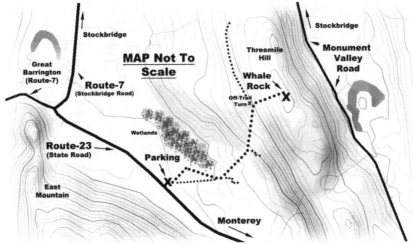

Thomas-Palmer Brook Reserve - Berkshire Natural Resources Council

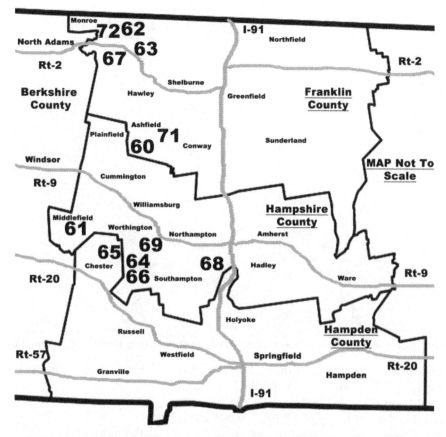

Western Massachusetts Glacial Erratics - Boulders

60. Balancing Rock. DAR State Forest-DCR: (Goshen)
61. Big Rock. (Middlefield)
62. Blue Dot Boulder. Monroe State Forest-DCR: (Monroe)
63. Elephant Head Arch-Deerfield River: (Zoar)
64. Fish Mouth Rock & Boulders. (Huntington)
65. Hiram's Tomb Boulder. (North Chester)
66. Leaning Rock. (Huntington-Knightville)
67. Mohawk Rock. Mohawk Trail State Forest: (Savoy)
68. Mt. Tom Reservation Boulder & Moss Rock-DCR: (Holyoke)
69. Old Man-in-the-Rocks. Chesterfield Gorge: (West Chesterfield)
70. Painted Rocks: Fish, Flag, Fish Mouth, Rock, Bear Rock
71. The Pebble Bullitt Reservation. (Ashfield)
72. The Titanic. Monroe State Forest-DCR: (Monroe)

60. Balance Rock - Goshen

Balancing Rock - Daughters of the American Revolution Forest. - Goshen, MA

Location: Cape Street / Route-112 DCR. Goshen (Hampshire County)
Parking GPS: N42° 27' 26.46" W72° 47' 27.03"
Trailhead GPS: N42° 27' 22.70" W72° 47' 24.90"
Destination GPS: N42° 27' 5.04" W72° 47' 7.47"
Wow Factor: 8 **Accessibility**: Moderately easy 0.4–0.5-mile hike
Fee: Vehicle fee to enter the state forest from Memorial Day to Labor Day
Additional Info: DAR (Daughters of the American Revolution) State Forest, 78 Cape Street, Goshen, MA 01032; (413) 268-7098
Trail map: https://www.mass.gov/lists/dcr-trail-maps

Description: The Goshen Balancing Rock is a truck-size, 14-foot-high boulder perched on an inclined slope of bedrock. Several smaller boulders lie about nearby, dwarfed and dominated by the immensity of the perched rock.

History: The Daughters of the American Revolution (DAR) donated 1,020-acres of land to the state of Massachusetts in 1929, which became the nucleus of the DAR State Forest. During the 1930s, extensive work was done by the Civilian Conservation Corps (CCC) to give the park its present-day look. Since then, another 750-acres of land have been acquired.

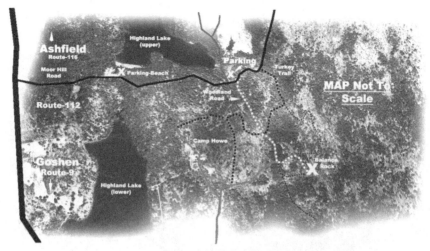

Balance Rock – Goshen, MA

Directions: From north of Goshen (junction of Route-9 & Route-112), drive north on Route-112 (Cape Street) for 0.7-miles. Turn right into the entrance for the DAR State Forest.

From west of Ashfield (junction of Route-112 & Route-116 East), drive south on Route-112 for ~5.2-miles. Turn left into the entrance for the DAR State Forest.

Approaching from either direction, follow Moore Hill Road east into the park for 0.7-mile and turn left into the parking lot at the southeast end of Upper Highland Lake.

From the parking lot, walk back up to Moore Hill Road, turn left, and walk east on Moore Hill Road for 100-feet. You will see a dirt road to your right that leads into the woods. Follow this road southeast for 0.3-mile (along the way passing by the Porcupine Trail at 0.2-mile) until you come to a junction, where the Tilton Farm Trail continues straight ahead, and the Balance Rock Trail goes left.

Follow the Balance Rock Trail east for 0.05-mile. Then bear right, continuing south on the trail for another 0.1-mile to reach the boulder, which is on the left side of the path.

61. Big Rock - Middlefield

Big Rock - Middlefield, MA

Location: Middlefield (Hampshire County)
Parking GPS: N42° 20' 53.0" W73° 00' 52.5" (Church/Senior Center)
Destination GPS: N42° 20' 49.1" W73° 00' 57.4"
Wow Factor: 6 Accessibility: Short walk 0.2-mile RT

Description: Big Rock is a 12-foot-high, stand-alone boulder that has been receiving visits from curiosity-seekers for centuries. It is nondescript as glacial erratics go, but it is "big" for the area.

History: Big Rock is often used during "Middlefield Days" as a hiking destination. The letters "M. H. Hill" are chiseled into one side of the boulder. Any idea who he is-was?

Directions: From Hinsdale (junction of Route-143 & Route-8), drive east on Route-143 (Maple Street) for 0.8-mile. Turn right onto Creamery Road/Middlefield/Road/Middlefield Skyline Trail and head southeast for ~8.6-miles to reach the center of Middlefield. Park to your right in front of a playground/senior center/church area at the corner of Skyline Trail and Town Hill Road.

From behind the senior center and church, follow signs and pink plastic ribbons left behind from previous past summer activities that show the way to the rock. Older red blazes are visible on some of the trees. The trail meanders somewhat for 150-yards west away from the road.

62. Blue Dot Boulder - Monroe

Blue Dot Boulder - Monroe State Forest - DCR, Monroe, MA

Location: Tilda Hill Road-Main Road. Monroe (Franklin County)
Parking GPS: N42°43' 12.69" W72° 59' 30.43"
Destination GPS: N42° 43' 10.1" W72° 59' 16.7"
Wow Factor: 8 **Accessibility**: Easy hike 0.6-mile RT

Description: Blue Dot Rock is a 20-foot-high boulder that was named for its close proximity to the blue-dot trail that parallels Dunbar Brook. This is a massive rock, with shallow shelter caves formed by overhangs on opposite sides of the boulder.

History: The Dunbar Brook Trail follows along Dunbar Brook—a mountain stream that tumbles 700 vertical feet in two miles. In the 1800's, the forest was a ribbon of farmlands and pastures. Now, only stone walls and cellar holes remain. Farming simply could not be sustained due to the land continuously giving rise to new crops of rocks and boulders.

In 1924, 1,600-acres of land were purchased by the State of Massachusetts and the Monroe State Forest established. Since its inception, the park has grown to over 4,000-acres. The state forest was named after James Monroe, the fifth president of the United States.

Directions: From North Adams (junction of Route-2 & Route-8 North), drive east on Route-2 for ~5.4-miles up into Florida and turn left onto Tilda Hill Road. Proceed north for 4.1-miles, and then turn right into the small parking area at the sign for the Monroe State Forest.

From the parking area, walk towards the Dunbar Brook bridge. Just before crossing the stream, turn left onto the blue-blazed Dunbar Brook Trail. Within a couple of hundred feet, you will come to the remarkably well-intact, stone walls of an abandoned sluiceway. Water was diverted from Dunbar Brook for hydropower here and then returned to the brook just below the stone walls. Follow the blue-blazed trail for less than 0.3-mile (all the time paralleling Tilda Hill Road, to your left and Dunbar Brook, to your right). Blue Dot Rock is impossible to miss, directly to your right, less than 50-feet from the trail. (See Chapter #72 *The Titanic* for local map)

63. Elephant Head - Mt Negus-Zoar

Negus Mountain Glacial Erratic – Zoar, MA

Location: Zoar (Franklin County)
Parking GPS: N42° 39' 10.4" W72° 57' 15.8" (The Gap-Zoar Bridge)
Destination GPS: N42° 39'18.6" W72°57' 08.2"
Elephant Head Arch: N42° 39' 16.68" W72° 57' 19.78"
Mt Negus Boulder Field: N42° 39' 13.4" W72° 57' 16.0"
Type of Formation: Large Boulder and Profile Rock **Wow Factor**: 6–8
Accessibility: *Mt Negus Erratic*: 0.5-mile hike; elevation change of 400-feet. *Elephant Head Arch and Boulder Field*: 0.1-mile hike along active railroad track.

Degree of Difficulty: *Mt Negus Erratic:* Difficult due to steepness and trail marking irregularity. *Elephant Head Arch*: moderate, no trail with a scramble the last 25 yards down a very steep river embankment *Boulder Field*: easily located in woodlands between the Elephant Head Arch and bottom entry point to Mt Negus.

Description: The Negus Mountain Glacial Erratic is a 12-foot-high, 15-foot-long glacial boulder located on the shoulder of Negus Mountain below its summit. The area below the boulder is steep, rocky and fairly barren of trees, creating terrific and exhilarating vistas.

Elephant Head Arch is situated on east side of the Deerfield River embankment just below the rapids known as "The Gap". From the river's edge, the profile appears to be an elephant head with trunk drinking from the river. This formation is rare and unique due to the large 4-foot eroded hole creating the arch which enhances the head and neck shape of this formation.

Boulder Field: a few large rocks with the largest and most significant being 14-feet-tall.

Elephant Head Arch - Deerfield River – Zoar, MA

History: The Mountain's name is pronounced "knee-gus." Some call it the "big little mountain" due to its surprisingly rocky summit and respectable height of 1,773-feet.

In the Ethiopian language of Amharic, *Negus* means "ruler" or "emperor." One could say, in summation, that this mountain rules.

Nearby, near Rowe, is *Pulpit Rock* which, according to the 1937 Federal Writers' Project's *WPA Guide to Massachusetts*, is "… a geological phenomenon resembling an old-fashioned canopied pulpit."

Directions: From Charlemont (junction of Route-2 & Route-8A), drive west on Route-2 for 2.2-miles and turn right onto Zoar Road just before crossing the Deerfield River.

From North Adams (junction of Route-2 & Route-8 North), drive east on Route-2 for ~16-miles. As soon as you cross over the Deerfield River, turn left onto Zoar Road.

Approaching from either direction, head northwest on Zoar Road for ~3.8-miles (or 1.0-mile beyond Rowe Road, which comes in on your right).

In Zoar, just prior to crossing over the Florida Bridge spanning the Deerfield River, look to your right for a short-paved access to the railroad tracks. Park here, making sure not to block the gate or barrier at the end.

Walk to the end of the access road and, after carefully crossing this active railroad track, follow the trail that starts directly across from the barrier. Within 300-feet into the woodland, this path will start to meander steeply uphill. The trail was not well marked. Essentially, if it looks rutted or eroded and goes up, that's the trail. In places you will want to make sure that you have three points of contact. Expect the ascent to take ~45 minutes. Pay attention on the way up, for that will make the descent that much easier. This hike will be short, but invigorating.

Elephant Head Arch: From the parking location, walk past the end of the access road barrier, do not cross the railroad track. Continue north along upper embankment of the Deerfield River next to the railroad track for 0.1-mile. Below and next to the river edge you will see the rock formation. Access to the river edge can be difficult requiring one to use caution scrambling down over loose gravel and stone.

Boulder Field: Located across the railroad tracks just east of the Elephant Head Arch location and set back within the woodlands above the track.

Be visually alert for trains whenever crossing or walking near the railroad tracks. The Deerfield River creates its own "White Noise" from the rushing water and the rapids easily masking the sound of any oncoming train.

64. Fish Mouth Rock - Huntington

Fish Mouth Rock (FR-6) – Huntington, MA

Location: Chester Wildlife Management Area. (Hampshire County)
Parking GPS: N42°19' 20.1" W72° 52' 13.1" (*Fish Mouth Rock* Rt-112)
Parking GPS: N42° 19' 01.8" W72° 52' 46.3"(*Boulder Field*-Goss Hill Rd)
Destination GPS: *FR-1* -- N42°19' 01.6" W72°52' 37.8"
FR-2 -- N42°19' 04.2" W72°52' 37.5" *FR-3* -- N42°19' 05.2" W72°52' 38.5"
FR-4 -- N42°19' 05.3" W72°52' 36.3" *FR-5* -- N42°19' 04.1" W72°52' 32.3"
FR-6 -- *Fish Mouth Rock* -- N42°19' 18.8" W72° 52' 19.1"
FR-7 -- N42°19' 21.3" W72°52' 22.6"
Westfield River Erratic -- N42°19'45.1" W72° 51'17.3"
Accessibility: *Fish Mouth Rock* – 0.1-mile hike; Upper *Boulder Field* –0.2-mile hike; *Westfield River Erratic* — 2.7-mile hike from Route-112 or when Knightville Dam Basin is open, a 2.0-mile drive, followed by a 0.7- mile walk from U.S. Corps Engineers Road interior gate.

Description: Fish Mouth Rock is a fractured, 8-foot-high rock that resembles a fish with its mouth agape. Adding to the illusion is a round eye that seems to be naturally formed by lichens.

Located on a plateau above Fish Mouth Rock is an impressive, but small boulder field. The largest rock, embedded in the hillside, looms at a height of over 25-feet (FR-2). There are other distinctive boulders as well, including a 10-foot-high stand-alone boulder, and a 6-foot-long rectangular rock that is balanced against a larger, somewhat more rounded boulder (FR-1). Because access from Fish Mouth Rock would require a 0.3-mile ascent up a steep hill through rugged woodlands, our suggested approach is from Goss Hill Road.

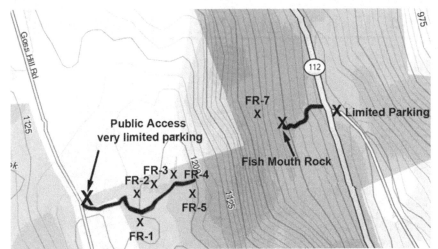

Fish Mouth Rock & Upper Boulder Field - Huntington

Directions: *To Fish Mouth Rock* – From Huntington (junction of Route-112 & Route-66), drive north on Route-112 (Worthington Road) for 3.6-miles. Park to your right at the gated entry road to the Knightville Dam, making sure not to block the entrance. Walk across the road and head west uphill bushwhacking into the woods for about 500-feet to reach the boulder. There is no real trail to follow. Another large erratic (FR-7) is located 300 feet farther north and uphill.

To Upper Boulder Field -- From Huntington (junction of Route-112 & Route-66), drive north on Route-112 (Worthington Road) for 1.2- miles. Turn left onto Kimball Road and head northwest for 0.5 mile. from here is a winter snowmobile trail. From the field, head east over a small knoll and down the other side. FR-1 will be seen to your right. Continue east for another 300-feet and FR-2 will be visible in the woods When you come to Goss Hill Road, turn right and proceed north for 1.4-miles. Park on your right, at the end of small dirt road which leads up to the end of a large pasture. This road provides a narrow public access corridor to state lands. Follow the road to the upper left corner of the field. Essentially, the only navigable trail leading off to your left, as well as FR-3 after another 150-feet, and FR-4, 150-feet beyond that.

The Westfield River Erratic is a large, 20-foot-high roadside boulder within the Knightville Dam Westfield River Basin (a flood control project) and hiking area over seen by the Massachusetts Fish & Game Management.

To Westfield River Erratic – Access is from the same parking spot used for Fish Mouth Rock on MA-112. Whether you drive or hike, start at the Old Worthington Road gate off MA-112. If the gate is open, drive down for 0.9-mile, turn at the first left onto the Army Corps of Engineers Road, continue on this dirt road for ~1.0-mile. At the next gate and parking area, continue on foot for 0.7-mile past the gate to reach the boulder, on your left.

65. Hiram's Tomb - North Chester

Hiram's Tomb – North Chester, MA

Location: Maynard Road. North Chester (Hampden County)
Parking GPS: N42° 18' 13.38" W72°55' 12.59"
Destination GPS : N42° 17' 56.5" W72° 55' 06.5"
Wow Factor: 8 **Accessibility**: Moderately easy uphill 0.8-mile RT

Description: Hiram's Tomb-Boulder is a 10-foot-high, 30-foot-long granite boulder that contains the terse inscription: "Hiram Smith, died 1873; Sarah Toogood, died 1869." There are actually two people entombed inside this rock—something that makes this boulder very unique for a Massachusetts rock which isolated deep and high atop a hill in the forest.

History: Hiram's Tomb Boulder is named for Hiram Smith and his sister, Isabell Toogood who are entombed within the boulder. Hiram was adamantly opposed to being buried in the ground, and chose the rock to serve as his mausoleum. Isabell it would appear, was either of like mind or having died first, had no say in the matter. Stories suggest that Hiram's aversion to interment beneath the ground was the result from seeing his parents' graves washed away during a torrential rain and flash flood, or from witness to a funeral where the burial site was awash with mud and water requiring the grave needing to be emptied before lowering the casket. In his will, Hiram had set aside enough money to have the road leading up to his tomb to be kept in good repair, but the money apparently was misspent by the trustee of this fund, which is why the old road is fairly obscure and slightly over grown today.

A close-up of the engraved epitaph for Hiram Smith and sister Isabell Toogood.

Directions: From Worthington Corners (junction of Route-143 & Route-112 South), drive northwest on Route-143 (Old North Road) for ~4.3-miles to West Worthington. Turn left onto River Road/East River Road and proceed south for ~10.5-miles, traveling next to the Middle Branch of the Westfield River, until you come to Maynard Hill Road, on your right.

From Huntington (junction of Route-20 & Route-112 North), head north on Route-112 North (East Main Street) for 0.2-mile. As soon as you cross over the Westfield River and a railway bridge, turn left onto Chester Hill Road (also known as the Skyline Trail) and proceed northwest for over 4.0-miles. When you come to East River Road, turn right and drive north for 2.0-miles to reach Maynard Hill Road on your left.

Follow Maynard Hill Road (a dirt road) uphill, going west, for 0.9-mile. Pull into an unimproved pull-off on you left (a discontinued log landing) where there is room enough for one car. Walk uphill along an old logging road for 0.4-mile to Hiram's Tomb Boulder, located in a small spruce grove at the top.

66. Leaning Rock-Knightville Dam-Huntington

November 2021

April 2015

Leaning Rock. Knightville Dam Recreation Area. Huntington, MA

Location: Route-112, Knightville Road. Huntington (Hampshire County)
Parking GPS: N42° 17' 21.87" W72° 51' 42.07"
Destination GPS: N42° 17' 22.63" W72° 51' 43.13"
Wow Factor: 8 **Accessibility**: Easy side of Moderate-No trail 300-foot
Additional Info: When open, the recreation area contains a universally accessible public restroom, picnic tables, fireplaces, and a pavilion.

Description: Leaning Rock is an enormous, 45–50-foot-high slab of bedrock that was featured in early twentieth-century postcards. It lies below the Knightville Dam on the southeast side of the outlet stream. The size of the rock is impressive, but diminished somewhat by the sheer enormity of the dam. Beneath it, the rock slab has formed a 20-foot-high, 10-foot-deep shelter cave that faces away from the dam.

History: The Knightville Dam Recreation Area encompasses 2,430 acres of land that is overseen by the U. S. Army Corps of Engineers. The dam was constructed from 1939–1941, impounding the East Branch of the Westfield River. Its creation was in direct response to the devastating flood of 1936.

Directions: From Huntington (junction of Route-20 & Route-112), drive north on Route-112 for 3.9-miles and turn right onto Knightville Dam Road.

From northeast of Worthington Corners (junction of Route-143 East & Route-112 North), drive south on Route-112 for ~16-miles and turn left onto Knightville Dam Road.

Proceed north on Knightville Dam Road for 0.5-mile, and then left into the entry for the Knightville Dam picnic/recreation area. (Note: The Army Corps of Engineer Road continues uphill to the top of the dam). Follow the picnic area road counterclockwise for 0.3-mile as it loops around in front of the dam. Be sure to take note of the large rock to your left at the apex of the loop. Picnic tables are located on both sides of it. Park off to the side of the road.

Walk west over to the long chain-linked fence that separates the picnic area from the steep slope leading down to the river. Look for a small opened gate where two sections of the fence come together at a right angle. Follow a fairly steep path that leads around and down to the river and to the base Leaning Rock in 100-feet.

Be aware that water levels can rise suddenly in this area, so be attentive.

Leaning Rock depicted in an old postcard as the *Devils Arm Chair*.

67. Mohawk Rock - Savoy

Mohawk Rock – Savoy, MA

Location: Route-2 Mohawk State Forest-DCR. Savoy (Berkshire County)
Parking GPS: N42°37' 59.90" W72°58' 16.60"
Destination GPS: N42°37' 57.14" W72°58' 14.58"
Wow Factor: 5 **Accessibility**: Easy side of moderately 0.3-mile RT

Description: Mohawk Rock is a 12-foot-high, 15-foot-long, metamorphic boulder that rests on the side of a hill overlooking the Cold River. The boulder's name comes from its close proximity to Route-2, a highway that historically has been called the Mohawk Trail; hence, *Mohawk* Rock. The 69-mile-long Mohawk Trail, which opened in 1914, is considered to be one of America's first and finest scenic highways. Apparently, this is a good boulder with easy access and has good route for boulderers.

Directions: From North Adams (junction of Route-2 & Route-8 North), drive east on Route-2 for ~11.3-miles to Black Brook Road. From here, continue east on Route-2 for another 0.2-mile and turn into a pull-off on your right. Initially from the northern end of the parking area, bushwhack up the steep embankment 100-feet to a shelf (a plateau-like area), and then follow a faint path east for 100-feet, paralleling the road below, continue east for another 200-feet to reach the boulder.

68. Mt. Tom Boulder - Holyoke

Mt Tom Boulder - Holyoke, MA

Location: On M&M Trail Holyoke (Hampden County)
Parking GPS: N42°13'49.1" W72°38'50.2"
Destination GPS: *Mt. Tom Boulder* -- N42°14' 11.6" W72° 38' 35.9"
Destination GPS: *Moss Rock* -- N42°14' 12.0" W72° 38' 50.3"
Type of Formation: Large Boulder   **Wow Factor**: *Mt. Tom Boulder* – 8;
Moss Rock -- 5   **Accessibility**: *Mt. Tom Boulder* -- 0.5-mile trek; *Moss Rock*
– 0.7-mile trek
Degree of Difficulty: Moderately easy

Description: *Mt. Tom Boulder* is a 16-foot-high, trap rock boulder that rests on top of a tiny hill. The surface of the boulder is rough-hewn, as though someone took a chisel and hammered at it, chipping pieces away. Bits of trap rock lay scattered about around the base of the boulder, further adding to the illusion that a mad sculptor once worked here.

The south end of the Whiting Street Reservoir can be seen downhill to the east when the foliage is sparse.

Moss Rock (a name we have given to the rock) is 15–20 feet tall and somewhat triangular shaped. It is mostly moss-covered—hence, the name. The surface of the rock is curiously rippled, and the lower right corner is riddled with potholes.

The rock, including several smaller ones, rests at the bottom of a sloping, 100-foot-high ridge. It is likely that all these pieces have broken off from the top of the ridge, and now lie about as talus at the base. Directly behind Moss Rock and 75 feet uphill, sections of the bedrock along the ridge line exhibit potholes, and one rock-face is stitched with a series of holes that form an L-shaped pattern—a clear sign of past quarrying.

History: Farther along the M&M Trail, roughly 0.7-mile uphill from where the path and old road join, is the south summit of Mt. Tom. Although there is little to suggest otherwise today (except for an occasional relic or artifact), at one time the mountain supported a summit hotel, ski area, amusement park, inclined railroad, and a number of summer cottages.

Farther south, near Holyoke, is *Dinosaur Footprints*—a Trustees of the Reservations' preserve— where the tracks from a 15-foot tall, bipedal carnivore dinosaur can be seen, captured 190-million years ago and preserved in slabs of sandstone.

Directions: From Interstate I-91 near Holyoke, get off at Exit-15A or Exit-15B and follow Route-141 (Easthampton Road) north for ~1.6-miles. Turn right into a pull-off, directly across from an animal hospital. This parking has been used for quick access to the M&M Trail north, there is a larger parking area 0.4-mile east towards Holyoke where the M&M Trail crosses Route-141 from its southern origins.

To Mt. Tom Boulder -- Follow the white-blazed Metacomet-Monadnock (M&M) Trail north for 0.5-mile, walking along an old, abandoned road. Look for the boulder to your left, only 20-feet from the trail.

From Mt. Tom Boulder to Moss Rock –Continue north on the M&M Trail for another 0.1-mile. You will reach a point where the M&M trail veers right from the road into the woods and begins to climb up Mt. Tom southern slope, continue straight ahead on the road, now heading west, for another 0.1-mile. Look to your right and you will see a ridge-line paralleling the road some 300-feet away. Head towards the ridge, keeping a sharp eye out for Moss Rock, which will be at the bottom of the escarpment.

69. Old-Man-in-the-Rocks-Chesterfield

Old Man-in-the-Rocks Profile - West Chesterfield, MA

Location: Chesterfield Gorge. Trustees of Reservations (Hampshire County)
Parking GPS: N42° 23' 35.6" W72° 52' 49.2"
Viewing Location GPS: N42° 23' 34.1" W72° 52' 47.8" (Profile View Point)
Wow Factor: 4 **Accessibility**: Easy 150-feet towards gorge from parking lot.
There is a parking/access fee for non-members.

Description: The Old Man-in-the-Rocks is the profile of an old man's face in the rock wall of the Chesterfield Gorge.

History: The Chesterfield Gorge is a long canyon formed by the East Branch of the Westfield River, with walls that rise vertically to as high as 60 feet. Elias Nason, in his 1874 *Gazetteer of the State of Massachusetts*, wrote that "in one place the water of the Westfield River has cut a channel thirty feet deep and sixty rods long through the solid rock as symmetrically as if done by art."

The town and, later the gorge, were named after the Earl of Chesterfield.

The nucleus of the Chesterfield Gorge Park was acquired by the Trustees of Reservations in 1929. Additional lands were purchased in 1949, 1950, 1955, and 1994 thanks to generous donors. The park now contains 166-acres.

High Bridge, whose abutments can be seen near the beginning of the gorge, lasted until 1835 when the Westfield River went on one of its periodic rampages, sweeping away the bridge and nearby grist and saw mills.

To view of Old Man-in-the-Rocks – Facing towards the gorge from the out-house end of the parking area, walk straight ahead for 150-feet. When you come to the side railing (GPS), look directly across the chasm to the opposite wall to see the profile. Its sharpness will depend upon such intangibles as lighting, weather, brush growth and viewing perspective. Sometimes, just a slight change in position is enough to create the required "ah HA!" response "I see it!"

Chesterfield Gorge Potholes - Chesterfield, MA

Directions: From west of West Chesterfield (junction of Route-112 & Route-143), drive southeast on Route-143 (Williamsburg Road) for 3.0-miles to West Chesterfield. Before crossing the Westfield River Bridge, turn right onto Ireland Street and drive south for over 0.8-mile. Then turn left onto River Road (a dirt road) and proceed south for 0.1-mile to the parking area for the gorge, on your left.

70. Painted Rocks-Western Massachusetts

Bear Rock - Granville, MA

Location: Route-57. Granville Road (Hampden County)
Destination GPS: N42° 4' 37.69" W72° 50' 39.18" (Roadside View Point)
Wow Factor: 5 **Accessibility:** Roadside viewing.
Directions: From the Granville Town Common and Library where Route-189 junctions with Route-57, head east on Route-57 for 1.4-miles. Rocky outcrop of *Bear Rock* will be seen on the right.

Pig Rock – West Granville, MA

Location: North Lane. West Granville (Hampden County)
Destination GPS: N42° 6' 39.10" W72° 55' 49.10" (Roadside View Point)
Wow Factor: 4 **Accessibility:** Roadside viewing.
Information: Unfortunately, the B&W does not provide the impact of this brightly painted pink rock. Only information obtained is the image was painted in humor for remembrance of a friend's passing. Fitting to the image is the rock to its left has also been painted with the word "Oink". Recently repainted (2019) with the name "Wendy" added. ??

Directions: From West Granville head east on Route-57 for 1.0-mile. Turn left onto North Lane and head north for 2.4-miles. Pig Rock is on the east side of the road part of small boulder cluster.

Fish Rock – Chester, MA

Location: Old Chester Road Chester (Hampden County)
Destination GPS: N42°14'34.10" W72°54'36.71"
Wow Factor: 6 **Accessibility**: Roadside Viewing-North side of road.

Information: Unlike many painted boulders, Fish Rock is symmetrical, allowing it to be viewed from either side, or head-on, while still retaining all of its features. In addition, evidently someone enjoys keeping this roadside point-of-interest looking sharp with a coat of paint frequently.

Directions: From Huntington junction of Route-20 and Route-112, drive northeast on Route-112, (East Main Street) for 0.1 mile. Turn left onto Basket Street and proceed west for 1.6-miles, following along the side of the West Branch of the Westfield River. At a fork, bear left onto Old Chester Road and continue west for another 0.3-mile until you come to the rock, on your right.

Flag Rock – Westfield River – Huntington. MA

Location: Middle Branch Westfield River Huntington (Hampshire County)
Parking GPS: N42° 14' 8.05" W72° 52' 22.30" (Route-112 Pull-Off)
Viewing Location: N42°14' 09.6" W72°52' 19.9" (Westfield River Edge)
Destination GPS: N42°14'8.66" W72°52' 18.32" (Flag Rock)
Wow Factor: 4 **Accessibility**: Park and easy walk to river side

Description: Flag Rock is a small painted rock of the American Flag that has been traditionally painted by a town resident for some time. Take note the Westfield River viewing location will vary according to seasonal water flow or water release from the Knightville Dam.

Directions: From Huntington (junction of Route-20 and Route-112), follow Route-112 (East Main Street/Worthington Road) north, through the town, for 0.4-mile.

Just before the first corner where the Westfield River comes into view, park on the right at the road-side pull-off across from a local strip mall *Huntington Shoppes*. From here, using caution, walk 200-feet north along Route-112, carefully climb over the guardrail, and then scramble down the small embankment to the river's edge. Flag Rock is visible across the river on the opposite bank. It will be easier locate and observe when trees and bushes have shed their foliage. Recently the person who might have originally painted this for patriotic reasons might have left town, time will tell if any one steps in and hopefully gives this rock a fresh coat of paint every now or then.

71. The Pebble - Ashfield

"The Pebble" Bullitt Reservation – Ashfield, MA

Location: Bullitt Road. Trustees of the Reservations. Ashfield (Franklin County)
Parking GPS: N42° 30' 7.17" W72°45' 22.29" (Trustees Parking Area)
Destination GPS: N42° 30' 09.8" W72° 45' 37.5" (The Pebble)
Wow Factor: 7 **Accessibility**: Moderately easy 0.4-mile hike; 170-foot elevation change

Description: The Pebble is a stand-alone, 16-foot-high, 18-foot-long glacial erratic boulder located on the southeast shoulder of a small mountain. The part of the boulder closest to the trail is squeezed tightly between two trees that have sprouted up around it, giving the rock the appearance of the head of a huge beast held snugly in a yoke.

Despite the name, which suggests a tiny, rounded stone, The Pebble is massive and imposing. A more fitting name—one giving a nod to its former property owner—would be "Bullitt Rock," or just plain "The Bullitt."

History: With the exception of The Pebble, the farmhouse (now a visitor center) is the main point of interest at the Bullitt Reservation. From 1839 to 1874, it served as the poor farm for the community of Ashford. Later, it became the summer retreat for the Bullitt family, most notably William C. Bullitt, Jr., who served as an ambassador to France and the Soviet Union during the Cold War.

Directions: In Ashfield at the (junction of Route-112 & Route-116 East), drive southeast on Route-116 (Main Street/Conway Road) for 3.1-miles and turn right onto Bullitt Road.

From Conway (junction of Route-116 & Sherburne Falls Road), drive west on Route-116 (initially River Road) for 4.7-miles and turn left onto Bullitt Road.

From either direction, proceed southeast on Bullitt Road for 0.6-mile, turn right into the Bullitt Reservation, and park next to a small white house that serves as the reservation's headquarters.

Proceeding on foot, return to Bullitt Road, walk past the pond, and then follow the trail to your left for several hundred feet that leads into the woods. When you come to the yellow-blazed, *Pebble Loop Trail*, head either clockwise or counterclockwise, with either direction taking you to the boulder in roughly 0.3–0.4-mile.

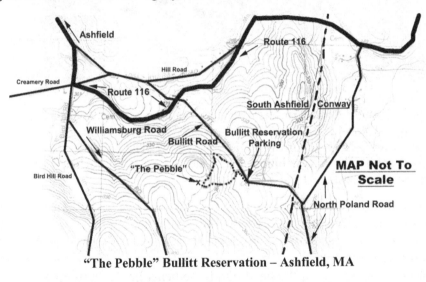

"The Pebble" Bullitt Reservation – Ashfield, MA

72. The Titanic - Monroe

"The Titanic"- Monroe State Forest – Monroe, MA

Location: Tilda Hill Road. Monroe State Forest-DCR (Franklin County)
Parking GPS: *Lower parking area* -- N42°4' 3'12.69" W72° 59' 30.43"
Upper parking spot; start of bushwhack -- N42°42' 53.9" W72° 59' 40.5"
Destination GPS: The Titanic -- N42°42' 54.0" W72°59' 28.2"
Wow Factor: 10

Boulder Field A: Lower Raycroft Road
A1 -- N42° 43' 05.7" W72° 59' 29.1" **A4** -- N42° 43' 01.4" W72° 59' 26.3"
A2 -- N42° 43' 03.4" W72° 59' 26.4" **A5** -- N42° 43' 00.9" W72° 59' 26.2"
A3 -- N42° 43' 02.3" W72° 59' 25.7" **A6** -- N42° 43' 00.2" W72°5 9' 28.2"

Boulder Field B: Middle Raycroft Road
B1 -- N42° 42' 39.6" W72° 59' 15.1" **B5** -- N42° 42' 43.4" W72°59'04.1"
B2 -- N42° 42' 39.1" W72° 59' 12.2" **B6** -- N42° 42' 42.2" W72°59'03.9"
B3 -- N42° 42' 42.8" W72° 59' 08.1" **B7** -- N42° 42' 35.8" W72°59'10.0"
B4 -- N42° 42' 44.0" W72° 59' 06.2"

Boulder Field C: Upper Raycroft Road
C1 -- N42° 42' 20.0" W72° 58' 50.7" **C4** --N42° 42' 10.8" W72° 58' 37.0"
C2 -- N42° 42' 09.1" W72° 58' 42.1" **C5** --N42° 42' 06.5" W72° 58' 35.7"
C3 -- N42° 42' 12.1" W72° 58' 37.9" **C6** --N42° 42' 05.0" W72° 58' 35.3"

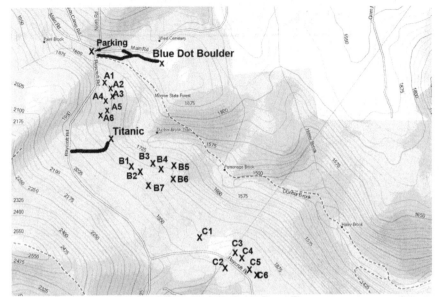

Boulder Fields of Monroe State Forest

Type of Formation: Large Boulder **Wow Factor**: *The Titanic* -- 10; *Other boulders* -- 4–8 **Accessibility**: *The Titanic* -- 0.4-mile walk (or drive) up road; 0.2-mile bushwhack from upper section of road; *Other boulders* – 0.2–0.8-mile trek **Degree of Difficulty**: Moderate-Moderately difficult (due to bushwhack)
Additional Info: Trail map: mass.gov/eea/docs/dcr/parks/trails/monroe.pdf

Description: The Titanic, also called Titanic Rock, is an enormous, 30-foot-high boulder that may well be the largest glacial erratic in western Massachusetts. It leans against a second, 20-foot-high boulder that is just as massive. This "smaller" boulder has fractured into two pieces that remain close together.

A cathedral-like, 8-foot-high shelter cave has formed between the Titanic and its companion boulder, the result of the Titanic's pronounced tilt. You can walk right through the opening to the other side. Tiny potholes adorn the Titanic's underbelly.

A small stream runs down the mountainside only 50-feet away from the back of the boulders.

The area containing the Titanic is a goldmine for rock enthusiasts, filled with a plethora of large boulders (but none quite matching the Titanic in terms of sheer size or height). Generally, the rocks are found on the hillside between Raycroft Road and Dunbar Brook. The GPS coordinates that we have listed are for some of the bigger boulders that are accessible by bushwhack from various points along Raycroft Road.

They are grouped into three areas: Boulder Field A, Boulder Field B, and Boulder Field C.

Directions: From North Adams (junction of Route-2 & Route-8 north), drive east on Route-2 for ~5.4-miles. When you come to Tilda Hill Road, turn left and proceed north for 4.1-miles. Turn right at the sign for the Monroe State Forest onto unpaved, unmarked Raycroft Road (also called South Road), head downhill for 100-feet, cross over the Dunbar Brook bridge, and park immediately to your left.

For those with 4-wheel drive vehicles, continue driving up the road from the lower parking area for 0.4-mile and turn into a pull-off on your right, just after crossing over a tiny stream that goes under the road.

For hikers, park in the lower parking area by the bridge, and continue uphill on foot for 0.4-mile. After going past a large boulder to your right, and heading downhill to where the road momentarily becomes level, look for where a small stream goes under the road.

From here, follow the creek downstream, bushwhacking for ~0.2-mile. Although the creek zigzags a bit, the way down is essentially a straight line. You will come to the backside of the Titanic, left of the stream, 0.1 mile before reaching Dunbar Brook.

B-5 one of many large erratics found along the ridgeline above Dunbar Brook.

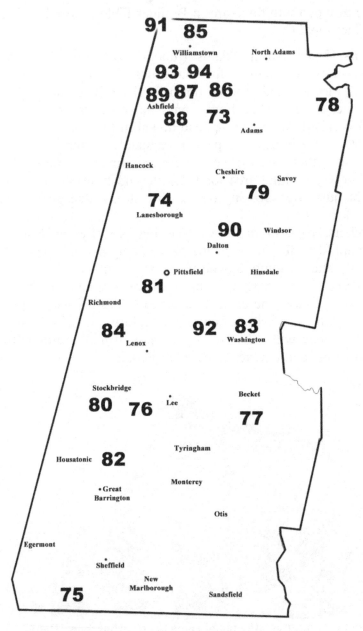

Berkshire Hikes and Vistas

Berkshire Hikes and Vistas

73. Adams Vista. Mt Greyock Reservation-DCR: (Adams)
74. Ashuwillticook Rail Trail – DCR: (Adams - Lanesborough)
75. Bartholomew's Cobble. Trustees of Reservations: (Sheffield)
76. Beartown State Forest CCC Ski Lodge: (Lee)
77. Becket Quarry. Becket Land Trust: (Becket)
78. Busby Knob-Spruce Hill. Hoosac Range-BNRC: (North Adams)
79. Cheshire Cobble. Appalachian Trail: (Cheshire)
80. Laura's Tower- Ice Glen. (Stockbridge)
81. Mahanna Cobble BNRC: (Lenox)
82. Monument Mountain. Trustees of Reservations: (Great Barrington)
83. October State Forest. Fountain DCR:(Washington)
84. Parsons Marsh. BNRC: (Lenox)
85. Pine Cobble Vista. (Williamstown)
86. Raven Rocks. Ragged Mountain. Mt Greylock Re-DCR: (Adams)
87. Robinson Point. Mt Greylock Reservation-DCR: (Williamstown)
88. Rounds Rock. Mt Greylock Reservation-DCR: (Lanesborough)
89. Stony Ledge. Mt Greylock Reservation-DCR: (Williamstown)
90. The Prairie. (Dalton)
91. The Snow Hole. (Petersburg, N.Y.)
92. Washington Mt. Lake Marsh Trail. October State Forest-DCR
93. Williamstown Vista: Mt. Greylock Reservation- DCR
94. Williams College Harris Cabin & Bernard Trail: (North Adams)

73. Adams Vista - Mt Greylock Reservation

From Adam's Vista - Mt. Greylock Reservation. Adams, MA

Location: Mt Greylock Reservation-DCR. Adams (Berkshire County)
Parking Cheshire Harbor Trail GPS: N42° 36' 38.57" W73° 9' 23.24"
Parking Gould Trailhead GPS: N42° 37' 8.47" W73° 9' 1.51"
Adams Vista- Summit Road GPS: N42°38' 5.58" W73° 9' 53.80"
Wow Factor: 9 Accessibility: Seasonal road-side or hike ~ 4.5-mile RT

Information: The Adams Vista is located on the Mt Greylock Summit Road just 0.3 mile up from the junction of Rockwell Road and Notch Road. You can drive up from either Lanesborough or the North Adams entry gates; it is 7.5-miles up from either gate to a small pull-off for 3-4 vehicles on the Summit Road. The view is guaranteed to be terrific!

For hiking, a popular access is via the Cheshire Harbor Trail; this trail originates from the end of West Mountain Road in Adams and winds 2.3-miles up to Rockwell Road. Note: that the trail does not go directly to the Adams Vista with the last 0.4-mile being on the narrow roadway which unless closed for the season will have vehicle traffic. In addition, this trail hosts the Mt Greylock Ramble an annual event on each Columbus Day. Hundreds of hikers have been participating since 1967 seeking the event's certificate of completion, prizes for the youngest, oldest hiker and fastest ascent.

One other trail, the Gould Trail (2.1-miles) also brings the hiker up to the junction of Rockwell and Notch Roads and then continues up the 0.3-mile on the Summit Road to the vista.

74. Ashuwillticook Rail Trail - Lanesborough

Rainbow on the Ashuwillticook (ash-oo-will-ti-cook) Rail Trail. Cheshire, MA

Location: Adams – Cheshire – Lanesborough, MA (Berkshire County)
Parking GPS: N42° 37' 27.95" W73° 7' 5.88" (Adams Visitor's Center)
Parking GPS: N42° 33' 14.86" W73° 9' 56.02" (Cheshire Lake - Route-8)
Parking GPS: N42° 32' 22.03" W73° 11' 1.21" (Farnam's Road - Route-8)
Parking GPS: N42° 29' 19.90" W73° 12' 13.18" (Lanesborough-Route-8)
Wow Factor: 9 **Accessibility:** Easy to moderate due to length. 11.2 miles

Information: This paved trail is perfect for biking, roller blades running, walking and during the winter, crossing-country skiing. The wide, 10-foot paved trail passes 11.2-miles through the towns of Adams, Cheshire and Lanesborough and is considered one of the most scenic in Massachusetts. It offers outstanding views of the wildlife and scenery as it proceeds by the Cheshire Lakes and the Hoosic River. (e.g. Geese, Swans, Blue Heron, Snowy Egret, Bear, Fox and Raccoons to name a few.) Free parking and restrooms are available at selected locations along the way at the Adams Visitor's Center, Farnam's Road and Lanesborough parking areas.
Directions: **Lanesborough** from junction of Route-8 and Route-9 in Pittsfield, 1.5-miles north on Route-8, left at lights onto Berkshire Mall Road, 150-feet west, trail parking lots on both sides of road.
Farnam's Road from junction of Route-8 and Route-9 in Pittsfield, 5.2 miles north on Route-8, turn left onto Farnam's Road.
Cheshire Lake (upper) on left side of Route-8 rest area in Cheshire.
Adams Visitor's Center follow Route-8 up into Adams, 1st right onto Hoosac Street after passing the President McKinley Statue.

75. Bartholomew's Cobble - Sheffield

Over-hanging Rock is a large escarpment on the Ledges Trail - Sheffield, MA

Location: Trustees of Reservations. 105 Weatogue Rd. Sheffield, Massachusetts 01257 (Berkshire County) westregion@thetrustees.org (413) 229-8600   Fee for non-members or for special programs

Parking GPS: N42° 3' 26.84" W73° 21' 2.85" (Visitor's Center)
Destination GPS: N42° 3' 21.9" W73° 20' 58.8" (Over-Hang Rock)
Destination GPS: N42° 2' 57.9" W73° 20' 36.2" (Fractured Rock)
Destination GPS: N42° 3' 4.60" W73° 20' 52.10" (Cottonwood Tree)
Destination GPS: N42° 3' 0.70" W73° 20' 48.60" (Spero Trail Boulders)

Information: Originally occupied by the Mahican tribe and later settled by Colonel John Ashley, a colonial revolutionary for whom Ashely Falls is named. The current reservation is only a part of a sprawling estate; the name comes from a series of Bartholomew's that owned the property after Colonel Ashley. In 1838 Wyllis Bartholomew purchased the Colonel John Ashley house and five and one quarter acres from the Ashley family. He owned it until his death in 1846 when Wyllis' son Hiram inherited it; Hiram sold it to his son George in 1852 who farmed it for many years. The reservation is named for George Bartholomew who expanded and purchased most of the fields and uplands in the late 19th Century. The Trustees acquired the Cobble in 1946. From 1963 to 2000, additional land, and the historic Ashley House, from where enslaved African American Mum Bett Freeman sued for her freedom has been incorporated into the reservation and hiking trail system.

Referred to as an ecological treasure, this preserve of 329-acres has 800 species of plants; geological cobbles consisting of quartzite and marble, immense boulders and the Housatonic River just to get started. Access to all its intricacies is through only five miles of mostly moderate hiking trails. The reservation also boasts one of the larger Cottonwood trees in the state found at the end of Bailey's Trail at the junction of the Spero Loop Trail.

The highest elevation which provides a panoramic vista to the north overlooking the Berkshire Mountains and the Housatonic River Valley is Hulburt's Hill accessible by a tractor path to the summit.

The Spero Loop Trail passes by Fracture Rock (above) and another 16-foot-tall boulder (below.) Along with other smaller rocks, this boulder cluster is at the southern end of the Cobble near the Massachusetts-Connecticut border.

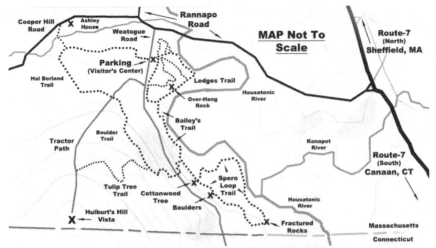

Trails of Bartholomew's Cobble Reservation.

Directions: From the junction of Route-7 and Route-41 just below the center of Great Barrington, MA, travel south on Route-7 for 5.5-miles into the center of Sheffield. From the center of Sheffield, continue south on Route-7 for an additional 2.0-miles. On the right, turn onto Route-7A (Ashley Falls Road) and head south for 0.5-mile. Turn right onto Rannapo Road, from the railway tracks continue south for 1.5-miles to where the road junctions with Cooper Hill Road on a sweeping left corner. Within 100-yards, Weatogue Road (a dirt road) is on the right, 100-yards down on the left is the entry and large dirt parking area for Bartholomew's Cobble.

In Canaan, CT from the junction of Route-44 and Route-7, head north on Route-7 for 1.2-miles. Turn left onto Route-7A prior to crossing state border and head towards Ashley Falls, MA. After 1.0-mile, turn left onto Rannapo Road and follow for 0.9-mile. Turn left onto Weatogue Road (a dirt road), 100-yards down on the left is the entry and large dirt parking area for Bartholomew's Cobble.

Vista from summit of Hulburt's Hill. Bartholomew's Cobble. Sheffield, MA

76. Beartown State Forest CCC Ski Lodge - Lee

Only Twin Chimneys of Beartown State Forest Ski Lodge remain. Lee, MA

Location: Beartown State Forest Pine Street. DCR Lee (Berkshire County)
Parking GPS: N42° 16' 18.70" W73° 16' 33.30" (Pine Street Entry)
Destination GPS: N42° 16' 21.95" W73° 17' 20.67" (Twin Chimneys)

Information: Built by the Civilian Construction Corps-CCC's as a recreational Ski Train destination in the mid-1930's, Beartown Ski Area growth, popularity and longevity (1935 to 1966) grew from (1) open slope and (2) trails to become one of the largest ski areas in Southern New England with (2) open slopes, (5) trails served by (3) rope-tows spanning 820-vertical-feet.

In 1951, Al Prinz, who also operated nearby Oak-N-Spruce resort, took over operations extending a rope-tow to the summit and some trail expansion. During the late 1950's a lack of snow and increased competition from newer ski slopes provided little incentive to invest or operate the Beartown Ski area. The other ski areas installed more comfortable and faster chairlifts along with snow-guns that were able to produce good ski conditions when Mother Nature would not. Eventually it would be surpassed by Jiminy Peak, Catamount, Bousquet and Brodie Mountain Ski areas.

From 1961-1966 the slopes were operated by William T. McCormack president of Beartown Associates, Inc. a.k.a. as the Beartown Ski Club, Inc a non-profit organization. By the end of 1966, the lack of resources and expansion led to the demise of this area to be reclaimed by the woodland forest as we find it today.

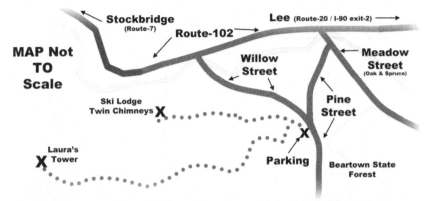

Old access road to remains of Beartown State Forest Ski Lodge.

Directions: Access is via the northern Pine Street entry of the DCR Beartown State Forest which is off Route-102 in South Lee. From Exit-10 from Interstate I-90, head west on Route-102 for 2.5-miles or in Stockbridge from the junction of Route-7, head east on Route-102 for 1.7-miles until turning onto Meadow Street which heads towards Oak & Spruce Resort. Shortly after crossing the old trestle bridge on the Housatonic River, turn right onto Pine Street, in 0.3-mile, Willow Street will merge from the right onto Pine Street. Within 100-yards from this junction, a small parking area on the right with a gated access road is found. Park here, do not block the gate. Across the street is a very tempting area to park, but is private property and is not an authorized parking area. Walk pass the gate and follow the wide trail 0.75-mile until reaching the twin chimneys on the trail. The trail is easy to travel with a short and mild upgrade.

The CCC's built the Chimneys with superb masonry craftsmanship. 1939.

77. Becket Quarry - Becket

Becket Quarry – Becket Land Trust. Becket, MA

Location: 456 Quarry Road. Becket, MA (Berkshire County)
Parking GPS: N42° 15' 3.85" W73° 1' 12.56" (Quarry Road)
Destination GPS: N42° 14' 39.27" W73° 0' 54.05" (Generator shed)
Destination GPS: N42° 14' 39.85" W73° 0' 55.60" (Compressor Truck)
Destination GPS: N42° 14' 42.17" W73° 0' 57.84" (Quarry-lower View)
Destination GPS: N42° 14' 34.00" W73° 1' 02.83" (Drill Test Tunnel.)
Destination GPS: N42° 14' 34.65" W73° 1' 00.65" (Compressor-Portable)
Destination GPS: N42° 14' 39.72" W73° 1' 01.06" (Winch-upper Quarry)
Wow Factor: 7 **Accessibility:** Easy-moderate, roadway trails. 2.0-mile RT

Information: This former Hudson-Chester Granite Quarry was once one of the largest of several quarries in the area and operated from 1850 until closing in the 1960's. The cut granite was shipped by a local railroad to nearby Chester, was polished and then sold throughout the region mainly for monuments or gravestones. Upon its closure, the quarry was left abandoned with derricks, drills, trucks and cut-stone left in place slowly rusting with nature reclaiming the surrounding landscape. The site has virtually remained the same creating a time capsule as a living museum with artifacts from an era where quarrymen harvested stone. Parking fee might be required.

The Becket Land Trust was founded in 1991 by Becket citizens to maintain the hill-town and rural nature of the Town of Becket. Then in 1999, a proposed purchase and reopening of the quarry, motivated citizens of Becket to purchase the quarry and donated it to the land trust. A self-guided tour is in store for those having interest, plaque

Old compressor truck and equipment part of the quarry's self-guided tour.

kiosks are in place and on-line maps are found if you Google the Becket Quarry Land Trust. Otherwise, imagination on who, what or how it was to work here will be augmented by many strange or unusual structures in place or hiding in over-grown bushes. In 2022, the Trustees of the Reservations acquired the 300-acres from the Becket Quarry Trust. A parking kiosk fee is now being utilized.

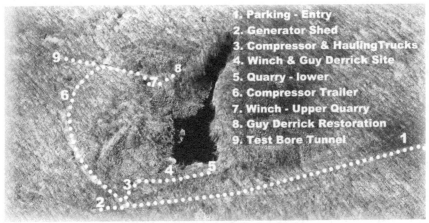

1. Parking - Entry
2. Generator Shed
3. Compressor & Hauling Trucks
4. Winch & Guy Derrick Site
5. Quarry - lower
6. Compressor Trailer
7. Winch - Upper Quarry
8. Guy Derrick Restoration
9. Test Bore Tunnel

Becket Quarry - Basic Layout.

Directions: From Interstate-90, Exit-10 in Lee. Turn onto Route-20 and head east for 14.0-miles (Route-8 will join Route-20.) At the junction where Route-8 turns left heading north, turn right on Bonny Rigg Hill Road. Drive 1.2-miles and turn left on Quarry Road, then drive for 1.0-mile, the parking and trail entry will be on the right. A parking/entry fee has been established along with strict parking regulations anywhere else on adjacent roads to reduce the liabilities and trash from beer and/or swimming parties at the quarry. From the parking area, the first 0.5-mile in on the access road is easy and will bring you into the four- corners where access to the upper and lower quarry and other aging or rusting relic's will be found.

This is the mast of a "Guy Derrick" also referred to as a "Boom Derrick. The vertical mast is 55-feet in height and is held upright by several cables, but still allowed it to rotate. At its base is a large 12-foot "Bull Wheel" it was connected through steel cables and pulleys; it could rotate the mast using a winch. Extending from the mast a large 50-foot "Boom" that could be raised, lowered, or tilted into position and was used to hoist the cut stone.

This Guy Derrick at the top level of the quarry is being restored, the mast is original, the broken boom requires repair or replacement and the bull wheel was corroded and in disrepair has been restored.

A similar derrick called a "Stiffed Leg Derrick" was also used; these had their masts supported not by guide wires, but by two or more "stiff" ridged beams keeping the mast upright. Both types of derricks were used here, reportedly; at least seven Guy Derricks and three Stiff Leg Derricks were in operation here. The technology is astounding and simple, although we would be hard pressed to find skilled laborers and operators who could perform under these working conditions today.

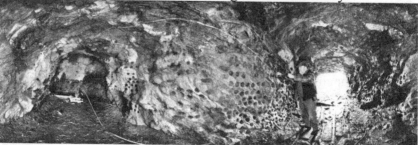

Inside the drill testing tunnel, the bore holes are recessed some 60-inches.

78. Busby's Knob - Spruce Hill

North Adams from Busby Knob - Spruce Hill. Savoy State Forest, Ma

Location: Center Shaft Road-Savoy State Forest-DCR. (Berkshire County)
Parking GPS: N42° 39' 29.20" W73° 3' 20.70" (Central Shaft Road)
Busby Trail Cellar-Hole GPS: N42° 40' 7.90" W73° 3' 48.40"
Destination GPS: N42°40'12.38" W73° 4'8.40" (Busby's Knob)
Wow Factor: 8 **Accessibility:** Moderate-plus, marked trail 3.0-mile RT

Information: Located on the southern end along the ridge line of the Hoosac Range, Spruce Hill provides a spectacular view of North Adams and Mt. Greylock Reservation. Access is from either Route-2 and down the Hoosac Range Trail or from with Savoy State Forest on the Busby's Trail which is the first approach illustrated here.

I prefer the Busby Trail starting from Central Shaft Road for the trail begins on a shaded woodland trail with a relatively level altitude and slow altitude gain for the first mile, although, this first mile can become very muddy. After arriving at remnants of an old cellar hole the trail will turn uphill beginning a steeper ascent for the next 0.3 mile with the last 0.1-mile ascent having the greatest required effort until you reach and break out onto the Spruce Hill out-cropping. The trail is popular and well-trodden with several steep segments having been improved with natural stone stairways greatly assisting the ascent.

The location is often used by environmentalists to observe and count hawks or owls during their migrations which can often be seen soaring on the thermal updrafts which the ridge is well noted for.

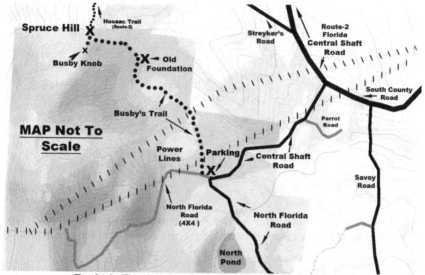

Busby's Trail to Spruce Hill – Savoy State Forest

Directions: Traveling east on Route-2 (Mohawk Trail) and from the crest of the hill above the iconic hair-pin turn, travel 0.6 mile turning right onto Shaft Road. Travel 0.4-mile, bearing right and following the main road as it becomes Central Shaft Road. Travel south for 2.0-miles, turn right and continue following Central Shaft Road. Continue 1.0-miles, you will enter into Savoy State Forest, just pass the DCR Park offices on your right and at the sweeping left turn is the roadside parking area kiosk at the trailhead for Busby's Trail.

(Note the 4x4 dirt road that heads west into the woodland, is not the Busby Trail.) From behind the kiosk a foot trail does lead onto the Busby Trail, it also originates as a gated road 100-feet down the road mentioned above. Follow the blue blazed Busby Trail north, in 0.1-mile pass under powerline #1, another 0.3-mile pass under powerline #2. Continue for another 0.6-mile reaching a fieldstone foundation. From here, the trek is uphill and west, the first 0.2-mile is relatively a moderate-plus. At a stone wall crossing there is a bench which will invite a short rest. The last 0.2-mile will be the steepest with a switch-back or two before breaking onto the ridgeline and joining with the Hoosac Trail. The best views are from the knob just a little further south on the ridge by passing through a small patch of brushy growth. *Caution: The outcrop has a steep drop-off and no barriers.*

Hiking the Hoosac Ridge (South) to Busby Knob

The Hoosac Range Trail after Sunset Rock travels south and will pass by a multitude of mossy covered stone ledges and lush green ferns patches.

Parking GPS: N42° 41' 47.30" W73° 3' 53.60" (Route-2, BNRC)
GPS: N42° 41' 31.80" W73° 3' 48.70" (Sunset Rock)
GPS: N42° 41' 31.00 W73 03 49.4 (Hoosac Trail south to Spruce Hill)
GPS: N42° 41' 18.00" W73° 3' 49.60" (Escarpment Wall)
GPS: N42° 41' 15.10" W73° 3' 49.20" (Egg Rock-Erratic on trail)
GPS: N42° 41' 03.60" W73° 3' 56.40" (The Marbles (2)-small erratics)
GPS: N42° 40' 42.10" W73° 3' 59.30" (Vista looking East-Charlemont)
GPS: N42° 40' 24.60" W73° 4' 9.60" (Vista looking West-North Adams)
GPS: N42° 40' 14.50" W73° 4' 6.80" (Junction with Busby's Trail)

With vehicles parked on each end it is sensible to hike one-way from Route-2, down the Hoosac Range Trail and finishing with the Busby Trail then out to Central Shaft Road in Savoy State Forest.

Parking is on Route-2, just pass the upper turn heading east, above the historic Hairpin Turn on the right. A large gravel parking area with room for a dozen vehicles is on the right. Behind the kiosk the trail begins heading south, the trail is blazed with a white-bar with a red-slash in the middle. The initial 0.5-mile segment of the trail will bring you to the junction for the loop trail up to Sunset Rock; either direction brings you to the small vista with a complete circle and back to the parking area providing you a 1.6-mile trek. The junction to continue south on the Hoosac Range Trail, is located 100-feet west from the Sunset Rock vista location.

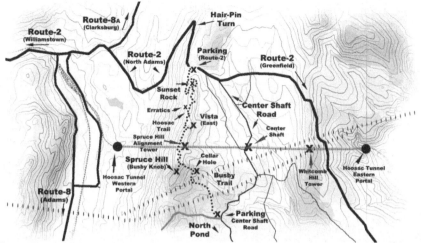

From Route-2 Hoosac Range Trail to Spruce Hill and Busby's Knob Vista. Out on the Busby's Trail to Center Shaft Road, Savoy State Forest.

From the BNRC Route-2 parking area, the 1st mile is uphill at a relatively moderate slope. Afterwards the trail is mostly level meandering along on top of the ridge for the next 1.8-miles until meeting the Busby's Trail on east side Spruce Hill. Surprisingly, there were few vistas, with the summer foliage providing a green canopy and cool breeze. There is a vista that looks off towards the east and Spruce Hill and Busby's Knob provides awesome views looking west.

The Hoosac Range Trail after Sunset Rock travels south. Here the trail passes in the vicinity where one of the Hoosac Tunnel Alignment Towers was situated.

These two small erratics are just off the trail 30-feet. Jim Boyle (Left) and Russell Dunn (right) provide dimension on how big the boulders aren't.

Reaching Spruce Hill, you will junction with the Busby's Trail blazed with blue dots. Descending down from Spruce Hill, the first 0.2-miles is relatively steep with some stone stairs being in place to assist, reaching a stone wall crossing and newly installed bench the last 0.2-miles is moderately easy. Reaching the old foundation means the trail on out is relatively easy and approximately 1.0-mile to reach Central Shaft Road and your parked secondary vehicle. As you venture out and pass beneath two different powerlines, after the second power line the roadway can be puddled or extremely muddy.

An old farm house foundation is located on the lower Busby Trail.

Directions: Parking for the BNRC Hoosac Range Trail is 300-feet east, on Route-2 from the crest of the hill above the iconic hair-pin turn and on the right.

79. Cheshire Cobble - Cheshire

Town of Cheshire from Cheshire Cobble

Location: Appalachian Trail, Cheshire Ma (Berkshire County)
Parking GPS: N42° 33' 22.00" W73° 8' 39.50" (Notch Road Parking)
Destination GPS: N42° 33' 1.00" W73° 8' 50.80" (Butt Rock)
Destination GPS: N42° 33' 2.90" W73° 8' 51.90" (Cobble Vista)
Wow Factor: 9 **Accessibility:** Moderate to strenuous 1.8-mile RT.

Information: Cheshire Cobble has a view unlike any other, so close and direct to Cheshire, that it feels like an act of surveillance or an intrusion of the town's privacy through binoculars or a telephoto lens. Although, the hike up to the rocky outcropping (0.8-mile) is relatively short, it definitely will provide your legs and lungs a cardio work-out for the uphill trail is moderate with steep sections most of the way.

Just below the parking area and trailhead, South Brook flows beneath the Notch Road Bridge and usually has a nice set of cascades forming a small waterfall along with a wading pool. This is a very nice location to decompress afterwards and enjoy the ambient white noise of the cascades along with a dose of tranquility.

Please respect the residential area at the end of Furnace Hill Road; while the Appalachian Trail does have access here, there is no parking at this location.

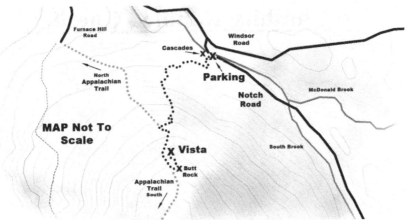

Cheshire Cobble from Notch Road. Cheshire, MA

Directions: From Cheshire center on Route-8 (North-South Street), at the traffic light head east on Church-Main Street for 0.5 mile. Shortly after passing by the Ashuwillticook Bike Trail and over a small bridge, turn right onto East Main Street. Continue east for 0.7-mile, the road will become Windsor Road as it heads uphill. As you crest the road top, turn onto Notch Road on your right, it drops downhill, just after you cross the South Brook Bridge, on your right, pull into the improved parking area for several vehicles.

From the parking area, the trail begins and starts its upward jaunt. Much of the lower section are old road beds and, in the spring, may have muddy segments. After the first 0.2-miles you will bear left onto a newer and more recent repositioning of the trail. (The older trail would lead to the Appalachian lower on the northern slope.) This newer section will join the Appalachian Trail higher up in about 0.3-mile. After joining the AT trail, you'll continue heading south, then a switchback or two as approach the cobble at its base. Continue up the rocky trail as if you seem to be going past, however at a higher point, the trail will turn left and up a small natural stone stairway. Note: at the top is "Butt Rock" a small boulder having a naturally carved U or dip for one to sit their butt down and rest. From here you leave the AT following the ridge-line back down and north for 0.1-mile until you break out onto the cobble. *Caution: there are no railings or barriers at the edge of the outlook and for safety of other hikers walking below never throw any objects off from the top.*

Trekking poles and good boots will make this hike much easier. Depending on the season and day, a jacket or wind-breaker will also be appreciated once on the top of the cobbles.

<u>80.</u> Laura's Tower-Ice Glen - Stockbridge

Looking towards Kripalu from Laura's Tower – Stockbridge, MA

Location: Park Street. Stockbridge, MA (Berkshire County)
Parking GPS: N42°16' 42.19" W73°18'26.96" (End of Park Street)
Destination GPS: N42° 16' 38.0" W73°18'19.7" (Shark Fin Rock)
Destination GPS: N42° 16' 26.9" W73°18'23.6" (Inscription Rock)
Destination GPS: N42° 16' 18.78" W73° 18' 7.58" (Laura's Tower)
Accessibility: Moderate short walk 2.0 miles RT

Information: *Ice Glen* is a fantastic, steep-walled gorge filled with large boulders, shelter caves, and toppled trees. In the early days, a hiker had to be fairly nimble to make it through the glen. Today, a more clearly defined path, with enhancements, exists.

Shark Fin Rock is a 12 to 14-foot-high, 16-foot-wide boulder that was named by somebody who believed that the rock resembled the menacing triangular dorsal fin of a shark lurking beneath the forest floor.

Inscription Rock is a 10-foot-high, moss-covered rock-face with letters carved into it. The inscription reads: "Ice Glen. The gift to Stockbridge of David Dudley Field 1891." Because the rock-face is moss-covered, it can be easily missed as you make your way into the glen.

Laura's Tower is a large 40-foot, steel observation tower at the summit. A steep stairway leads to the top which will probably the most strenuous portion of this hike. A tremendous view will be the reward for those persevering to the tower's top platform.

History: Ice Glen has been intriguing hikers and adventure-seekers since the early 1800s. It was originally called Ice Hole, undoubtedly because some of its crevices and talus caves would hold onto ice until the middle of summer. In 1891, 40-acres of land, including the Ice Glen, was donated to the Laurel Hill Association by David Dudley Field, a prominent New York attorney.

It was during this time that revelers carrying torches and dressed in fantastic costumes would make their way through the glen to celebrate special occasions. The procession would start at the Stockbridge House (today known as the Red Lion Inn) and move to the foot of Laurel Hill where a huge bonfire awaited. After much dancing, singing, and frivolity, the gatherers would pick up kerosene-soaked torches and march up to the Ice Glen, from where they would make their way through its narrow passageways, eventually reaching an open field at the other end.

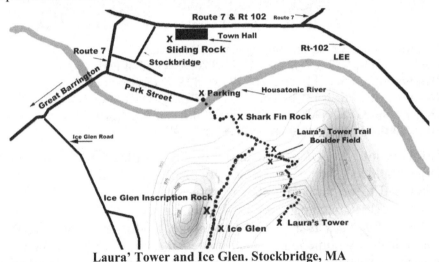

Laura' Tower and Ice Glen. Stockbridge, MA

Directions: From Stockbridge at the Red Lion Inn (junction of Route-7 & Route-102), drive south on Route- 7 (South Street) for 0.2-mile. When you come to Park Street, turn left and head southeast for 0.3-mile to a cul-de-sac parking area at the end of the street.

Proceeding on foot, walk across the historic 1936 Laurel Hill suspension footbridge that spans the Housatonic River. Afterwards cross over the railroad tracks and up into the woodlands.

To *Shark Fin Rock* - Head uphill for 0.1-mile. Look to your left to see Shark Fin Rock, 50-feet into the woods. After another 0.1-mile the trail splits; left for Laura's Tower and right for Ice Glen.

Shark Finn Rock on the way to Laura's Tower – Ice Glen. Stockbridge, MA

Ice Glen - When you come to the junction with the Laurel Hill Trail, bear right onto the Ice Glen Trail and continue south for over 0.1-mile. Inscription Rock can be seen to your right and slightly off trail, just as the Ice Glen begins. Passing by Inscription Rock, follow a 0.2-mile trodden path that winds its way through a boulder-filled gorge. Some caution will be required for scrambling over damp and mossy boulders. Ice is notably found in the small nooks and crannies under these boulders well into June and sometimes July. In addition, a remarkable coolness within the glen will be felt during the hot and humid summer days

*Laura's Towe*r - Hiking up the Laura's Tower Trail from the junction with the Ice Glen Trail, you will encounter a field of large boulders as the trail zigzags up the 600-feet of elevation gain to the summit and to the tower.

Inscription Rock is highlighted by smearing ice & snow into its script.

81. Mahanna Cobble - Lenox

Mahanna Cobble-Berkshire Natural Resources Council - Lenox, MA

Location: Mahanna Cobble-BNRC Lenox (Berkshire County)
Parking GPS: N42° 25' 8.00" W73° 16' 35.60" (Bousquet Ski Resort)
Destination GPS: N42° 24' 41.20" W73° 16' 47.80" (Trail Turn - A)
Destination GPS: N42° 24' 31.10" W73° 17' 23.40" (Cobble Spur Trail)
Destination GPS: N42° 24' 30.00" W73° 17' 20.70" (Mahanna Cobble)
Wow Factor: 7 **Accessibility:** Moderate 2.8-mile RT

Information: Hiking up to Mahanna Cobble on the southern end of Osceda Mountain-Bousquet Ski resort is a venture well worth the exertion. Looking south from Mahanna Cobble the landscapes of Kennedy Park, Yokum Ridge, central Berkshire County and on a clear day Monument Mountain looming in the far distance all free from the clutter of roadways and structures. Fall foliage seekers here will be guaranteed a meditative environment free from interruption.

Bousquet Ski Resort is allowing access for three seasons in use of their trails. (No access in winter due to skiing.) In my opinion this is a great option; there is plenty of parking, the trail ascends at a moderate slope on the eastern slope of Osceda Mountain. The return trip provides an awesome view of Pittsfield from the top of Bousquet's ski slopes. In addition, Mahanna Cobble is one of five notable cobbles with public access, the others being; Pine Cobble, Cheshire Cobble, Tyringham Cobble, and Bartholomew's Cobble.

The Mahanna Cobble is one of the more recent additions to Berkshire Natural Resources Council BNRC properties. In 2007, Bousquet Ski Area owner the late George W. Jervas was selling the cobble to BNRC, a conflict arose when a land developer who was to purchase the ski area, also made claim that the cobble was to be part of that transaction, with their intent to develop the mountain top into a resort and restaurant. In 2010, the courts affirmed BNRC's right to purchase the 233-acres land. Actually, Mahanna Cobble is within the township of Lenox while the northern parts are within the city of Pittsfield boundaries. At the cobble, a stone bench is dedicated to George Wislocki who served as BNRC first director from 1967 to 2001 and thanks him for his vision or determination to protect this ridgeline and the many other locations throughout the Berkshires.

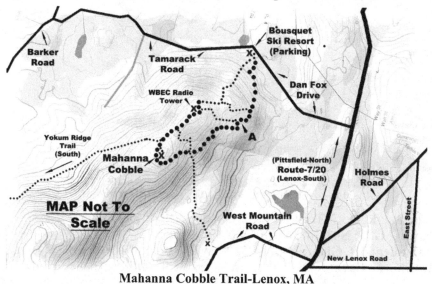

Mahanna Cobble Trail-Lenox, MA

Directions: Bouquets Ski Area parking is located off Dan Fox Drive which is just north the Pittsfield-Lenox boundary off Route-7 and Route-20. Turn onto Dan Fox Drive and head west for one mile. The Bousquet's Ski Lodge and parking area will be on you left.

Start pass and behind the waterslide, turn left (walking up with the Condo's on your left.) Bear left until reaching trail junction-A at 0.6-miles, turn left at what looks like a small turnaround, within 25-feet, right rear, a foot-path will begin. The trail will gradually transverse the slope, continue up for 0.7-mile to where it will merge onto the blue-blazed, West Mountain Road trail. Shortly, within 0.1-mile, the spur trail will turn off and, on the right, out to the cobble.

Return back to the West Mountain Road trail, turn right, stay on this trail north for 0.5-mile, it will pass two trail junctions which head south, stay north pass the radio tower reaching the top of the ski slopes. Follow the service paths down to the lodge and parking.

82. Monument Mountain - Great Barrington

Old-Man-of-Monument Mountain. Great Barrington, MA

Location: Route-7, Trustees of Reservations (Berkshire County)
Parking GPS: N42°14' 36" W73°20' 07" (Route-7)
Monument Mt. Giant: N42°14' 52.8" W73°20' 16.5" (On the Hickey Trail)
Hawthorne Cave: N42°15' 03.7" W73°20' 25.8" (Off the Hickey Trail)
Inscription Rock: N42°14' 59.84" W73°20' 28.94"
Devil's Pulpit: N42°14' 45.0" W73°20' 22.2" (View point)
Old Man-of-the-Mountain: N42°14' 45.0" W73°20' 22.2" (View point)
Submarine Rock: N42°14' 27.4" W73°20' 06.9" (Mohican Monument Trail)
Wow Factor: *Monument Mt Giant—8;--- Hawthorne Cave – 4; Inscription Rock – 3; Devil's Pulpit – 5; Old Man-of-the-Mountain – 5; Submarine Rock – 6*
Accessibility: *Monument Mt. Giant – 0.4-mile hike; Hawthorne Cave – 0.6-mile hike; Inscription Rock – 0.8-mile hike; Devil's Pulpit – 1.2-mile hike; Old Man-of-the-Mountain – 1.3-mile hike; Submarine Rock – 0.2-mile hike.*
Degree of Difficulty: Moderate to strenuous

Description: *Monument Mt. Giant* a.k.a *Kissing Rock* is a massive, 20 to 25-foot-high, trail-side boulder that is part of a large field of boulders and talus that have collected along the east side of the mountain. Good spot to suggest a rest and a power kiss to energize!

Hawthorn Cave is a 6-foot-high, 4-foot-deep shelter cave with a tiny stream flowing over it that has formed at the head of a small ravine. The cave is historically significant, for it was here that Nathaniel

Hawthorne, Herman Melvin, and a party of friends took shelter from a storm while hiking up the mountain in 1850.

Inscription Rock is a small boulder that bears the following inscription:

THIS RIDGE AND THE CLIFFS
OF MONUMENT MOUNTAIN WERE CONVEYED
TO THE TRUSTEES OF PUBLIC RESERVATIONS
BY DEED BEARING DATE OCTOBER 19 A.D. 1899
IN FULFILMENT OF A WISH OF ROSALIE BUTLER
THAT SUCH PORTIONS OF THIS MOUNTAIN
MIGHT BE PRESERVED TO THE PEOPLE OF BERKSHIRE
AS A PLACE OF FREE ENJOYMENT FOR ALL TIME

Inscription Rock at junction Hickey and Mohican Monument Trails.

The Devil's Pulpit, also called Pulpit Rock, is an enormous, 80–100-foot-high detached rock pillar of white quartzite located on the east side of Monument Mountain's Peeskawso Peak (1,642').

Old Man of the Mountain, also called Profile Rock, is the rock profile of an old man's face—Massachusetts's version of New Hampshire's now defunct Old-Man-of-the-Mountain.

Submarine Rock (our name) is a massive rock 7-feet-in-height and nearly 40-feet-in-length. The trail-side end of the rock harbors a tiny shelter cave. The opposite end is flat and smooth, suggesting that this rock column broke off from its base, perhaps starting off higher up on the mountain until it toppled over and slid downhill to its present location

History: Monument Mountain is the centerpiece of a 503-acre preserve overseen by the Trustees of Reservations since 1899. The original parcel of land was gifted, with endowment, in 1897 by Miss Helen C. Butler as a memorial to her sister, Rosalie Butler. Additional parcels of land were acquired by the State in 1980, 1985, and 1986.

The top of the mountain is an elongated, nearly 1,650-foot-high ridge of pinkish quartzite, narrow or barely wider than 15-feet in spots.

The mountain's name comes from William Cullen Bryant's poem, *Monument Mountain*.

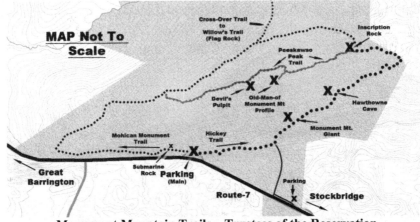

Monument Mountain Trails – Trustees of the Reservation

To Monument MT. Giant – Go 0.4-mile until you come to the Monument Giant, directly next to the trail on your left.

To Hawthorne Cave – At 0.6-mile, you will reach the turn-off on your left to Hawthorne Cave. A 100-foot-long spur path leads to it.

To Inscription Rock – Inscription Rock is reached at 0.8-mile. The boulder is located at the junction of the Peeskawso Peak Trail, Hickory Trail, and Mohican Monument Trail. From Inscription Rock, begin following the red-blazed Squaw Peak Trail south:

To Devil's Pulpit Overlook -- Go 0.3-mile. At the point where the Peeskawso Peak Trail bears right and descends to a lower shelf, turn left and follow a spur path uphill and then southeast to the Devil's Pulpit overlook. Although not obvious at first, the overlook bluff forms the Old Man-of-the-Mountain profile, which can only be seen farther south looking back.

To view Old Man-of-the-Mountain – Climb back down the spur path to the junction. Instead of following the Peeskawso Peak Trail downhill (straight ahead), bear left and continue on an unmarked, but well-worn trail south for over 0.1-mile until you reach the Devil's Pulpit. From here, look north to view the Old Man-of-the-Mountain profile.

Caution; is paramount while traveling across the Peeskawso Peak Trail. There are no barriers along the eastern side of the impressive, but dangerous cliffs. Slippery rocks, strong gusts of winds and poor judgment have and can contribute to incidents of injury or death.

In addition, on the back side of Monument Mountain, off the Mohican trail there is now a blazed cross-over connecting trail for Willow's Trail and Flag Rock Vista destination. (See Chapter #49.)

Monument Mt. Giant a.k.a Kissing Rock on the Hickey Trail.

Hawthorne Cave - Off the Hickey Trail. Great Barrington, MA

Directions: From Stockbridge (junction of Route-7 south & Route-102), go south on US 7 (South Street) for ~3.1-miles and park to your right off Route-7 within a large evergreen grove. There is no parking fee for Trustees of Reservations members, but will need their current membership pin number. Others will need to use the parking kiosk and display the ticket on the dash of the vehicle.

From Great Barrington (junction of Route-23 east & Route-7), go north on Route-7 for ~3.0-miles and park on your left.

From the north end of the parking area, follow the orange-blazed Hickey Trail uphill northwest: this direction is the fastest and steep ascent. The Mohican Monument trail is longer, but not as strenuous, both trails junction at Inscription Rock.

83. October State Forest Fountain

Sandwash Reservoir Aerator – Fountain. October Mountain State Forest

Location: October Mt State Forest-DCR. Washington (Berkshire County)
Parking GPS: N42° 22' 37.72" W73° 9' 2.03" (AT Trailhead-Beach Road)
Parking GPS: N42° 21' 33.54" W73° 10' 50.99" (Lenox-Whitney Road)
Destination GPS: N42° 22' 1.21" W73° 10' 20.90" (Sandwash Fountain)
Wow Factor: 7 **Accessibility:** Moderate short hike woodland road.

Information: Situated in the eastern side of October Mountain State Forest at the base of Sandwash Reservoir Dam is what is known as the Sandwash Fountain. Actually, it's an aerator that assists in the oxygenation of water or to dispel gaseous elements e.g. carbon dioxide or tannic acid from the reservoir's lower level of decaying vegetation. While it is not the *Trevi Fountain* found in Rome, it is a unique item to be found deep within the woodlands.

Early 1800's till about the Civil War, quartz sand that was quarried from near here was washed in this brook, ergo the name *Sandwash*, and put in barrels where it was driven down the mountain via Roaring Brook Trail and turned into glass in Lenox Dale. In places you can still see on the trail the remnants of white quartz sand that spilled during the trip down the mountain. This silica-quartz sand was found it to be 99.99 percent pure and only needed to be washed before crushing which dictated the need for water to wash the silica before being shipped worldwide. During the 1930's the Sandwash Dam was built creating the reservoir which through two separate aqueducts supplies water to each the Ashley Lake and Farnham Reservoirs part of Pittsfield's watershed located within October Mountain State Forest.

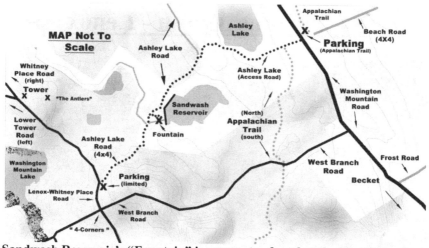

MAP Not To Scale

Whitney Place Road (right)
Tower
X X "The Antlers"
Lower Tower Road (left)
Washington Mountain Lake
Ashley Lake Road (4x4)
Lenox-Whitney Place Road →
Fountain
Sandwash Reservoir
Parking (limited)
West Branch Road
" 4-Corners "
Ashley Lake Road
Ashley Lake (Access Road)
Ashley Lake
Appalachian Trail
X Parking (Appalachian Trail)
Beach Road (4X4)
Washington Mountain Road
(North) Appalachian Trail (south)
West Branch Road
Becket
Frost Road

Sandwash Reservoir's "Fountain" is an aerator found at the base of the dam.

Directions: In Pittsfield, at the junction of Dalton Division Road and Washington Mountain Road, travel south 4.5-miles on Washington Mountain Road to where the Appalachian Trail crosses and the junction of Beach Road on the left. Across the road, a small dirt access road to Sandwash Reservoir heads west, follow this access road, in 0.3-mile you will pass Ashley Reservoir on your right, continue west, uphill for
0.5-miles. At the top of the hill, an older segment of Ashley Lake Road junctions and comes in from the right. Continue left, downhill for 0.7-mile, past the 1st levee of the Sandwash Reservoir and downhill towards the base of the dam. At the small brook, turn left and walk up-stream to where the fountain is located towards the base of the dam.

From four corners in October Mountain State Forest, head north on Lenox-Whitney Place Road for 0.2-mile. On the right, Ashley Lake Road heads east. Follow this unmaintained road for 0.7-mile to the base of Sandwash Dam. At the brook, turn right, upstream towards the base of dam the "Fountain" should be found.

(From Chapter #92) Four corners are best approached off Washington Mountain Road turning onto West Branch Road (N42°21' 57.19" W73° 8' 36.82") and drive west for 2.2-miles. The other, is off Route-8 below North Becket, turning onto County Road (N42°18'52.76" W73° 5' 40.02") Follow County Road west for 0.9-mile, bear right at the fork staying on County Road. Continue north for 3.75-miles, (the pavement ends ~ 2.0-miles) at the next fork, bear right, County Road becomes Lenox-Whitney Place Road with an additional 1.2-miles to 4-Corners.

84. Parsons Marsh - Lenox

Looking over Parson Marsh from raised observation deck - Lenox, MA

Location: 170 Under Mountain Road. BNRC. Lenox (Berkshire County)
Parking GPS: N42° 21' 51.97" W73° 18' 17.84" (Under Mountain Road)
Destination GPS: N42° 21' 51.95" W73° 18' 3.30" (Observation Platform)

Information: Berkshire Natural Resources Council (BNRC), the Town of Lenox, and private landowners have partnered to conserve 183 acres for wildlife habitat, and recreation. Hunting or fishing is allowed.

Designed and built in 2018, the Parson's Marsh Trail was designed to be readily accessible by wheelchairs or "senior friendly" for people with limited mobility. The first 600-feet of trail has a crushed stone surface which joins with a raised section of wooden trail that raises up and outward over the marsh and with a 900-feet wide boardwalk terminating with an observation deck.

Along with the viewing platform there is a picnic area, signs with descriptions of the natural and human history of the area and a place frequented by a variety of animal or bird species and allows people of all abilities to experience our beautiful woodlands and wild places.

Directions: At the junction of Route-7A and Route-183 in center of Lenox, head west on Route-183 south (West Street) towards the main entry Tanglewood. Continue for 1.4-miles turning right onto Under Mountain Road. The trailhead is 0.9-miles down the road on the right.

85. Pine Cobble - Williamstown

Williams College from Pine Cobble - Williamstown

Location: Williamstown (Berkshire County)
Parking GPS: N42° 42' 58.02" W73° 11' 6.86" (Pine Cobble Road)
Tree GPS: N42° 43' 18.40" W73° 10' 4.90" (On trail)
Destination GPS: N42° 43' 15.60" W73° 9' 57.90" (Pine Cobble Vista)
Wow Factor: 8 **Accessibility:** Moderate to Strenuous 4.5-miles RT

Information: Pine Cobble is located on land owned by the Massachusetts DCR, Williams College and Williamstown Rural Lands Foundation. This rocky outcrop is a popular hiking destination; the views of Williamstown and North Adams are exceptional, especially during the fall foliage. The trailhead from Pine Cobble Road parking lot has room for several vehicles; from there the blue blazed trail is a well-worn path that meanders on the easy-side of moderate for the first mile. While the climb does become steeper, only the last 0.5-mile becomes slightly strenuous with seasoned hikers finding this last heft only moderate.

At the top, a spur trail off to the right will venture out onto the rocky ridge with some great panorama views of the valley below and of the Mt. Greylock Range to the south. Williamstown seen to the west will be closer and to the east North Adams will be observed better if you brought binoculars. Where the spur trail junctions, if you continue north, within 0.5-miles you will summit on top of East Mountain and further along join up onto the Appalachian Trail. The Long Trail also begins at the Vermont and Massachusetts border which travels the length of Vermont.

(Above) An unusual oak tree sits on the trail just 300-feet below the spur trail to the cobble. The story told: after this oak tree was originally cut down, three shoots sprouted around the edges of the old stump while the center rotted away creating a bowl. Often water collects in the bowl, which for many a pup has enjoyed after the trek uphill. A reminder to bring water, unless you do not mind sharing.

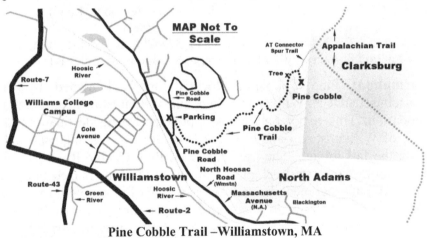

Pine Cobble Trail –Williamstown, MA

Directions: From the eastern end of the traffic rotary and park at the junction of Route-2 and Route-7, head east on Route-2 for 0.6-mile through Williams College Campus to the first and only traffic light. Turn left onto Cole Avenue, travel 0.75-mile to its end, turn right onto North Hoosac road. Traveling east for 0.4-mile taking the first left onto Pine Cobble Road. Drive uphill for 0.1-mile to the parking area on your left. The Pine Cobble, blue blaze trail starts slightly uphill and across the road at the trail sign. Over time this area has become more residential, please be respectful of their privacy as you pass near some of their property.

<u>86.</u> Raven Rocks - Mt Greylock Reservation

Looking towards Mt Fitch and Mt Williams from Raven Rocks Vista.

Location: Mt Greylock Reservation - Adams (Berkshire County)
Parking GPS: N42° 37' 39.20" W73° 8' 15.30" (Greylock Glen-Thiel Rd)
Parking GPS: N42° 40' 24.37" W73° 8' 21.00" (Notch Road-North Gate)
Destination GPS: N42° 39' 3.30" W73° 8' 23.60"

Information: Remoteness, lack of marked or maintained trails make the venture to ***Raven Rocks (***Also known as ***Big Rock)*** suitable only for those prepared for a physically strenuous hike and the skills to navigate between GPS coordinates or dead reckoning.

Ascent up the ***Thunderbolt Trail*** from Thiel Road in the Greylock Glen is steep with a matrix of turns to reach Ragged Mountain's Vista #1. From Vista#1, there is **no marked, blazed or maintained trail** to *Raven Rocks* until returning back to Point B on the Thunderbolt Trail and down to the Thiel Road parking. Essentially this approach makes a 6.5-mile loop and is considered strenuous.

All the next destinations are best achieved with a GPS unit, a compass and pre-reconnoitering of topographic maps or Goggle Earth. A dose of common sense along with preparing for unknown situations by being self-sufficient is essential for safety and enjoyment for this day long trip. While all the trails leading to Ragged Mountain are well marked, it is the unmarked trails from Vista #1 to Vista #2, Vista#2 to Raven Rocks and from Raven Rocks down to point B which will be the biggest challenge. The GPS index map will provide a GPS configured route. (See page 194.)

The other approach to Ragged Mountain's trail junction at point **G** is not as steep. The trailhead for the ***Bellows Pipe Trail*** is off Notch Road at the sharp bend 0.2-mile below the Mt Greylock north gate. The hike to point **G** is 2.2-miles on the *Bellows Pipe Trail*. This approach works best when another car is left at the Thiel Road parking area. After reaching *Vista#1*, the approach to *Raven Rocks* and back down to the Greylock Glen will be same as the Thunderbolt Trail loop approach which is discussed first.

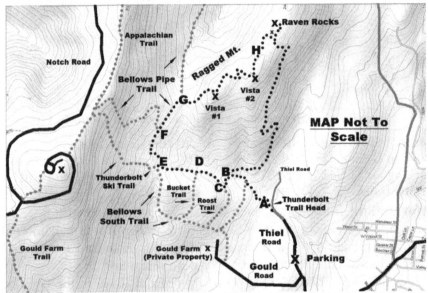

Trail Map to Raven's Rock on Ragged Mountain. Mt Greylock, Adams

Greylock Glen-Parking Theil Road: N42° 37' 39.20" W73° 8' 15.30"

Presently, there are concrete barriers at this location and in the future parking may be closer or slightly back at the junction of Gould and Thiel Road. From the barrier, walk up Thiel Road 0.5-mile, presently it starts as pavement and becomes dirt. At the end Thiel Road will bear right, continue straight, a slender metal sign indicates ***Thunderbolt Road*** along with older wooden signs nearby labeling it as the ***Thunderbolt Ski –Foot Trail.***

A: Thunderbolt Rd Trailhead GPS: N42° 38' 1.44" W73° 8' 26.8"

Heading up-hill on the *Thunderbolt Trail*, Hoxie Brook will be on you right, continuing 0.4-mile to point **B** where the *Roost Trail* turns uphill on your left. Towards the right is a wash-out of a trail which continues across Hoxie Brook and is the location where you will return back to from Raven Rocks.

B: Roost Trail GPS: N42° 38' 9.90" W73° 8' 45.70"

The *Thunderbolt and Roost Trails* continue uphill southerly away from Hoxie Brook for 0.1 mile. At point **C,** the *Thunderbolt Trail* will turn sharply right and back towards Hoxie Brook, while the *Roost Trail* will bear left toward *Bellows South Trail* and Gould Road.

C: Thunderbolt Trail GPS: N42° 38' 5.70" W73° 8' 43.90"

The *Thunderbolt Trail* continues north and uphill for the next 0.6-mile, pass point **D,** until the *Bellows Pipe Trail* junction at point **E.**

D: Bucket Trail GPS: N42° 38' 12.20" W73° 8' 57.30

Here the Bucket Trail descends south from the *Thunderbolt Trail* to the lower *Bellows South Trail.* (No turns, point of reference only.)

E: Thunderbolt onto Bellows Pipe GPS: N42° 38' 15" W73° 9' 15.65"

At point **E,** turn right and head north on the *Bellows Pipe Trail.* (The *Thunderbolt Trail* will continue uphill steeply and will eventually connect with the Appalachian Trail and to the Mt Greylock summit in about 1.1-miles.) Continue north towards point **G** for 0.5-mile. (Along the way on the left, you will pass point **F,** the *Bellows Pipe Summit Trail* which leads to the summit.) Continue straight towards point **G.**

F: Bellows Pipe Summit Trail GPS: N42° 38' 26.20" W73° 9' 15.80"

G: to Ragged Mt GPS: N42° 38' 37.30" W73° 9' 7.20"

While *Bellows Pipe Trail* will continue straight for 2.2-miles to the Notch Road in North Adams, at point **G** turn right, head east and onto the *Ragged Mountain Trail* for 0.3 mile to reach Vista #1.

X: Ragged Mt Vista #1 GPS: N42° 38' 39.40" W73° 8' 49.70"

Here ends the well-trodden trail with approximately 0.5-mile to the next destination, Vista #2. The good news is that the long steep uphill trekking is basically done.

Mt Greylock Summit as seen from Ragged Mt Vista #1.

Continuing onward to Vista #2 the usage of a GPS will certainly help. Although, this is not all that difficult even without a GPS unit, but that said, even a seasoned woodsman can get turned around due to different seasons or a misconception in direction or distance traveled.

It is not too much to say Mother Nature treats everyone equal, but you are hiking in New England a northern jungle and those who prepare will have greater enjoyment in such adventures. This part of the adventure is broken down into 3-segments: *Vista #1 to Vista #2, Vista #2 to Raven Rocks* and from *Raven Rocks the return to Greylock Glen.*

GPS Points To Vista #2: Refer to GPS trail points map. (Page 194)

#0: N42° 38' 39.40" W73° 8' 49.70" Vista #1: (end of marked trail) Return back up the access trail and head northeast across Ragged Mt southernmost knoll-summit for ~0.1-mile (northeast 30°). Look for a faint trodden path or occasional blue-dot on saplings especially at the Start. (Originally there was a trail over to Vista #2.)

#1: N42° 38' 46.63" W73° 8' 44.22" Turn right, (east 110°) heading downhill for 0.1-mile onto a flatish area between two knolls.

#2: N42° 38' 45.47" W73° 8' 39.70" Bear left (northerly 33°) for 0.1 mile, over a small knoll and down into another valley.

#3: N42° 38' 46.30" W73° 8' 35.10" Continue (easterly 100°) for 0.1 mile, up onto a knoll where Vista #2 sits further on down to its southern ledge.

#4: N42° 38' 44.62" W73° 8' 31.24" 114° Vista #2

View of Adams and East from Ragged Mountain Vista #2. GPS: H

The view from Vista #2 has a very nice panoramic view spanning north from Clarksburg, directly overlooking Adams, and to Cheshire. It is a terrific view during the fall foliage season and for that matter anytime is good.

View of Raven Rocks from point #6 the northern most point on "The Spine"

From Vista #2 the route to Raven Rocks is essentially heading north ~0.4 mile, following the rocky *"Spine"* of the ridge north from Vista #2. Half-way there is a descent which brings one off the ridge down to the forest floor. Within 0.2 mile at the base of the Raven Rocks is a talus cave and from here a short steep climb up to the vista is worth the effort.

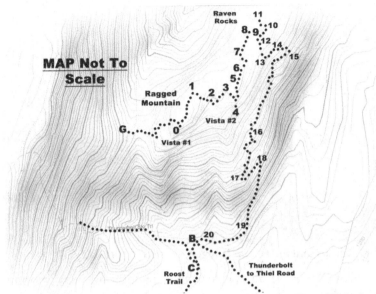

GPS index from Bellows Pipe Trail, Point G to point B on Thunderbolt Trail

#5: N42° 38' 52.02" W73° 8' 29.53" Approximately the half-way point walking on the Spine of Ragged Mountain, on its western edge with some open vistas of Mt. Greylock, Mt. Fitch and Mt Williams. Continue north for 0.1 mile.

#6: N42° 38' 53.82" W73° 8' 28.65" On the northern tip of the rocky Spine towards Raven Rocks. Wonderful view of Raven Rocks some 0.2 miles away (as the "Raven" flies) north 20°. Descend down on a winding path, (not that difficult) onto the woodland level.

#7: N42° 38' 55.16" W73° 8' 29.08" Continue north for 0.1-miles (north 15 to 20°)

#8: N42° 39' 0.80" W73° 8' 27.00" Begin a sweeping right easterly turn (60° to 75°) almost to Raven Rocks base.

#9: N42° 39' 1.83" W73° 8' 23.72" Raven Cave is found at the base of Raven Rocks. Going to the top is best by starting east in a sweeping uphill left turn. (95° to 110°)

#10: N42° 39' 01.5" W73° 08' 22.1" Continue in a left-counter clockwise sweeping for up through the brush until reaching the lower-level rocky tier of the vista. Turn right, continue north up rocky slope to the top.

#11: N42° 39' 03.4" W73° 08' 23.6" Enjoy the vista you are halfway.

Within Ragged Mountain's Raven Rocks Talus Cave.

The way home: If you came in from Notch Road via the Bellows Pipe Trail and did not place a 2nd vehicle in Greylock Glen on Thiel Road, you will have to retrace your steps back to Vista#2 & #1 and return on the Bellows Pipe Trail. If needed or want, returning the way you came up the Thunderbolt is still an option. You came in this way and have the GPS coordinates.

If you did leave a vehicle on Thiel Road or originally came up the Thunderbolt Trail approach, the next section will continue the adventure from *Raven Rocks* down the east side of Ragged Mountain. This will return back to point **B** where the junction of the Roost Trail and the Thunderbolt Trail takes you down to Thiel Road and the vehicle.

Fortunately, the return back down from Raven Rocks is not that hard for an old cart road or "Herd" path is very apparent once found. The path is a blessing, but it follows the very steep downside on east side of Ragged Mountain.

#10: N42° 39' 01.5"   W73° 08' 22.1" Finding this old herd path is your chore in the initial decent from Raven Rocks, returning down from the vista to #10, the base of Raven Rocks will be on you right westerly, but not directly to its base. From this point, head southerly (195°) for 200-feet. The terrain will flatten some and funnel through a rocky area.

Looking east off Ragged Mountain very steep east side from the "Herd" path.

#12: N42° 38' 59.10" W73° 8' 23.10" Continue easterly and sweeping somewhat left (165°) for 300-feet.

#13: N42° 38' 56.50" W73° 8' 22.40" The brim of the steep slope should start to become apparent along with the beginning of the path. The path is unmarked and begins getting rather steep as it turns more north (~70°) for a short distance.

#14: N42° 38' 57.5"W73° 8' 18.6" The trail returns easterly downhill.

#15: N42° 38' 57.1"   W73°   8' 16.2" The path at #15 is a switch-back towards the right and turns downhill heading southerly as it traverses the hillside for the next ~1.2-miles. This is a good old path with steep terrain bordered by rocky ravines, but has no technical or 3-points of contact climbing and is not that bad.

#16: N42° 38' 36.07" W73° 8' 26.5"   Just 0.5-miles below #15, on the left, down in a parallel ravine are some super boulders and have become known as "King Kong Ravine"

#17: N42° 38' 26.51" W73° 8' 29.02" Important to note: You need to be aware of this Hair-Pin turn junction which has 3 directions, it is very easy to walk pass the turn you want that come up low or an angle and can be easily missed. You want to sharply turn left and downhill.

#18: N42° 38' 30.05" W73° 8' 23.3" Another switch-back, 0.1-mile downhill turning back south. Continue heading downhill southerly for 0.3-mile.

#19: N42° 38' 14.20" W73° 8' 27.20" Turn right westerly for ~0.3 mile until you cross Hoxie Brook returning to point **B.**

King Kong Boulders #16 East side of Ragged Mt. Mt Greylock Res. Adams, MA

#20: N42° 38' 11.74" W73° 8' 45.10" If you came from Notch Road, turn left on the other side of the brook going downhill ~0.4-mile on the Thunderbolt until reaching Thiel Road, continue straight until reaching pavement in 0.1-mile, only 0.3-mile more to reach the parking barrier and the vehicle.

Directions: *Thiel Road* from the President McKinley Statue on Park Street in Adams, follow Maple Street west 0.4-miles; turn left onto West Road for 0.4-mile turning right onto Gould Road, drive uphill pass the apple orchard for 0.3-mile, turn right at the fork onto Thiel Road, park near the barrier. (Gould Road turns left towards Pecks Falls.)

I hope the above is not overly complicated with having an emphasis on GPS coordinates, compass bearing degrees or distances. The lack of marked trails and remoteness of the terrain found on Ragged Mountain will provide different experiences for each individual. Hopefully providing more information to those who know how to utilize the data is better for safety and a more enjoyable adventure.

NOTE: Seems like the Ragged Mt Vista #2 is being called Raven Rocks. Having been told in the 1970's by a Mt Greylock DEM, Mountain Maintenance Mentor, that Raven Rocks cannot be seen from the Town of Adams, and is best seen from the Greylock summit. The northerly, larger vista & cave is often known as "Big Rock." To my understanding, having worked on Mt Greylock myself, it is known by many, as Raven Rocks for having a more grandiose view than Vista #1 or Vista #2 and has the talus cave. It is confusing point of contention, for a TOPO map, does place a labeled location on the east side of Ragged Mountain. However, the label "Raven Rocks" is placed at a much lower elevation and is not located near either location.

87. Robinson Point - Mt Greylock Reservation

Robinson Point looking west into the "Hopper" Mt Greylock Reservation.

Location: Mt Greylock Reservation. Williamstown (Berkshire County)
Parking GPS: N42° 38' 34.51" W73° 9' 47.69" (Notch Road trailhead)
Destination GPS: N42° 38' 43.20" W73° 9' 54.40" (Robinson's Point)
AT Spur Trail GPS: N42° 38' 31.50" W73° 9' 45.60" (To Notch Road)

Wow Factor: 8 **Accessibility:** Moderate to Strenuous 0.5-mile RT

Information: This vantage point is somewhat obscure and has very limited parking, but provides a guaranteed "Wow" from its small rocky perch looking west, out and over of the Hopper compared to looking east and into the Hopper from Stony Ledge. This location will provide a spectacular view of The Hopper, Mt. Prospect and Mt. Fitch especially during fall foliage season with far less effort than accessing the Stony Ledge Vista. The trail is steep and easy to follow, but can have sections in less than pristine condition. Reaching Robinson Point can be a matter minutes down dropping 270-feet, 0.2-miles, with returning back up slightly more in time and effort.

A definitive person on who this particular location is named after has been difficult to specify. Reported in *Appalachian Trail Names: Origins of Place Names Along the AT* by David Lillard. It was either "Judge Arthur M. Robinson" from Williamstown who served 13-years of service to the reservation or for "George D. Robinson" serving in Massachusetts Congress 1877-1884 and then Massachusetts Governor 1884-1887." Many advocate that the honor goes to Judge Arthur M. Robinson with bonds directly tied to the Mt. Greylock Reservation.

It does stand up to scrutiny, as many honorariums and accolades that define the Mt. Greylock Reservations landscape are from previous individuals who had close community and developmental ties with the reservation. e.g. Williams College President Ebenezer Fitch (*Mount Fitch*) climbed Greylock in 1799, probably over a rough route cut by a local pioneer farmer Jeremiah Wilbur (*Wilbur's Clearing.*) *Bascom Lodge* was named in honor of John Bascom, a Williams College professor and Greylock Reservation Commissioner. *Rockwell Road* built in 1906-07 was named for Francis W. Rockwell of Pittsfield, one of the original Greylock Commissioners and chairman from 1910 to 1925.

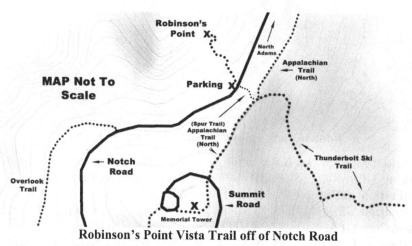

Robinson's Point Vista Trail off of Notch Road

Directions: From the Lanesborough southern entry and the Mt Greylock Visitor's Center gate, head north uphill on Rockwell Road for 7.0 miles until it junctions with the Notch Road just below the Mt Greylock summit. Turn left and heading north on Notch Road for 1.0 mile. On your left, the small 1-2 car pull-off parking and trailhead of Robinson's Point will be found.

From North Adams northern entry, at the Notch Road gate, head uphill and south for 4.7-miles until on your right, the small 1-2 car pull-off parking and trailhead of Robinson's Point will be found.

From Mt. Greylock Summit when parking on Notch Road is limited, hiking north on the Appalachian Trail for 0.3-mile the from the summit parking area, will bring one to s short 0.1-mile spur trail which heads west and down to the Notch Road and trailhead for Robinson's Point. Use caution crossing the Notch Road to trail head.

88. Rounds Rock - Mt Greylock Reservation

Rounds Rock – looking southwest from Vista #2

Location: Mt Greylock Reservation - Cheshire (Berkshire County)
Parking GPS: N42° 35' 36.10" W73°11' 50.11" (Rockwell Road)
Destination GPS: N42° 35' 21.60" W73° 12' 5.80" (View Point #1)
Destination GPS: N42° 35' 21.90" W73° 12' 11.40" (View Point #2)
Destination GPS: N42° 35' 23.07" W73° 12' 10.66" (Northrup Trail-Spur)
Destination GPS: N42° 35' 26.80" W73° 12' 10.00" (Airplane Crash Site)
Wow Factor: 8 **Accessibility:** Easy side of moderate 1.2-mile RT

Information: Rounds Rock is a knoll having one the lowest points of elevation (2,500-feet) found on the Mt. Greylock Reservation. Yet, provides a couple of excellent viewpoints looking south and west towards Pittsfield or Brodie Mountain. Plus, towards the end of July or early August, low-bush blueberries will sweeten the trek if not over-picked prior to your arrival (It is not a secret any longer.)

On the north leg of the loop trail, while sad and intriguing, is the 1948 crash site of a twin-engine Cessna aircraft. In August 1948, the aircraft piloted by John Newcomb from Albany, New York was reported missing. Despite search and rescue over a large area which included Mt. Greylock Reservation, the crash site wasn't discovered until 4 months later by hunters on December 7, 1948. Some parts of the air-frame and engine are still in place along with a memorial.

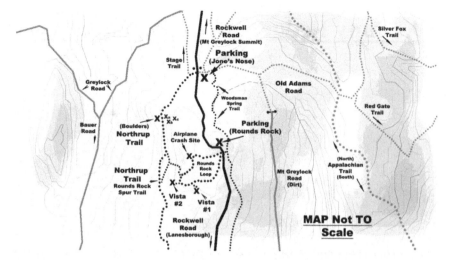

Directions: From the Lanesborough southern entry for Mt. Greylock Reservation from Mt. Greylock Visitor's Center gate, head north uphill on Rockwell Road for 3.0-miles. As you crest over the knoll of Rounds Rock a roadside parking area will be on the right for several cars.

Across the road and up a small slope is the Rounds Rock trailhead. You will not walk very far into the woodlands until you come to where the loop trail forks, to the right the northern leg and crash site, to the left the south leg which passes by the two vista locations first.

Either way you will pass everything one way or another.

There is the spur trail down to the Northrup Trail which is important if you are planning the 2.5-mile loop from Jones Nose, down the Woodsman Spring Trail south 0.7-mile, cross over to Rounds Rock Loop Trail and down the Northrup spur trail onto the Northrup trail north returning to the Jones's Nose parking area.

John Newcomb crash site of a twin engine Cessna aircraft. August 12, 1948

89. Stony Ledge - Mt Greylock Reservation

Stony Ledge commands a view of Mt. Prospect "Hopper" Williamstown, MA

Location: Mt. Greylock Reservation - Williamstown (Berkshire County)
Mt. Greylock Visitor's Center 30 Rockwell Road. Lanesborough, MA 01237
(413) 499-4262
Destination GPS: N42° 38' 39.09" W73° 11' 37.15" (Stony Ledge Vista)

Information: Mt. Greylock's western entry consists of hiking trails passing through the area known as the *Hopper*. The Hopper's name is derived from its bowl-shaped valley made up with steep slopes and reminiscent of a four-sided funnel, which delivered grains to the mill wheel of an old-fashioned gristmills. Stony Ledge is one of the premier viewing locations to take it all in, especially during fall foliage season. Looking north and naming clockwise from Stony Ledge, the summits and ridgelines of Mt. Prospect, Mt. Williams, Mt. Fitch, Mt Greylock, Saddle Ball Mountain and back to Stony Ledge Vista create this beautiful and unique wilderness area.

There are several hiking trails that will provide exhilarating hiking experiences to Stony Ledge or with proper connections all the way to Mt Greylock summit. The Hopper Trail is one of the oldest vintage hiking trails on Mt Greylock Reservation being created in the 1830's by Williams College students as a horse trail. Along with The Haley Farm Trail, Roaring Brook Trail, and Stony Ledge Ski Trail all are well maintained, marked and well-trodden for Stony Ledge access and can be fashioned to create a desirable loop trail.

Previously, the 1930's Civilian Conservation Corps Camp was located on Sperry Road, a gravel road off of the Rockwell Road which comes up from southern access gate in Lanesborough and is where the

Mt. Greylock Reservation Visitor's Center is located. The old CCC camp eventually evolved into the Greylock Sperry Road Wilderness Campground. There used to be full access to Stony Ledge via Sperry Road, but for environmental concerns Sperry Road has been closed to vehicles with hiking into the campground sites or Stony Ledge being the main manner for accessibility.

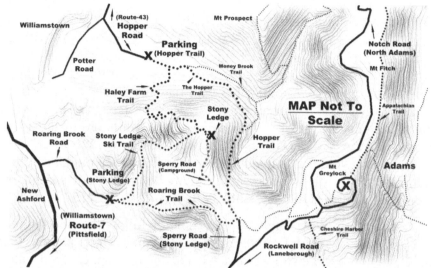

Hopper -Haley Farm - Stony Ledge Ski Trail or Sperry Road to Stony Ledge.

Sperry Road Parking GPS: N42° 37' 27.90" W73° 11' 26.53"
Moderate hiking on gravel road. 3.2-miles total round trip.

Directions: Sperry Road junction is off Rockwell Road, 5.5-miles up from the Mt Greylock Visitor's Center. On the right, parking is for several vehicles at the Dynamite Trailhead. Caution as you cross Rockwell Road walking down Sperry Road for traffic is in both directions. Follow the road; heading north, in 0.6-mile you reach the campground entry, continue north through the campground for another 0.6-mile, continue north, then uphill 0.4-mile until reaching Stony Ledge. The campground is often occupied please respect their privacy, including a group camp site out near Stony Ledge.

Hopper Road Parking **GPS:** N42° 39' 19.58" W73° 12' 17.38"
Haley Farm Trail is a moderate to strenuous uphill 2.0-miles to Stony Ledge, down Sperry Road campground and back down the lower Hopper Trail for a 5.2-miles total round trip.

Directions: Haley Farm Trail and The Hopper Trail From the center of Williamstown. At the junction of Route-2 and Route-43, head south on Route-43 (Water Street) for 2.5-miles (becomes Green River Road.) Turn left onto Hopper Road at "Sweets Corner", cross over the bridge and follow Hopper Road for 1.4-miles, bearing left and staying on Hopper Road for another 0.75-mile to the large dirt parking lot on the right.

Walk east from the parking area for 0.2-mile, pass the gate, for the *Haley Farm Trail* **(GPS: N42° 39' 16.70" W73° 12' 1.20")** will turn right and will quickly cross a field entering into the forest; avoid the HFT loop trail by staying with the blue blazes at all times. While the trail will be essentially uphill, it is well maintained and worn, easy to follow. Just below the destination to Stony Ledge, the Haley Farm Trail and Stony Ledge Ski Trails meet with 0.1-mile left of the ascent arriving at the vista. **(GPS: N42° 38' 43.00" W73° 11' 42.50")** Depending on your conditioning, some will find this a moderate climb with some places strenuous, reaching Stony Ledge in 1.5 to 2.5-hours. *Stony Ledge Vista* **GPS: N42° 38' 39.09" W73° 11' 37.15"**

You can return down the way you came or follow the Sperry Road south, down through the campground for 0.9-mile. Here, just pass the latrine, between campsite #1 and #3, the lower Hopper Trail enters Sperry Road and will continue up an additional 1.75-miles as the upper Hopper Trail to the Mt. Greylock summit from the campground if you desire a trip to the summit.

Hopper Trail- Lower **GPS:** N42° 38' 1.50" W73° 11' 20.60"
Turn left and follow the lower Hopper Trail down, it is steep, with a remarkably straight and consistent gradient. From the campground, ~1.0-mile down, the Money Brook spur trail will be off to the right, stay straight with the Hopper Trail. Within an additional 1.0-mile, the main Money Brook Trailhead will junction off the Hopper Trail to the right, continue on the Hopper Trail west and in 0.1-mile you will return to where the Haley Farm Trail branched off and will be almost back to the Hopper Road parking area. Well done!

Roaring Brook Road **Parking GPS**: N42° 38' 11.02" W73°13' 7.8"
Stony Ledge Ski Trail is moderate to strenuous-up 1.9-miles to Stony Ledge; return down Sperry Road campground and down the Roaring Brook Trail. 4.6-miles total round trip.

Directions: <u>**Roaring Brook and Stony Ledge Ski Trail**</u> From the junctions of Route-7 and Route-43 (Green River Road) just south of Williamstown, head south on Route-7 for 1.6-miles.

Turn left onto Roaring Brook Road a dirt road and head east for 0.6-miles. Here head-in parking is on the left for several vehicles.

Note: The Goodell Hollow a.k.a Mt Greylock Ski Club is at the end of the road. The common road etiquette for the final section of Roaring Brook Road leading up to the Ski Club is narrow. For safety, it is one-way up until 2:30 PM and one-way down after 2:30 PM on ski days. Please plan your visit around 2:30 PM to the ski club. Just be aware of this rule.

From the parking area, head east on the Roaring Brook Trail (RBT) for 0.3-mile (cross the brook bridges which are usually intact) to where the Stony Ledge Ski Trail branches off and heads north while the Roaring Brook Trail continues east. From this junction the *Stony Ledge Ski Trail* **(GPS: N42° 38' 6.10" W73° 12' 49.3")** is ~ 1.5-miles to where it joins the *Haley Farm Trail* from the Hopper Road access. **(GPS: N42°38'43.00" W73°11'42.50")** At this point it is only a short 0.1-mile up to *Stony Ledge Vista.* (*GPS*: **N42° 38' 39.09" W73° 11' 37.15")**

You can return down the way you came or follow the Sperry Road south, down through the campground for 1.0-mile to where just down the road from where the lower Hopper Trail enters and across from campsite#1 a small road leads 0.1-mile towards the Ash Group sites. The trailhead for the Roaring Brook Trail is located across the bridge spanning Roaring Brook and takes a quick right following the brook downstream. **(GPS: N42° 37' 56.19" W73° 11' 18.91")**

Continue heading down stream for 0.1-mile to where the trail will cross the brook again, a spur trail on the left goes down steeply to the Deer Hill Falls; continue on the RBT, heading downhill for 1.2-miles to where it will re-join the Stony Ledge Ski Trail. Pass here in another 0.3-miles west and your back to the parking area.

Looking towards Mt Greylock summit from the Arthur "Kelly" Hooks bench. Dedicated in 2003 at Stony Ledge Vista, brush and tree growth has hidden its setting/view more and more each year. GPS: N42° 38' 40.14" W73°11' 36.88"

90. The Prairie - Dalton

"The Prairie" – Dalton

Location: Chalet Wildlife Management. Dalton (Berkshire County)
Parking GPS: N42°29'20.36" W73° 8'52.20"
Destination GPS: N42°30'41.8" W73°08'51.8"
Type of Formation: Unique Boulder Field
Wow Factor: 6 **Accessibility**: Moderate to difficult 5.0-miles RT
Difficulty: The hike is on trails not marked or maintained and approaches
~5.0 miles and could be considered difficult for unprepared hikers.

Description: The Prairie is an immense expanse of exposed Cheshire
Quartzite bedrock that covers an area 0.05-mile by 0.05-mile across.
The bedrock is slightly tilted and relatively barren of flora except for
occasional brush and areas of moss. Of particularly interest are the
numerous small-to-medium-sized boulders (including tiny stones and
pebbles) that lie scattered about—literally a graveyard of glacial
boulders. This is a very unique site, unlike anything else we have
described in western Massachusetts. The largest boulder is 6-feet in
height, located at the northwest corner of the boulder field, but there
are many 2–4-foot-high boulders scattered about that are equally as
interesting to view.

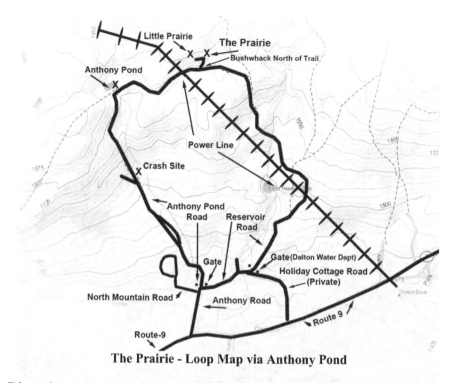

The Prairie - Loop Map via Anthony Pond

Directions: From Dalton (junction of Route-8A/Route-9 & Route-8), go northeast on Route-8A/Route-9 (North Street) for 0.9-mile. Turn left onto Anthony Road and drive north for 0.3-mile (or 0.05-mile past North Mountain Road). At a fork or sharp right corner, Anthony Road continues straight, as a smaller, gated dirt road. (This is commonly known as Anthony Pond Road). Pull off to the side of the road making sure not to block the gate. From here, proceed on foot, following the old Anthony Pond Road (to your left) heading steadily uphill northwest for 1.5-miles. Note, there are no major turns and Anthony Brook will be off on your right. (*Refer to map*). If you happen to see a faded cross-shaped marker to your right, 1.0-mile along the way, (N42°30' 04.4" W73°09' 26.1") it marks the site where a small aircraft crashed in 1999 and you're on the correct trail. When you come to Anthony Pond (N42°30' 28.6" W73° 09' 32.4"), turn right, and begin following a continuation of an old wood's road/trail, now heading east for 0.5-mile until you reach the power lines. The road continuing east passes under the power lines and re-enters into the woods directly across. At or about 0.1-mile (N42°30' 37.9" W73°08' 52.8") turn left and bushwhack uphill, going north, for 300 to 500-feet to reach the lower edge of The Prairie.

Nearby, is Little Prairie—also an inclined expanse of quartzite bedrock roughly 200 feet west through woods from the top edge of The Prairie. As titled, the Little Prairie is smaller in area and lacks any significant boulders.

The map included shows how the hike could be made into a loop. From the Prairie, continue east. At a junction, turn right, and precede steadily downhill, first southeast, and then southwest, to return to your car. Either approach or return is ~ 2.3 miles each way.

91. The Snow Hole - Petersburg Pass

"The Snow Hole" – Taconic Crest Trail – Petersburg, N.Y.

Location: Taconic Ridge Trail. Petersburg, N.Y.
Parking GPS: N42° 43' 23.61" W73° 16' 40.19" (Petersburg Pass Parking)
Junction GPS: N42° 45' 27.50" W73° 16' 53.10" (Snow Hole Spur Trail)
Destination GPS: N42° 45' 32.40" W73° 16' 50.10" (The Snow Hole)
Wow: Factor: 9 **Accessibility:** Taconic Crest Trail; 6.0-mile RT

Information: The *Snow Hole* is a cave-like 50-foot crevasse off the Taconic Crest Trail in New York State near the southern Vermont border. It is said, that snow can be found down inside at the base of the depression even during the summer months, our escapade in late June did find a thick layer of icy-snow at the bottom, conceivably it could exist easily into July or maybe longer. The earthen fissure is readily accessible at its eastern end by a ground level entry point and along with a 60-foot, narrow sloped pathway down into the interior. A lush green velvety moss clings to the rocky surfaces and along with the cooler temperatures as you descend will provide a surreal sensation, especially if the ambient air temperature above is hot and humid. The crevasse edges are unprotected, use caution at its edges to prevent falling in or knocking stuff down onto companions below. While walking inside some of the ice and snow hidden beneath leaves and can be slippery.

The Snow Hole – Taconic Crest Trail

Directions: In Williamstown, from the junction of Route-7 and Route-2, head south on Route-2 for 2.2-miles, turn right as Route-2 heads uphill and west, (Route-7 continues south.) Continue on Route-2, up 4.0-miles, on top of the hill, on the left is a dirt parking area. Across the road, up a small embankment is the Taconic Crest Trail trailhead, heading north, the trail is well maintained, easy to follow and is a moderate trek of 2.7-miles to the Snow Hole spur trail. The spur trail will descend east for 0.2-miles to your destination. Note: On some topo-maps at 1.5-miles from the start, might be marked as the "Snow Hole" this is not the location you seek; it refers to a ravine with the same name only.

Even if no snow is present, this unique geological wonder has been visited over many years with carved names and dates as far back to the late 1800's

92. Washington Mountain Lake Marsh Trail

Passing through reeds on the Washington Mountain Lake Marsh Trail.

Location: October Mountain State Forest. Washington (Berkshire County)
Parking GPS: N42° 21' 9.73" W73° 11' 16.60" (Schoolhouse Road #2)
Destination GPS: N42° 21' 11.24" W73° 11' 16.28" (Trailhead)
Accessibility: Trail is a level, moderate 2.8-miles RT; Trail planks are in need of repair or replacement in places where the trail crosses streams or coves. Beaver dams and high spring waters can be problematic engulfing bridges or trail segments, best trekking during drier summer months, but bring insect repellant.

Information: Located in October Mountain State Forest the trail follows the perimeter of what is called Washington Mountain Marsh. It was to be Washington Mountain Lake, but the dam built for its creation did not hold water due to a geological fissure, the dam was ripped out once and built twice in 1970's and cannot successfully hold the water safely.

This particular area was settled by many Dutch farmers who later in the 1890's sold their farms to William C. Whitney who purchased over 24-farms. Whitney at that time fenced in this area with a 12-foot-high barrier and stocked with exotic game, moose, elk as a personal game preserve. When clearing the land for the lake and dam project, older trees were found with pieces of fencing still attached

Crossing over at the beaver dam on the western side of the Marsh Trail.

In addition, you may notice at the trailhead or around the area that large tracts of mature spruce plantations exist. These were planted as seedlings by the CCC's in the 1930's and have begun to be harvested for their timber. In progressive forest management, the logging of these swaths of timber, opens up that area for forest regrowth and renew forest habitat for other species creating a healthier forest.

Washington Mountain Lake Marsh Trail - October Mountain State Forest

Directions: Your first task is to locate what is known as 4-Corners in October Mountain State Forest. Most roads through-out the forest are graded dirt and gravel roads with no markings. Four corners is best approached off Washington Mountain Road turning onto West Branch Road (N42°21'57.19" W73° 8'36.82") and drive west for 2.2-miles. The other, is off Route-8 below North Becket, turning onto County Road (N42°18'52.76" W73° 5'40.02".) Follow County Road west for 0.9-mile, bear right at the fork staying on County Road.

Continue north for 3.75-miles, (the pavement ends ~ 2.0-miles) at the next fork, bear right, County Road becomes Lenox-Whitney Place Road with an additional 1.2 miles to 4-Corners.

From 4-corners, head west on West Branch Road for 0.5-mile. Park at the next junction where road goes straight and/or turns sharply left and down towards Schoolhouse Lake #2. Park on the corner, the trailhead, along with an entry into an old cemetery is adjacent back across the road and 50-feet towards 4-corners.

Washington Mountain Lake Marsh Trail. October Mountain State Forest

Transition zone between the woodland and that of the marshland growth.

93. Williamston Vista - Mt Greylock

A sail plane passes at eye-level and very near to the Williamstown Vista.

Location: Mt Greylock Reservation Mt. Prospect (Berkshire County)
Parking GPS: N42° 40' 9.62" W73° 10' 3.92" (Notch Road)
Destination GPS: N42° 40' 21.96" W73° 10' 26.37" (Williamstown Vista)
Wilber's Clearing Shelter: N42° 40' 4.07 " W73° 10' 12.52" (Shelter)
Wow Factor: 10 Accessibility: Easy side of moderate 1.2-mile RT
Contact: Mount Greylock Visitor's Center   30 Rockwell Road, Lanesborough MA
www.mass.gov   413-499-4262   mount.greylock@state.ma.us

Information: Mt Prospect is within the Mt Greylock Reservation and can be approached from 3-directions. The *Appalachian Trail* and the *Prospect Trail-Hopper Trail* both junction at the *Williamstown Vista* and is a great resting spot with a magnificent view. From Vermont, the Appalachian Trail south ascends 0.9-mile up the northern slope of Mt Prospect with a strenuous and continuous steep upgrade topping out before the vista. The *Prospect Trail* upward is also a steep and steady ascent 1.0 mile to the summit with a 0.8-mile trek across its ridge to the vista. Descending Mt Greylock's summit and heading north on the Appalachian Trail will also pass by the Williamstown Vista. Great views which only gets better with fabulous sunsets, fall foliage, spectacular storm clouds or the sudden appearance of a sail plane silently in-flight, along with constant comings and goings of AT hikers with distant north or south quests. Williamstown Vista will provide a dynamic experience for every beholder every time.

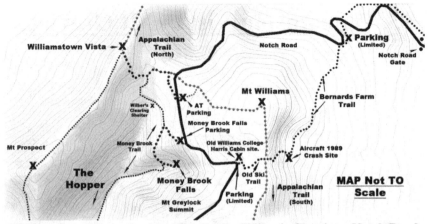

Williamstown Vista -Appalachian Trail - Wilber's Clearing - Notch Road

Directions: The easiest and best starting point for the Williamstown Vista is following the AT north from Wilbur's Clearing parking, only ~ 0.6-mile, 2/3 less stamina needed and much quicker. From the bottom gate on Notch Road, drive 2.2-miles up to a small parking area for several cars on the left, marked with a kiosk and spur trail to the AT south. Being on the Appalachian Trail the trail is well marked and maintained.

Across from the parking area, a spur trail goes 0.1-mile joining the AT trail north. (can go back down the road to where the AT crosses Notch Road and taking a left. Follow the AT north, it will junction in 0.2-mile with the Money Brook Trail and to the *Wilbur's Clearing* lean-to shelter. Stay on the AT north, for a short 0.2-mile moderate up-hill climb to Prospect Mt and Williamstown Vista.

Wilbur's Clearing is named after Jeremiah Wilbur, the farmer that owned and farmed 1,600-acres of land along the northern flank of the mountain. By the early 1800's, Mr. Wilbur had cleared most of the area for pasture and hay production. The shelter is used both by local as well as AT hikers.

94. Williams College Harris Cabin – Mt. Greylock

Chimney of the Harris Cabin – Mt Greylock, Williamstown, MA

Location: Mt Greylock Reservation Williamstown (Berkshire County)
Parking GPS: N42° 40' 28.09" W73° 8' 29.81" (Notch Road-Gate)
Parking GPS: N42° 39' 47.90" W73° 9' 39.10" (Notch Road-upper, 4th turn)
Destination GPS: N42° 39' 48.90" W73° 9' 37.50" (Harris Cabin)
Destination GPS: N42° 39' 49.61" W73° 9' 27.67" (Appalachian Trail)
Destination GPS: N42° 39' 50.80" W73° 9' 20.10" (Bernard Trail-Aircraft)
Wow Factor: 6 Accessibility: moderate with short 1.2-mile RT

Information: In 1932, a cabin was built between Mt. Williams and Mt. Fitch. This cabin, built by the CCC, had a living room with fireplace, a kitchen with stove, a bunk room and a loft. The Williams Outing Club purchased the cabin in memory of Norman Harris a Williams Graduate (1931) who perished in a car accident shortly after graduating. Organized Outing Club trips and individual Outing Club members used the cabin extensively in the mid-late 1940's and into the early 1950's. In addition, the Harris Memorial Cabin was used by Appalachian Trail hikers until October 1962, when it was burned down by vandals during Halloween.

From the chimney, head uphill east on the blue blazed trail for 0.3-mile until it junctions with the Appalachian Trail and the Bernard's Farm Trail. Continuing down and east on the Bernard's Trail for 0.2-miles, there is aircraft wreckage from a 1989 crash site on the east side of Mount Williams. Some parts of the plane remain including a large section of fuselage, the pilot whose plane crashed in 1989 near the Bernard Farm Trail survived, although two passengers did not.

The remoteness and steep terrain field of debris the debris field highlights the trauma of the impact and rescue operations that went on here at that time

Aircraft wreckage from 1989 crash, Bernard Farm Trail. North Adams, MA

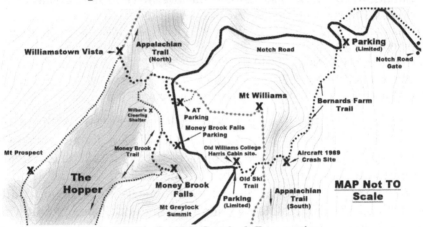

Notch Road of Mt Greylock Reservation.

Directions: The Notch Road is a seasonal road, from the bottom gate on Notch Road, drive 2.9-miles up to a small paved parking area for 2-3 cars on the left. The chimney of the Harris Cabin is 150-feet in from this trailhead; the old ski trail is off on the right, follow it up and over the AT onto Bernard Farm Trail and down to the crash site.

Bernard Farm Trail does begin at the Notch Road gate, the trail is essentially an all up-hill trek until reaching the AT Trail. In the summer, you can shorten the trail by starting at the trailhead located on the 4th switchback curve. A small unmarked, unimproved parking spot for only 1 to 2 cars will be found 0.9-mile up on the left going up.

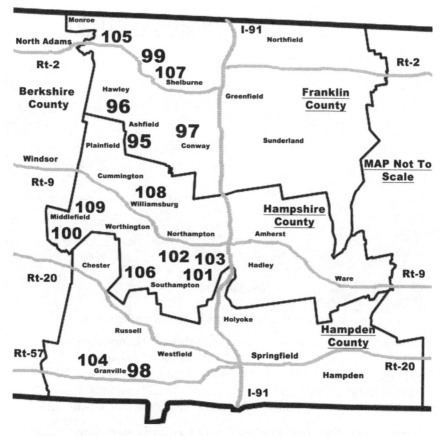

<u>Western</u> **Massachusetts Hikes and Vistas**

95. Chapel Ledge. Trustees of the Reservations: (Ashfield)
96. Charcoal Kilns. Hawley State Forest-DCR (Hawley)
97. Conway Station Dam. South River: (Conway)
98. Drake Mountain – Granville Reservoir. (Granville)
99. High Ledges. Audubon Sanctuary: (Shelburne)
100. Keystone Bridges. (Becket-Middlefield-Chester)
101. Manhan Rail Trail. (Northampton-Easthampton)
102. Northampton- Haydenville Bikeway (Northampton)
103. Norwottuck Rail Trail. (Northampton-Hadley-Belchertown)
104. Phelon Memorial Forest. North Lane: (Granville)
105. Raycroft Look Out. Monroe State Forest-DCR: (Florida)
106. Stevens Property. Hilltown Land Trust: (Huntington)
107. Stone Fire Tower. Massaemett Mt: Shelburne MA
108. Williamsburg 1874 Dam Trail (Williamsburg)
109. WWII Aircraft Crash Memorial. Garnet Hill: (Peru)

95. Chapel Ledge-Ashfield

Climbing Wall at Chapel Ledge – Ashfield, MA

Location: Trustees of the Reservations. Ashfield (Hampshire County)
Parking GPS: N42° 28' 57.22" W72° 45' 36.86" (Williamsburg Road)
Destination GPS: N42° 28' 59.68" W72° 45' 42.29" (Climbing Wall)
Destination GPS: N42° 29' 1.73" W72° 45' 43.22" (Summit Vista)
Wow Factor: 7 **Accessibility:** Moderate trail to summit 1.1-mile RT

Information: The well-known Chapel Falls is very popular, the trail that heads in the opposite direction and uphill is also well known by rock-climbing enthusiasts. As a sport within the Berkshires, Chapel Ledge is sanctioned by the Trustees of the Reservations and provides an excellent rock escarpment for beginners to learn or to practice their skills. Following the trail west and uphill for 0.1-mile will bring you to the "climbing wall." However, if you do not want to take the cliff-face short-cut, you can continue pass this location and by continuing another 0.3-mile to reach the summit of Chapel Ledge.

Directions: From Ashfield center, travel east on Route-116 for 1.5 mile into South Ashfield, at the sharp bend/fork in Rt-116, bear right taking Williamsburg Road south for 2.2 miles. There is a Trustees of The Reservations sign for Chapel Brook, park here or across the road where a small lane is located.

From Williamsburg center, off Route-9, follow Ashfield Road, north (becomes Williamsburg Road), for 6.7-miles until the parking area is on your left. (Chapel Falls chapter #29 for map and directions.)

96. Charcoal Kilns - Hawley

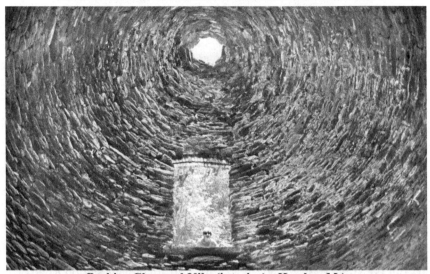

Beehive Charcoal Kiln (interior) - Hawley, MA

Location: Kiln Road-Hawley State Forest-DCR. (Franklin County)
Parking GPS: N42° 33' 39.83" W72° 52' 39.88"
Destination GPS: N42° 33' 47.49" W72° 52' 46.05"
Wow Factor: 8 **Accessibility:** Easy level short walk 0.4-mile RT

Information: In Hawley, is one of oldest beehive-shaped charcoal kiln in New England. Built in 1870, the historic kiln is constructed with flagstone measuring 25-feet in diameter by 25-feet in height and designed to hold 35-cords of wood. Making charcoal in New England was once a thriving and necessary industry. Charcoal was used in the home to heat and cook, while iron forges and blacksmiths used it to heat their metal to shape and fashion tools. In a baking process, a kiln is used to transform wood that is not suitable for lumber into charcoal becoming a fuel source. It was also used to make potash which is used in making fertilizer, glass, soap, dyeing fabrics or gunpowder.

Directions: In the center of Plainfield, off Rt-116, head north on North Central Road for 0.4-miles. Bear right onto North Union Street; continue on the main road for 1.75-miles, still following the main road bear left onto North Street. Continue on North Street which will change into Plainfield Road, within 2.1-miles, but before the Hawley Fire Station and across from Ashfield Road is a large DCR dirt parking area. From the back of the lot, past the kiosk, bear right following the dirt road 0.2-mile to the kiln which is near the backside of the field.

97. Conway Station Dam - Conway

Old Dam at the Conway Station Hydroelectric Site. Conway, MA

Location: Conway Station Road. (Franklin County)
Parking GPS: N42° 32' 23.60" W72° 40' 5.40" (Conway Station Road)
Destination GPS: N42° 32' 19.90" W72° 40' 1.90" (Hydro-Dam)
Wow Factor: 8 **Accessibility:** Steep Stairs- short walk 0.4-mile RT

Information: Conway was developed around its South River which flows through and into the Deerfield River. The lower South River is now a state forest has some unique historic sites which have come and gone leaving enough relics to stimulate your imagination. Conway as a bustling mill town by the 1890's had an electric trolley which ran above South River for 5.9-miles down to where it jointed the Deerfield River.

Conway Station, on the high southern bluff above the rivers was the terminus of the Conway Electric Street Railway. In addition, here was where the New York, New Haven & Hartford Railway junction with the Boston & Maine Railway, another separate steam railway, across Deerfield River on the north side at South Station. Both the Conway Station and South Station were connected by the tallest railroad trestle (175-feet) in Massachusetts at that time. Dismantled in the 1930s, the massive abutments still remain and presently are used to support "Polly's Crossing" a fiberglass foot-bridge on the Mahican-Mohawk recreation trail that runs along the Deerfield River.

The High Trestle 1894 Train Trestle Abutments on South River, portions in use supporting "Polly's-Crossing" foot bridge on the Mahican-Mohawk Trail.

Electricity that powered the Conway Electric Street Railway was generated by large 50-foot by 132-foot dam and reservoir located 0.5-mile upstream on the South River. A penstock from the reservoir supplied water to a powerhouse turbine generator below the dam. Originally built of timber in 1897 and later replaced with concrete in 1910, today the dam remains totally silted in, but supplies a very picturesque over-flow. Access is by parking on Conway Station Road and descending 0.1-mile down a steep set of railway tiers stairs (125-steps) to the brink of the dam, one can get further below the dam where cascades and remnants of the penstock may be seen. Continuing following South River downstream below the dam within 100-yards an impressive series of cascades empties into a large pool.

Parking GPS: N42° 32' 30.40" W72° 39' 34.60"(Conway Station Road-End)
Destination GPS: N42° 32' 26.54" W72° 39' 30.51" (Bridge Abutments)

Following Conway Station Road to its very end, goes to an unimproved parking-picnic area, the trail down to the abutments is 0.2-miles down a steep section of the Mahican-Mohawk trail. The South River State Forest can be reached by taking Bardswell Ferry Road to Conway Station Road. Conway Station Road is a maintained seasonal dirt road and ends at the very point where freight yards and a passenger station existed. Here is where electric trolley and steam rails met and where the South River enters the Deerfield River one hundred feet below. Immense granite bridge abutments, remnants of the High Bridge, still stand down in the South River. If you walk down to the abutments, you can notice and imagine the various track layouts where trolleys and trains merged or turned around heading back into Conway. Detailed answers and historic insight can be discovered at the Shelburne Trolley Museum near the Bridge of Flowers in Shelburne.

You may take 125 giant steps down and then back-up. Conway, MA,
(Jan & I had different counts of 125 or 126-steps, we did not repeat the climb.)

Directions: From the center of Conway, head north on Route-116 towards Ashfield. Bear right at the green highway sign, either turn immediately right onto Shelburne Falls Road or straight on Baptist Hill Road-Emerson Hollow Road which will merge onto Shelburne Falls Road in 0.6-mile. Driving north for 1.75-mile, bear right onto Bardwells Ferry Road. Continue for 1.5-miles, Conway Station Road will veer off on the right. Road surface will become a wide dirt road, continue 1.1-mile for the Conway Station Dam. There were no signs, but there is a small parking area on the left, the stairway which is becoming worn will be down on the right. The road will continue for an additional 0.5-mile will end above the Deerfield River which is part of the Deerfield River Recreation Area.

Looking up South River to "Polly's Crossing" on the Mahican-Mohawk Trail.

98. Drake's Mountain – Granville Reservoir

A painted Indian Head on the main gravel service road. Granville Reservoir.

Location: Granville Reservoir. Old Westfield Road. (Hampden County)
Parking GPS: N42° 6' 7.80" W72° 51' 20.10"(Old Westfield Road-Gate#1)
Destination GPS: N42° 5' 42.30" W72° 50' 57.60" (Indian Head Rock)
Destination GPS: N42° 5' 35.50" W72° 50' 34.00" (Awesome Boulder)
Destination GPS: N42° 5' 43.54" W72° 50' 30.10" (Yellow Dot-East End)
Destination GPS: N42° 6' 08.55" W72° 50' 41.37" (Balance Rock)
Destination GPS: N42° 5' 48.15" W72° 50' 7.74" (Amazing Boulder)
Destination GPS: N42° 5' 54.80" W72° 50' 9.90" (Trail Side Boulder)
Destination GPS: N42° 6' 0.15" W72° 50' 1.58" (Look-Out Rock)

Information: Drake's Mountain boundaries towards the east are the city of Westfield and Southwick with Granville on its western slope. Granville Reservoir is located here which is also Westfield's water supply. Being watershed property, it is posted against: "No bathing, Swimming, Shooting, Fishing, Fires, Camping or all other acts which may pollute the water supply or injury to the property are prohibited." Otherwise, walking, hiking, mountain bicycle, running and x-country skiing all seem to be legal activities judging by the encounters of numerous people in these activities. There is a kiosk just inside Gate#1 which also talks about the necessity to clean-up after your dog.

Within the surrounding woodlands of Drakes Mountain and the reservoir are some WOW sized boulders along with a small balanced rock and a painted *Indian Head Rock*. These destinations make hiking to each location an interesting ramble, but a difficulty arises due to the lack of a structured trail system. A couple of service roads, paths along with many meandering mountain bike trails make exploration tedious due their unmarked and indirect approaches.

Therefore, GPS coordinates during some bushwhacks will sharpen your woodsman skills to find these geo-cashes and the treasures are yours if you can carry them out.

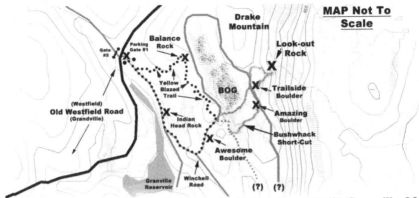

Drakes's Mountain–Balance Rock via the Yellow lazed Trail. Granville. MA

Parking at Gate #1 off Old Westfield Road has room for 1 or 2-cars, make sure not to block the gate. From here, pass by the gate heading south; down the main gravel access road for 0.6-mile reaching the painted Indian Head Rock on the left side. It is unique being painted on both sides having a different look from left, right or straight on.

From here, continue south, within 100-yards bear left onto a smaller dirt road (Winchell Road) and continue uphill for 0.3-mile, at the crest of a hill; a smaller dirt road turns left while Winchell Road continues straight. This old washed road is a well-used ATV/mountain bike trail. Heading northeast, uphill 0.1 mile, on the right, 50-feet off road and shrouded by evergreen trees is a large boulder, but 25-feet behind this first boulder is the much larger *Awesome Boulder* (shown below) and a small cluster of rocks nearby.

On the right, set back and unseen from the dirt road, a smaller boulder in front obscures a much larger 18-foot, Wow 8, presently known as Awesome Boulder.

Back onto the dirt road, uphill another 0.2-mile to where it levels off with typical New England stone walls and was once a prosperous farm. Here is the cross-road for a few of the trails, on the left, crossing the stone wall is the yellow blazed trail. It is well-trodden, but <u>poorly marked</u> with faded yellow marks on trees. Following it requires some vigilance for sometimes as if the trail was re-routed, the blazes are not present, but do eventually reappear. Used primarily by mountain bikes it will pass directly by the small *Balance Rock* after snaking through the woods for a good 0.6-mile. If you do follow the yellow blazed trail pass the *Balanced Rock* it will eventually return down towards the main gravel service road near Gate #1 in 0.7-mile. Again, a few unmarked trails junction with it, you will need to have some sense of direction to maintain the proper downhill direction.

A small roundish Balance Rock just off and next to the yellow blazed trail.

Again, back onto the dirt road to where it levels off and the start of the yellow blazed trail (refer to map.) If you continued straight the road runs north, parallel to the yellow blazed trail, within 0.6 mile the *Balanced Rock* would be adjacent to the road only 100-feet west, off on the left. Proceed on the road; which by now is more of an ATV trail with some puddles, the road will sweep to the right in a dogleg fashion with it rising to the Drake's Mountain ridgeline going south. Following this ridge trail south ~1.1-mile will pass by the *Trail Boulder,* another 0.2-mile south is the *Amazing Boulder* which is slightly off the trail some 75-feet west.

However, back to where the road levels off, not far beyond where the yellow blaze trail starts, on the right, an unmarked mountain bike trail heads southeast. (Across from its beginning, there is a steering wheel stuck into a tree.)

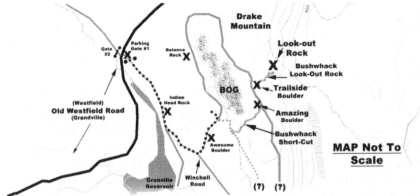

Drakes's Mountain-Granville –Balance Rock via the Yellow-Blazed Trail.

Instead of ~1.75-miles to the *Amazing Boulder* via the "road trail" a short bushwhack will only be 0.3-mile (65°NE), across Drake's Brook and up a mild slope to reach the ridge trail and the *Amazing Boulder*. Beware that there is a Bog that if you go too far north could mire the shortcut into a most undesirable ordeal. Going south 0.1-mile on unmarked bike path will help prevent such an experience. This is really not too hard utilizing the GPS coordinates or a compass that will save the extra steps if you "somehow" go too high or too low. In addition, remember that bushwhacking will be required on the return trip and back down to the dirt road used for the access into the area.

"Amazing Boulder" located 75 feet, west off the Drake's Mt. Ridgeline Trail.

After visiting the *Amazing Boulder*, return back onto the Drake's Mt. Ridgeline Trail, head north for 0.2-mile until arriving to *Trail Side Boulder*. Just north of the boulder, head into the brush and once again bushwhack towards the Look-Out Rock. 0.15-mile, 50° northeast. You should past a small boulder ~ 50-yards east of the *Trail Side Bolder*.

"Trail Side Boulder" a landmark directly on the Drake's Mt. Ridgeline Trail and is where the bushwhack heading northeast to *Look-Out Rock* will begin.

Continue 0.1 mile, crossing a bike trail that runs between a couple of rifts. Again, while there are mountain bike trails which travel to the Look-Out Rock, their origin, routing and destinations are undocumented meandering through Mountain Laurel brush. In places the Mountain Laurel is thick, walking northeast and continue towards the Look-Out Rock. The top of the rock is visible from a good distance away. Returning from *Look-Out Rock,* follow a bike trail north for a short distance, make corrections back to *Trail Side Boulder* where needed. Eventually reaching the TSB continues westerly and bushwhack downhill and back to the dirt road. Avoid the Bog!

Bushwhack right just pass this *Trail Side Boulder* to *Look-Out Rock*

As mentioned at the beginning, the trails have no apparent signage, organization, maintenance all which can be overwhelming, especially if you do not have a GPS device and the knowledge to use it correctly.

Front of *Look-Out Rock*, a few mountain bike trails do converge here, but slither of in unknown directions and destinations.

Backside of *Look-Out Rock*, the hillside starts to drop down steeply.

Directions: Grandville Common, junction Route-57 (Main Street) and Route-189. Head east on Route-57 for 0.2 mile, turn left onto Old Westfield Road, head north for 2.6-miles. Gate #1 will be on the right with Gate #2 directly across the street.

99. High Ledges & Wolf's Den – Shelburne

Shelburne Falls as seen 1.5 miles from High Ledges. Shelburne, MA

Location: High Ledges Audubon Sanctuary Patten Road (Franklin County)
Parking GPS: N42° 37' 9.80" W72° 42' 30.20" (Sanctuary Road-Main Lot)
Main Gate GPS: N42° 37' 8.10" W72° 42' 36.30" (Kiosk-Main Gate)
Destination GPS: N42° 37' 11.80" W72° 43' 15.20" (High-Ledges Vista)
Destination GPS: N42° 37' 32.40" W72° 43' 15.30" (Wolf's Den)
Wow Factor: 8 **Accessibility:** Moderate, marked trails 3.5 miles-RT

Information: High Ledges is a Massachusetts Audubon Society 587-acre wildlife sanctuary located in Shelburne, Massachusetts. The property located on a portion of Massaemett Mountain and is noted for its western view overlooking Shelburne Falls. A geologic feature "Wolves' Den" is where local lore has it that the last wolf in the region was exterminated. A diversity of native orchid species, ferns, mountain laurel and wildflowers, along with vernal pools which support wood frogs or the spotted salamander can be also be seen here.

The property was donated by Ellsworth and Mary Barnard, their stewardship is steeped in generations of the family farm which was established in 1790, with over 400-acres being donated their gift is a great portion of this sanctuary. The chimney of their cabin is located at the Ledges, enjoy the view or hike along the many maintained blazed and labeled trails to locate many species of flora and fauna found here. Sanctuary access for Audubon members is free with a small fee for non-members.

High Ledges has terrific views of Deerfield River Valley. Shelburne, MA

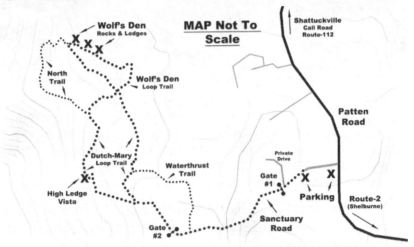

High Ledges Audubon Sanctuary Trail Map. Shelburne, Ma

From the parking lot, begin walking down the roadway for 0.1-mile. The main gate with a kiosk with information and a hiking trail map will be found here. Following the roadway, passing through another gate and in 0.7-mile the cabin chimney and High Ledge vista will be reached. Bring binoculars and/or telephotos lenses especially on clear crisp days.

To the Wolf Den Ledges, from the vista, follow the west leg of the Dutch-Mary Loop Trail down for 0.4-mile joining the Wolf Den Loop Trail which will loop around pass the Wolf Den Ledges (0.6-mile) and back to the Dutch-Mary Barnard Trail junction, taking the east leg of the Dutch-Mary Barnard Loop Trail will return to the roadway below the High Ledges vista, essentially creating a large figure-eight.

The trails are well marked with signs at trail junctions stating the trails name and color-coded discs attached to trees along the trail.

In the middle of the ledges, this boulder juts uphill on the Wolf's Den Trail.

Wolf's Den Loop Trail has large boulders, outcrops and ledges. Shelburne, MA

Directions: From Interstate I-91, use Exit-43, follow Route-2 west for 5.3-miles; turn right onto Little Mohawk Road. Continue on Little Mohawk Road for 1.3-mile, turn left onto Patten Road, in 0.5-mile bear left, then the next right. Stay on Patten Road for another 0.75-mile. On the left the sanctuary road entry which is dirt will be found. There is an overflow parking area at the very beginning of the road, but a closer and main parking area is down another 0.2-miles and is closer to the entry gate. Parking areas may become snowy or mud from December to May.

100. Keystone Arch Railway Bridges

Southern Keystone Arch Bridge (65-feet) circa 1841. Becket - Middlefield

Location: Chester-Becket-Middlefield (Berkshire-Hampshire County)
Parking GPS: N42° 18' 41.13" W72° 59' 33.53" (Herbert Cross Road)
Keystone Bridge-Double Arch GPS: N42° 18' 46.60" W72° 59' 38.7"
KAB Trail Head GPS: N42° 18' 50.68" W73° 0' 3.21"
Keystone Bridge GPS: N42° 18' 36.80" W73° 0' 11.40" (Still in use)
Destination 65' South Bridge GPS: N42° 18' 19.90" W73° 0' 19.47"
Destination 70' North Bridge GPS: N42° 18' 31.90" W73° 0' 51.70"
Wow Factor: 9 **Accessibility:** Moderate 5.0-mile RT marked trail.

Information: The design and construction of the Keystone Arch Bridges (KAB) took place during the late 1830's, with the railroad opening in 1841. Civil engineer Major George Washington Whistler, a West Point graduate and father to the famous painter James Abbott Whistler, presided over the project which in the day was a major accomplishment of engineering, a railroad through the rugged rivers and gorges of the Berkshire mountains.

The five magnificent bridges are constructed with hand-fitted granite blocks, each being laid in place without any mortar. A vast amount of manpower of skilled craftsmen can only be envisioned building scaffolding, moving then raising the granite blocks into position with block and tackle. With the final "keystones" being the last stones placed into the arch which continues to hold these remarkable bridges in place for over the past 180-years. Incredible!

Northern Keystone Arch Bridge (70-Feet) circa 1841 Becket-Middlefield, MA

A Double Arch Keystone Bridge still in use. Chester, MA

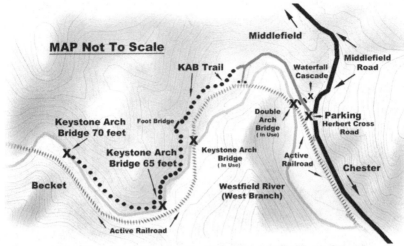

Keystone Arch Bridge Trail-Becket-Middlefield-Chester

Directions: Take Route-20 into the town of Chester. From the center of town, off Route-20, turn onto Middlefield Road and head north for 2.5-miles towards Middlefield. After crossing the railway tracks and where Middlefield Road turns and begins a steep uphill ascent, th KAB information sign for the arches is seen on your left at the entrance to Hebert Cross Road. This is where you should park.

Walk downhill, shortly you will cross a steel grate bridge with a small cascading waterfall, the Westfield River is on the left and the location of the first Keystone Bridge (still in use) can be seen from the river embankment nearby. Continue on this river-side road for 0.4 mile, the road sweeps left and begins to go up a slight rise, bear right and follow the road to the trailhead of the KAB trail. (Do not venture onto the railroad track by foot or vehicle)

Following the Keystone Arch Bridge Trail (KAB) will keep one legally off the active railway, the first 0.4-mile is through the woodlands and after crossing a wooden foot bridge it will bring one down to an access road, turn right and head west for 0.2-mile to the southern 65-foot Keystone Bridge located on the abandoned narrow-gauge railway. Continuing north from this bridge and following the old rail-bed west, through the rail-cut for 0.5-mile will bring one to the north 70-foot Keystone Bridge. There are no railings or barriers on top of the bridges, embankments are steep and not encouraged to venture onto them for environment erosion can result. Return back on the KAB Trail to the parking area.

Manhan Rail Trail – Northampton-Easthampton, MA

Location: Northampton-Easthampton (Hampshire County)
Parking GPS: N42° 20' 5.20" W72° 37' 16.10" (Damon Rd-Norwottuck)
Woodmont Road Tunnel GPS: N42° 19' 41.42" W72° 37' 56.60"
Manhan-Oxbow Spur Turn GPS: N42° 16' 36.50" W72° 39' 21.50"
Parking GPS: N42° 17' 12.87" W72° 37' 1.81" (Route-5 Oxbow Spur)
Parking GPS: N42° 15' 3.60" W72° 41' 42.90" (Coleman Rd Park-End)
Contact: information, maps or directions visit the Friends of the Manhan Rail web site; https://manhanrailtrail.org or info@manhanrailtrail.org

Information: Due to the ever-increasing rivalry from car and trucks the decline of passenger or freight trains resulted in the closure and abandonment of many railroad lines throughout New England. Other than ripping up the rails themselves for scrap metal, the value of these long right-of-ways were deemed as having little commercial value. Fortunately, their recreational desirability has great merit for they continue to grow as a community resource being extensively used by bicyclers, rollerblades, x-country skier's, walkers or hikers.

Officially, there are (3) rail-trails that merge or "spoke" out from Northampton. The *Norwottuck*, The *Manhan* Rail Trails and the *Northampton Bikeway* all intersect in the vicinity of King Street and Woodmont Road in Northampton. For brevity and my personal preference for parking and provides access to all three rail trails, is from the original western Norwottuck Rail Trail parking area on Damon Road. From here heading east, the Norwottuck Trail, crosses the Connecticut River on a fabulous bridge, through Hadley, Amherst and presently ends in Belchertown.

Heading west on its 2007 expansion, is a short paved 0.75-mile to Woodmont Road and the 2017 R&R pedestrian tunnel which allows safe passage beneath the present active railroad and to the trailhead for the Manhan Rail Trail or the Northampton Bikeway.

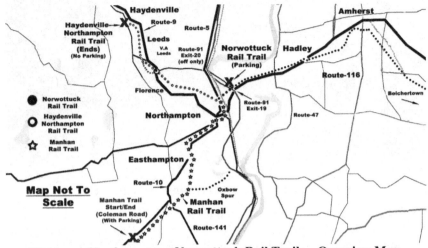

Manhan – Northampton - Norwottuck Rail Trails – Overview Map.

The Manhan Rail Trail is 7.5-miles from its start in Northampton from the western side of the Woodmont Road Tunnel. The first 1.5-miles through urban Northampton, then 6-miles south through Easthampton to Coleman Avenue just over and into Southampton. Further south past Easthampton center it becomes more residential with large shady trees.

In addition, there is the Manhan-Oxbow Spur Trail branching off the main trail just 100 yards north of the intersection of Pleasant Street and Ferry Street in Easthampton. This segment runs 2.3-miles to a small parking area on Route-5/Northampton Street, 300-feet north of East Street near ear a large electrical sub-station.

The Manhan Trail is fully paved; is well marked and relatively flat. The landscape pedaling through the back areas of Northampton or Easthampton is open and more exposed to the heat of the sun. It is exciting to note the past industrial heritage and its transformation into shops and eatery's which are easily accessible from the trail and provide rest stops for refreshment and browsing. Small parks with flowers, sculptured landscape and murals can be found along the way. Presently, there is limited roadside parking and no restrooms at the trailhead on Coleman Avenue in Southampton.

However, across the street and passing through the screening of roadside brush, one will enter beneath the tree canopy where old railroad tracks will be found. This undeveloped section indicates that each trail has great expansion potential and are works in progress. Hopefully, the will along with the means of expanding into an interconnected and extended network of recreational trails will continue grow throughout New England.

Heading south from Easthampton, future plans call for a trail to be developed through Southampton which will one day connect into the Westfield's Columbia Trail in Westfield, Southwick Rail Trail in Southwick, MA and the Farmington Canal Heritage Trail Northern Section in Connecticut. The New Haven & Northampton Canal Rail Trail is a long-term commitment for an 84-mile multi-use trail from New Haven, CT to Northampton, MA. In Connecticut the trail is referred to as the Farmington Canal Heritage Trail and in Massachusetts as the New Haven & Northampton Canal Rail Trail, although each town currently has their own name for the trail segments.

The vision is for the Manhan Rail Trail to continue from Coleman Ave through Southampton into Westfield's Columbia Trail to develop an 84-mile trail from New Haven Connecticut to Northampton, Massachusetts.

Directions: <u>Norwottuck Trail</u>; *Going north* on Interstate I-91, use Exit-25, at the end of the off ramp, go half-way around the traffic circle, taking the 2nd right, onto Damon Road. Within 100-feet, quickly turn right into the Connecticut River Greenway State Park-Mass Central Rail Trail- Norwottuck Branch. There is parking, air, water and seasonal rest rooms here.

Heading south on I-91 use Exit-26, at the end of the ramp, at the first set of traffic lights, turn left onto Damon Road. Stay on Damon Road for 0.9-mile turning left (before the traffic circle) into the Connecticut River Greenway State Park-Mass Central Rail Trail- Norwottuck Branch.

Manhan-Ox-Bow Access; Take Exit-23 off Interstate I-91 to Route-5, head south on Route-5 for 1.3-mile, on the right, next to electrical-distribution sub-station is a small parking area for several cars.

Manhan-Coleman Avenue Access; From the junction of Route-10 and Route-141 in the Center of Easthampton, travel south on Route-10 for 1.7-miles. Turn left onto Coleman Avenue, within 0.2 mile the Manhan Rail Trailhead will become apparent.

Additional parking is available at the Easthampton Public Safety Building at 32 Payson Ave., at Millside Park off of Ferry Street, at the Northeast Center for Youth and Families (203 East Street) and ample free public parking near the trail in the center of Easthampton.

The Manhan Rail Trail has a few elevated bridge spans that cross-over and above busy roadways or streams.

Rail Trail Etiquette
* Signal or Alert others when passing.*
Share the trail, stay to the right unless passing.
Share the trail, ride or roller blade in single file.
Stop and look both ways at road crossings.
Please don't litter: bring out what you bring in.
Keep dogs on a leash and pick up waste.
Wear a helmet (state law for bicyclists 16 and under).
Respect private property along the trail.
No unauthorized vehicles allowed on the trail.

102. Northampton – Haydenville Bikeway

Northampton – Florence - Leeds – Haydenville – Northampton Rail Trail,

Location: Northampton-Florence-Leeds-Haydenville. (Hampshire County)
Parking GPS: N42° 20' 5.20" W72° 37' 16.10" (Damon Rd-Norwottuck)
Woodmont Road Tunnel GPS: N42° 19' 41.42" W72° 37' 56.60"
Parking GPS: N42° 19' 39.16" W72° 38' 1.11" (Route-5, King St Access)
Look Park Entry GPS: N42° 20' 36.80" W72° 40' 53.60" (Rt-9 Circle)
Mill River GPS: N42° 22' 8.00" W72° 42' 5.60" (Haydenville-Terminus)

Information: Northampton-Haydenville Bikeway travels from King Street/Route-5 in Northampton through Florence residential neighborhoods and across upper side streets, but mainly under cool shade tree canopy until reaching the Look Park entry off the Route-9 traffic circle. The bike path can be shunted through Look Park and returns back onto the bike path or continue westerly on Route-9. Off Route-9, within 0.1 mile, the pathway will begin ramping up the old railroad bed until it is elevated and supported by elegantly engineered sloped embankment walls and keystone bridge portals entering into Leeds, continuing along the Mill River to its present terminus just over the Williamsburg border below Haydenville, but with no definitive ending here a U-Turn will be required back down the bike path or onto other public roadways.

The "master" plan is to continue the trail north via along South Main Street to Main St (Route-9) in Haydenville. A paved trail will be built alongside Route-9 heading northwest into Williamsburg. This will occur when the state rebuilds Route-9, possibly by 2025. This Trail segment is an awesome ride as this is a Work-In-Progress.

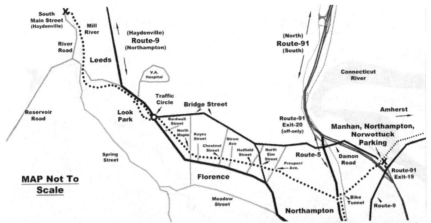

North Hampton to Haydenville Rail Trail. - Mass Central Rail Trail Coalition

Directions: Parking at the <u>Norwottuck Trail</u>; Going north on Interstate I-91, use Exit-25, at the end of the off ramp, go half-way around the traffic circle, taking the 2nd right, onto Damon Road. Within 100-feet, quickly turn right into the Connecticut River Greenway State Park-Mass Central Rail Trail- Norwottuck Branch. There is parking, air, water and rest rooms here.

Heading south on I-91 use Exit-26, at the end of the ramp, at the first set of traffic lights, turn left onto Damon Road. Stay on Damon Road for 0.9 mile turning left (before the traffic circle) into the Connecticut River Greenway State Park-Mass Central Rail Trail- Norwottuck Branch.

At the Connecticut River's planked R&R Bridge, turn left head west 0.75-mile, beneath Route I-91 to the Woodmont Road R&R Track underpass. Through the tunnel, left, up and right onto the King Street/ Route-5 cross over to continue point of entry. There is a small parking lot here also.

Continue west for 2.75-miles to Look Park and Bridge Street traffic circle; either enter Look Park with the bike trail which will rejoin the bike trail west or follow Route-9 west for 0.1-mile, where bike lane will shortly veer away from Route-9.

103. Norwottuck Rail Trail - Northampton

Norwottuck Rail Trail, Damon Road – Northampton, MA

Location: Northampton-Hadley-Amherst-Belchertown. (Hampshire County)
Parking GPS: N42° 20' 5.20" W72° 37' 16.10" (Damon Rd-Norwottuck)
Railroad Street GPS: N42° 20' 36.41" W72° 35' 38.63" (Access-Hadley)
Tunnel Route-9 GPS: N42° 20' 59.14" W72° 34 '1.23"
Station Road GPS: N42° 20' 30.92" W72° 29' 12.81" (Access-Amherst)
Warren Wright Rd GPS: N42° 19' 46.41" W72° 27' 49.08" (Belchertown)
Contact: DCR 446 Damon Rd. Northampton, MA 01060 United States
www.mass.gov/locations/norwottuck Rail-trail (413) 586-8706 ext. 3

Contact: Massachusetts Central Rail Trail Coalition. 413-575-2277
62 Chestnut Street Florence, MA 01062 Craig@MassCentralRailTrail.org

Information: For many railroads, the shifting economic trends away from railroad service just allowed them to disappear gradually. It was the 1938 Hurricane that ravaged Boston & Maine already ailing rail infrastructure, in time this defunct rail bed was acquired by the state in 1985 and developed into the trail in early 1992. The Norwottuck Branch Rail Trail is a large 11-mile segment maintained from Northampton east to Belchertown. The Mass Central Rail Trail Coalition has succeeded to reclaim 47-miles in a resurrection of the 104-mile corridor from Northampton to Boston. The vision of a statewide greenway as a combination bicycle or pedestrian paved right-of-way extends to Northampton, Hadley and Amherst, to Belchertown, Massachusetts This section was opened in 1992, and is now part of the longer Mass Central Rail Trail. Of the 104-miles desired, about 80% has been secured for public access, with 20-miles in undetermined ownership or other issues.

Starting from Northampton heading east the sections that are completed for the Mass Central Rail Trail includes; Norwottuck East Mass Central Rail Trail to Belchertown, Mass Central Rail Trail in; New Braintree-Hardwick, Mass Central Rail Trail; Barre-Rutland, Mass Central Rail Trail; Holden-West Boylston & Mass Central Rail Trail; Sterling in the towns of Belchertown, Braintree, Hardwick, Barre, Oakham, Rutland, Holden, West Boylston and Sterling. The trail today is growing exists in many unconnected sections and with differing surfaces. In Cambridge the last section of the Mass Central Rail Trail has been completed and is referred to as the Fitchburg Cutoff.

From the parking area, head east to cross the Connecticut River by an eight-span steel lattice truss bridge. It crosses above Elwell Island in the middle of the river; there is no access to the island riding over the bridge. It was built in 1887 by the R. F. Hawkins Ironworks Company and is has a span of 1,492-feet.

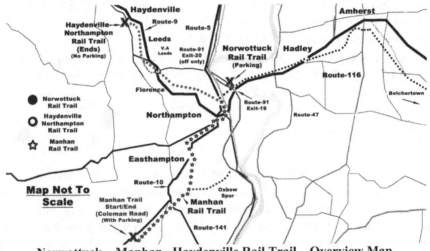

Norwottuck – Manhan –Haydenville Rail Trail – Overview Map.

Directions: In the two previous chapter's directions to Damon Road and the Connecticut River Greenway State Park - Mass Central Rail Trail-Norwottuck Branch can found just up-stream of the Calvin Coolidge Bridge which Route-9 uses to cross the Connecticut River.

Going north on Interstate I-91, use Exit-25, at the end of the off ramp, go half-way around the traffic circle, taking the 2nd right, onto Damon Road. South on I-91 use Exit-26, bottom of ramp, turn left onto Damon Road, 0.9-miles, parking on the left, before the traffic circle.

104. Phelon Memorial Forest-Granville

A sweeping panoramic view from the summit of Blueberry Hill. Granville, MA

Location: North Lane Granville. (Hampdem County)
Parking GPS: N42° 5' 51.80" W72° 55' 40.00" (North Lane -Entry)
Destination GPS: N42° 5' 42.52" W72° 55' 31.84" (Blueberry Boulder)
Contact: New England Forestry Foundation 32 Foster Street, Littleton, MA
PO Box 1346   01460   (978) 952-6856   www.newenglandforestry.org |

Information: Two donations made by Mr. Douglas M. Rice and Mr. Russell E. Phelon between 1973 and 1984 created the 954-acres Phelon Memorial Forest overseen by the New England Forestry Foundation.   A short walk uphill leads to a barren ridge with an expansive view, a picnic table and a large glacial erratic call Blueberry Boulder. This forest does have many paths and trails for X-Country skiing, mountain biking, but this the forest is selectively logged and the blueberries are commercially harvested, so enjoy the view and leave the blueberries alone. Migrating Raptor survey count done here.

Directions: In Granville at the junction of Route-57 and Route-189, follow Route-57 (Main Road) west 4.1-miles. Turn right onto North Lane Road, head north for 1.5-mile, on the right a small dirt parking and entry for 2-3 cars.

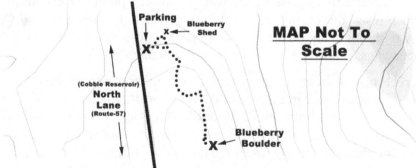

Phelon Memorial Forest to boulder and panorama view. Granville, MA

105. Raycroft Lookout - Monroe

Overlooking Bear Swamp Hydroelectric System. Florida, MA

Location: "Raycroft Lookout" Hunt Hill, Florida (Berkshire County)
Parking GPS: N42° 41' 34.70" W72°59' 37.14" (Monroe Road Parking A)
Turn Off GPS: N42° 41' 38.85" W72° 59' 12.48" (Hunt Hill Spur Road)
Parking GPS: N42° 41' 31.53" W72° 59' 4.63" (Hunt Hill Parking)
Destination GPS: N42° 41' 19.82" W72° 58' 53.56" (Observation Point)
Wow Factor: 7 **Accessibility:** Easy down, moderate up. 0.6-mile RT

Information: Located within the Massachusetts DCR's 4,000-acre Monroe State Forest which is primarily in Franklin County, the lookout is physically in the town of Florida just over the southernmost border of the forest. Built as a fire tower observation post in 1934 by the Civilian Conservation Corps Camp S-69, the stone masonry is more of a balcony lookout point located 0.3-miles down a foot-trail on the eastern slope from the summit of Hunt Hill. Its location provides a commanding view of the Deerfield River and the Bear Swamp hydroelectric plant. The Bear Swamp complex pumps water up to the upper reservoir during off-peak hours which is then released back down through its turbines during peak hours generating over 600 megawatts of power for up to 6 hours each day.

Directions: Access to Hunt Hill is by either seasonal dirt Monroe Road from Route-2 in Florida or by Raycroft Road entry off Tilda Hill Road in Monroe, both reach, the same short dead-end dirt road out to Hunt Hill summit. Raycroft Road is 2-miles longer and is in much poorer condition, having a 4x4 vehicle will definitely give better passage. The Monroe Road access off of Route-2 (Mohawk Trail) is a better choice and our directions focus upon that entry.

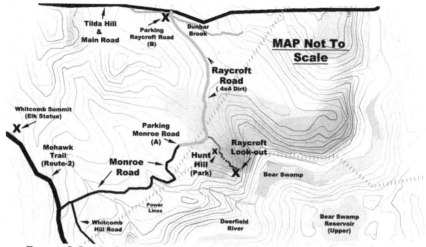

Raycroft Look-Out. Monroe State Forest-DCR Monroe-Florida MA

From Whitcomb Summit head south on Route-2 (Mohawk Trail) for 0.4-mile, turn left onto Whitcomb Hill Road. Head, downhill for 0.15-mile, on the sweeping right curve, Monroe Road will branch off on the left. (Whitcomb Hill Road continues steeply downhill.)

Monroe Road is well maintained for the next 1.75-miles and does get plowed during the winter months until just pass the last dwelling on the left. Shortly, after the last dwelling the road enters into the Monroe State Forest, off season this may not be passable due to mud or snow. In approximately 0.4-mile, a small dirt road on the right will lead out to Hunt Hill. This road dead ends in 0.2-mile with the trailhead for the Raycroft Look-out heading downhill and southeasterly for 0.3-mile.

Tilda Hill Road begins off Route-2 at the Florida Fire Station and heads north, in 4.1-miles it becomes Main Road as you enter into Monroe. Raycroft Road is on the right and is the DCR forest's northern entry; the first 0.1-mile is passable as it crosses over Dunbar Brook by a small bridge. A large dirt parking area is located here for access to the adjacent Dunbar Brook Falls Trail, Blue Dot or the Titanic Boulder. Continuing uphill, Raycroft Road is rough for the next 2.0-miles until reaching the small dirt road turning off on your left and out to Hunt Hill parking for the Raycroft Look-Out trail.

106. Stevens Property - Huntington

Split Boulder – Stevens Property. Huntington, Ma

Location: Pisgah Road - Hilltown Land Trust (Hampshire County)
Parking GPS: N42° 19' 7.70" W72° 49' 43.70" (Pisgah Road)
Destination GPS: N42° 19' 12.50" W72° 49' 36.40" (Trail Junction A)
Destination GPS: N42° 19' 11.30" W72° 49' 34.22 (Split Rock)
Destination GPS: N42° 19' 9.89" W72° 49' 32.98" (Trio Boulders)
Destination GPS: N42° 19' 3.60" W72° 49' 32.30" (Big Boulder)
Destination GPS: N42° 19' 3.91" W72° 49' 30.58" (Flat Boulder)
Destination GPS: N42° 19' 7.66" W72° 49' 28.06" (Overhang Boulder)
Destination GPS: N42° 19' 14.48" W72° 49' 29.84" (Giant Boulder-#2)
Destination GPS: N42° 19' 13.83" W72° 49' 34.33" (Giant Boulder-#1)
Wow Factor: 8 Accessibility: Moderate. Red Dot-Outer Loop 1.5-mile RT
Contact: 332 Bullitt Rd, Ashfield, MA 01330 (413) 628-4485

Information: For its size the Stevens Property's 1.3-mile short loop trail from Pisgah Road provides outdoor enthusiasts with a variety for flora-fauna and several very large boulders to behold. From the parking area, follow the red dot trail northerly parallel to the road, shortly the trail will shift towards the east and up a small sloped ridge. Uniquely, is an abundance of a large field stone rock pile, not just one, but several large piles in close proximity to each other. I have been told that Native Americans built them as trail markers or early farmers would cover large deceased animals as in graves or just simply the efforts of a farmer clearing their field of rock. No way of really telling, Native Americans normally did not create many structures from stone, farmers normally created stone walls to mark their boundaries or keep the livestock enclosed.

Moving on over the ridge you will reach trail junction-A for the loop trail, continuing right (counter-clock-wise) south the trail quickly encounters the first on trail boulder and clearly named Split *Rock*. The trail swings around and continues south. Seems like every tenth-of-mile a boulder, trail junction or foundation will be encountered, shortly past this Split Rock, the spur *Overlook Trail* will be on the left. This trail is a short dead end, while not much of a panorama view is found, *Trio-Boulders* will be found, one having a triangular shape and being some 18-feet in height.

Trio Boulder at end of Overlook Trail, Stevens Property – Huntington, MA

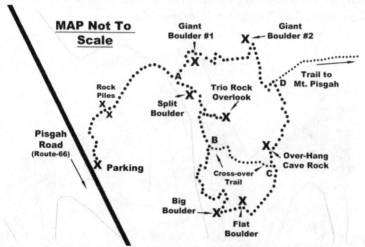

Red dot short loop trail. Stevens Property-Hilltown Land Trust. Huntington.

Returning to the trail, continue south, past trail junction-B for the cross-over trail which is only a small short-cut. Pass this point, next on the trail is *Big Boulder,* this boulder is actually on private property, do not climb or destroy the lichen for it takes decades to grow on rock. Shortly passing this location, on the left is *Flat Boulder*, small and not overly significant, but beauty is in the eye of the beholder. Further along, on the right a small rock foundation reportedly a sugar-shack to boil the maple syrup. Just past the other end of the cross-over trail at junction-C and now heading north is *Over-Hang Boulder*. While not easily seen from the trail side, the downhill side of this boulder has a rudimentary shelter cave, always a wonderful discovery for the young.

Big Boulder – Short Loop Trail. Huntington, MA

Continuing north, still on the red dot trail northerly, soon and on the right, the cut-off for the Long Loop Trail to Mt Pisgah will be on the right, marked with blue dots at trail junction-D.

Overhang - Cave Boulder, Stevens Property. Huntington, MA

Continue on the short loop, slight downward and across a small brook, off trail 50-yards on the right and pass a small field stone foundation *Giant Boulder #2* can be found. Back on the trail, headed westerly the trail will begin to ascend. Half-way uphill is *Giant Boulder #1,* a very large 16-foot-tall boulder with large "Lemon Squeeze' crack, it also looks like the front nose had a "Boulder Quarrying" attempt, although it is difficult to see any feather drill marking. Continue the ascent up, reaching the top and back to trail Junction-A, bear right and back to the Pisgah Road parking

Giant Boulder #1 – Stevens Property. Huntington, Ma

Directions: On Route-112 in Huntington, below Knight Ville Dam-Reservoir, and above Huntington Center, turn east onto Route-66. Travel east 5.5-miles on the left turn north onto Allen Coit Road. Go 0.4-mile turning onto Pisgah Road. Go 2.4-miles turning into the small parking area for 2-3 vehicles marked with a Hilltown Land Trust kiosk and a break in stone wall on the right. Trail begins north and behind of the kiosk.

Rule no motorize vehicles , camping or campfires

107. Stone Fire Tower – Shelburne

Stone Fire Tower (L) - circa 1920's (R) - 2019. Shelburne, MA

Location: Massaemett Mountain. Shelburne, MA (Franklin County)
Parking GPS: N42° 36' 10.50" W72° 43' 49.40" (Halligan Avenue)
Destination GPS: N42° 36' 24.60" W72° 42' 59.50" (Stone Fire Tower)
Wow Factor: 8 **Accessibility:** Moderate to strenuous uphill. 2.6-miles-RT

Information: The Tower Trail climbs uphill for 1.3-miles to the historic stone fire tower erected in 1909 on the top of Massaemett Mountain. The trail is well trodden, well-marked with white blazes and is well maintained. Shortly after starting on the lower access, hikers do have to make a choice. The option is either continue on the original trail (white blaze) which becomes increasingly steeper for a short distance or to take a slightly longer trail (orange-white) with an easier gradient slope. This secondary trail is only a bypass and rejoins shortly back onto the white blazed trail which continues uphill to the stone tower.

While the ascent is mainly uphill, the trail passes quickly arriving at the stone tower, a spiral cement stairway is open to the top level; there is no access into the top fire tower. The fire tower is still activated and studying the old photo clearly shows the top has been replaced.

The tower cab and ground cabin were destroyed by lightning and fire in 1944. As a result, a new tower cab and lightning arresting system was installed on the tower. A newest (the current) tower cab was built in 1967.

Interior spiral stairway of the 65-foot Stone Fire Tower

In Addition: This is one of only 2 remaining stone towers in New England still in active use. First date of operation was August 30, 1911. A stone cab was constructed on top its 65-foot, tower structure by 1912. Stone fire towers of this height are a rarity in the U.S. This prominent lookout was constructed by the Massaemett Tower Committee beginning construction in 1909. The 65-foot tower wooden cab on its top has been upgraded several times. It is operated by the Massachusetts Bureau of Forest Fire Control.

Trailhead Kiosk on the corner of Route-2 and Halligan Avenue. Shelburne, MA

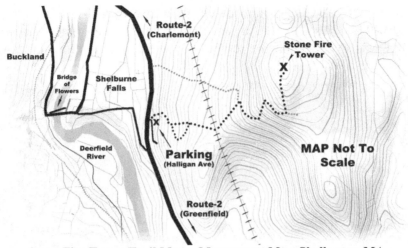

Stone Fire Tower Trail Map – Massaemett Mt. - Shelburne, MA

Directions: From the Greenfield traffic rotary, Exit-43, head west on Route-2 for 8.5 miles. Halligan Avenue will be on the right. The trailhead is at the kiosk located on the corner of Halligan Avenue and Route-2 in Shelburne. Parking on is permitted near the trailhead entry. The road is a dead end and residents appreciate turning around at the roadway entry and not their driveways. Parking on the right side of the road without blocking or impeding traffic. Parking is limited to about 3-4 cars facing downhill on Halligan Avenue.

108. Williamsburg 1874 Mill River Dam

Williamsburg Reservoir 1874 Dam Ruins -West End. Williamsburg, MA

Location: East Branch Mill River. Williamsburg (Hampshire County)
Parking GPS: N42° 25' 44.54" W 72° 44' 23.07" (Ashfield Road)
Destination: N42° 25' 43.49" W72° 44' 13.23" (1874 Dam Trailhead)

Destination GPS: N42° 26' 3.50" W72° 43' 53.30"3 (Dam Ruins-East)
Destination GPS: N42° 26' 4.20" W72° 43' 56.90" (Dam Ruins-West)
Wow Factor: 7 **Accessibility:** Moderate narrow trail. 1.8-mile-RT

Information: Prior to and during the Civil War, large factories and small milling business flourished along many of the rivers in New England. Flowing water turned the water-wheels which in turn created the mechanical power needed in producing items such as paper, guns, woolen, cotton linen and the many products used by the communities that flourished around these enterprises. However, low summer or seasonal water flow decreases or stops the output for many these businesses along the smaller rivers.

The Williamsburg Reservoir Company was formed in the 1860's with the intent to build a reservoir on the Mill River which would provide better water control year around. Built in 1864, the Mill River Dam appeared to be the solution to the manufacturing interests of the day by creating a large 45-feet deep, 100-acre lake, that would provide enough water power during the dry summer months.

Civil engineering and men calling themselves "Engineers" often had little qualifications or little experience in larger scale projects such as this. As business men, the cost of a structurally sufficient design was overwhelming high, deciding to go with the lower bid and to build the dam themselves, it was not a good choice.

Completed in 1866, the dam consisted of a narrow stone wall that stretched 600-feet between the hillsides and was supported by banks of packed earth to provide added strength. Unfortunately, there was a lack of federal or state regulations on dam construction and public safety standards. This allowed for poor design, when coupled with shoddy construction practices and along with no continuous repair or maintenance inspections, created a recipe for disaster.

On May 16, 1874, the cheap and shoddy dam began to collapse. The dam keeper George Cheney saw a large section of the earthen embankment separate from the stone dam facing. Water began to leak increasingly through the poorly grouted stone facing. It was inevitable that the dam was about to collapse releasing over 600-million gallons on the unsuspecting communities downstream. Racing on horseback ahead of a 40-foot wall of water, many villagers and factory workers were spared. Sadly, in the end, 139 lives were lost, along with over 740 left homeless, with the villages or factories in the communities of Williamsburg, Skinnerville, Haydenville and Leeds being devastated.

In the aftermath there were no federal or state disaster assistance programs, clean up and relief was managed by local committees who relied upon hundreds of volunteers and donations. An unprecedented inquest investigating the disaster's cause named five parties at fault: the reservoir company which owned the dam; the contractors who built it; the engineer for providing an inadequate design; the county commissioners who inspected and approved it; and the Massachusetts legislature which chartered the reservoir company without requiring any validation or assurance that it was safe.

In 1875, Massachusetts passed its first legislation in public safety regarding reservoir dam design, construction, and liability with public safety weighing in against the self-interests of manufacturers and businessmen.

Inadequate design, shoddy construction and no inspections along with little maintenance created a recipe for disaster. The communities downstream that laid in the path of a 40-foot wave of wreckage or other debris obliterated houses and factories along with a large toll of injury and death. Remnants of both ends of the dam and the lower stone wall channel (shown in the photograph) still can be found within the regrown forest. Scattered kiosks on site or along the trail illustrate relevant details of the event. Photograph view point is looking from the west end of dam across to the east side.

Directions: From Route-116 in South Ashfield, take Williamsburg Road south for 6.3 miles (pass Chapel Falls.) The parking area for Williamsburg Historic Dam Trail is on your left next near a fire pond and a defunct hydrant. The hydrant even has a sign "Hydrant out of service. OK to Park." From Route-9 in Williamsburg center, take North Street (towards Ashfield) (which becomes Ashfield Road) for 2.75-miles with the parking area being on your right. From the parking area head east on the dirt road, through a small field for 0.1-mile, the trailhead kiosk will be off on your left set back 100-feet.

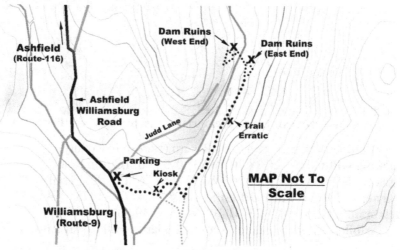

The Williamsburg Historic 1874 Dam Trail.

The trail is new and at the beginning passes through light woodlands, across 2 bridges, then after crossing the brook the trail ascends for a short distance and will travel northerly along the hillside above the brook below. The path is well trodden and marked with postings that there is no public access off the trail. You will be over half-way there when you pass a large glacial erratic on the trail. At the dam site, small trails loop, one end visits the eastern remnants of the dam, the other to the western end and the spillway. There are panel kiosks along the way describing the over-all nature of the historical significance of each location. Venturing off the trail will jeopardize the permissions for this access trail that the Williamsburg Historical Commission has secured from neighboring land owners and have collaborated with the Northampton Water Department for this permission. **Important:** This trail is closed during the winter.

109. WWII Aircraft Crash Memorial

WWII Aircraft Crash Memorial - Peru State Forest. Peru, MA

Location: Peru State Forest – DCR Peru (Berkshire County)
Parking GPS: N42° 23' 38.20" W73° 0' 55.60" (Curtin Road)
Parking GPS: N42° 23' 47.26" W73° 2' 57.76" (Skyline Trail)
Garnet Hill Road Turn Off GPS: N42° 23' 47.07" W73° 1' 43.38"
Destination GPS: N42° 23' 31.10" W73° 1' 39.80"
Accessibility: Moderate unmarked road (Garnet Hill Road) 2.0-mile RT

Information: On August 15, 1942, a large Douglas C-53 U.S. Army transport aircraft crashed with the loss of 16 paratroopers in the vicinity of Garnet Mountain. The aircraft flying from Fort Bragg, North Carolina and heading for Rhode Island, it lost its direction in the foggy darkness. While 3 paratroopers survived the crash with severe burns, Sargent Robert Lee from Ohio walked through dense underbrush and directed personal to the crash site. In the memory of the men who perished that night, a stone monument was erected in 1950 with a bronze plaque listing all those who gave their lives while serving their country. All traces of the crash site have regrown since then, only small traces of melted metal from the aircraft or other small pieces have been placed a top of the monument

Directions: From the top of the hill in Peru Center, travel east on Route-143 for 0.1-mile, turning right onto Curtin Road. Travel south on Curtin Road, the pavement will become gravel within 1.0-mile. After 1.8-miles bear left, staying on Curtin Road which will become more of a seasonal woodland road as it enters into Peru State Forest.

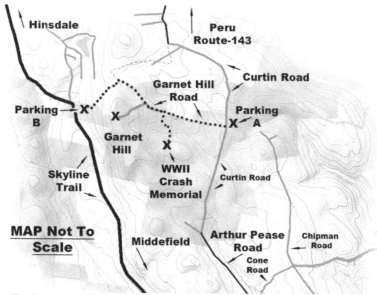

Trail map of WWII Aircraft Memorial in Peru State Forest. MA

After an additional 1.5-miles you will arrive to where Garnet Hill Road will be on the right. Park here without blocking the road, access is limited to just a few vehicles.

Walk west on Garnet Hill Road for 0.7-miles. Turn left and trek downhill on an old logging road, at the bottom, the road can become boggy with large muddy puddles, a recent bypass trail has developed on the right and heads south. The trail is unmarked, following the trodden path you should reach the monument clearing within 0.3-mile, set within a spruce grove.

From the Skyline Trail in the center of Middlefield, drive east on Bell Road, bearing left for 0.75-mile until you reach Arthur Pease Road. Turning left and head northwest for 0.9-mile, just past the last house on the left the road will become a seasonal dirt road as it heads north into woodlands. Continue 2.1-miles, where it becomes Curtin Road as you reach the Peru State Forest boundary then Garnet Hill Road on your left. Follow the above directions to the memorial.

There is access from the other end of Garnet Hill Road from an unmarked road off the Skyline Trail (GPS). Being uphill along with a matrix of unmark ATV trails makes this approach requiring more effort. After reaching the summit, follow the Garnet Hill Road heading east until reaching the old logging road turn-off (GPS) that will be on your right and then follow the same directions to the monument as above.

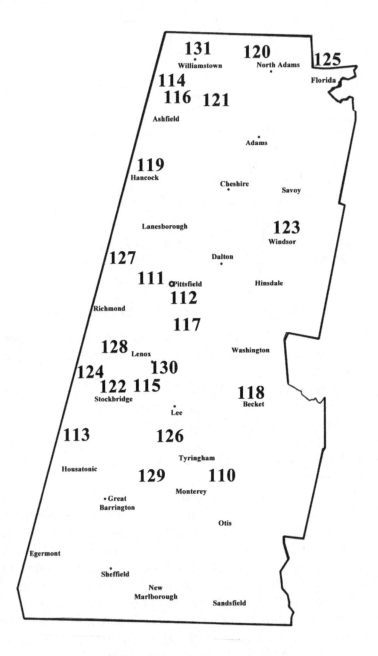

131 Williamstown
120 North Adams
125 Florida

114
116 **121**
Ashfield

Adams

119 Hancock

Cheshire
Savoy

Lanesborough

123 Windsor

127
Dalton

111 Pittsfield
Hinsdale
112

Richmond
117

128 Lenox
Washington

124
130
122 **115**
Stockbridge

118 Becket

Lee

113
126

Tyringham

Housatonic
129 **110**
Monterey

Great
Barrington

Otis

Egermont

Sheffield
New
Marlborough
Sandsfield

Berkshire Points of Interest

Berkshire Points of Interest

110. Ashintully Gardens. Trustees of Reservations: (Tyringham)
111. Berkshire Carousel. (Pittsfield)
112. Berkshire Museum. (Pittsfield)
113. Chesterwood. (Stockbridge)
114. Clark Art Institute. (Williamstown)
115. Edith Wharton's The Mount. (Lenox)
116. Field House. Trustees of Reservations: (Williamstown)
117. Herman Melville Homestead. (Pittsfield)
118. Jacobs Pillow. (Becket)
119 Jiminy Peak Mountain Resort. (Hancock)
120. Massachusetts MOCA. (North Adams)
121. Mt. Greylock Veterans Memorial Tower. DCR: (Adams)
122. Naumkeag. Trustees of Reservations: (Stockbridge)
123. Norman Rockwell. Rt-183: (Stockbridge)
124. Notchview Reservation. Trustees of Reservations: (Windsor)
125. Railroad History. Hoosac Tunnel,
125a. Hoosac Tunnel Alignment Towers.
125b. Rowe Alignment Tower.
125c. Whitcomb Hill Alignment Tower. (Florida)
125d. Spruce Hill Alignment Tower. (North Adams)
125e. West Mountain Alignment Tower. (North Adams)
126. Santarella a.k.a. The Gingerbread House. (Tyringham)
127. Shaker Village. (Hancock)
128. Tanglewood. (Lenox)
129. The Bidwell House. (Monterey)
130. Ventfort Hall. (Lenox)
131. Williams College Museum of Art. (Williamstown)

110. Ashintully Gardens – Tyringham

Ashintully Gardens (lower) – Tyringham, MA

Location: Sodom Road/Main Road Tyringham (Berkshire County)
Parking GPS: N42° 12' 54.98" W73° 10' 36.88" (Parking-lower Gardens)
Destination GPS: N42° 12' 47.37" W73° 10' 26.03" (Estate Ruins)
Contact: www.thetrustees.org (413)298-3239 westregion@thetrustees.org

Information: In 1903, Robb and Grace de Peyster Tytus purchased 1,000 acres at the southern end of Tyringham Valley, known as *Ashintully*. During 1910-1912, Tytus built a white, Georgian-style mansion which came to be known as the *Marble Palace*. Situated on a hillside bluff it was opulent and luxurious very similar to the many "Gilded Age" Berkshire cottages built during that era. With 35-rooms, 15-fireplaces, 10-baths and 4 impressive classical Greek Doric columns, these columns are massive and being the only imposing remnants from its remaining architecture. Sadly, the Marble Palace was destroyed by fire on April 20, 1952.

In 1937, John McLennan (Jr.) inherited the estate, but later after the fire, moved into the farmhouse at the bottom of the hill. The nearby barn was renovated into a music studio where during his 30-year career of composing he created contemporary orchestral music, chamber music and pieces for piano or organ. In 1985, his music compositions won an American Academy of Arts and Letters music award.

In 1966, John and Katherine began creating the gardens. The *Ashintilly Gardens* blended several natural features enhanced by stone walls, paths, stairs, a fountain pond and ornamental bushes or statues. In 1997,

Ashintully Gardens received the H. Hollis Hunnewell Medal, created 1870 by the Massachusetts Horticultural Society. A garden map and trail map is on site.

The Marble Palace ruins- Ashintully Gardens. Tyringham, MA

Through a gate at the top of the garden a 0.5 mile a woodland path will lead to terrific northerly view up the Tyringham Valley from the from site where the *Marble Palace* ruins which are easily found.

Starting with 446 acres, John McLennan Jr. began donating acreage of the Ashintully estate to the Trustees of Reservations in 1977, with additional 148 acres, creating the Mclennan Reservation to 549 acres by 1995. Lastly in 1996, John McLennan Jr. donated 120 acres to the Trustees. This land, included the Audio Studio *Ashintully Gardens*, *Marble Palace* ruins and the farmhouse.

Open on **Wednesdays and Saturdays only** from 1 to 5 PM, starting the 1st Wednesday in June through 2nd Saturday in October.

Please do not visit on days or times when the gardens are not open to the public.

Admission for members of the Trustees is free. Group garden tours of 15 or more are offered by prior appointment. No camping, picnic or fires. Please note: There are no restrooms at this reservation.

Directions: In Lee, at the junction of Interstate I-90 Exit-10, follow Route-20 east, an immediate right onto Route-102, and west for 0.10 mile and quickly turn left at the lights onto Tyringham Road which will become Main Road. Go south 6.8 miles, pass Santarella and through Tyringham Center. From Tyringham Center continue south on Main Road for 2.6-miles. At the junction of Sodom Road, just as the Main Road takes a sweeping turn to the right. A small parking area will be on the left for a few roadside vehicles in front of a fence.

111. Berkshire Carousel - Pittsfield

Berkshire Carousel-Pittsfield

Location: 50 Center St, Pittsfield, MA 01201 (Berkshire County)
Destination GPS: N42° 26' 48.51" W73° 15' 29.25"
Contact: berkshirecarousel.com (413) 499-0457 BerkshireCarousel@yahoo.com

Information: In its beginning, a stampede of ideas to fund raising, unexpected solutions from corporations or people, and after 12 years, the army of volunteers had refurbished the carousel itself, completed all hand-carving the wooden horses, painting and final installation. Then on July 4th 2016, the premier spin of the Berkshire Carousel was here. Indeed, over 5,000-riders in the 1st 4 days and by the end of the year 39,000-riders. The Berkshire Carousel is a not-for-profit, 501(C)3 venture that was designed to create an authentic classic wooden carousel that is both a work of art and a wonderful form of family fun and entertainment. The carousel building is air conditioned and heated operations or visits. There is Gift Shop and Concessions Stand that offer drinks, goodies, ice cream, popcorn, as well as an off-street parking lot for visitors to park in.

Unfortunately, the burst of operation, mired quickly, almost to a complete stop. The original crews aged or were unable to maintain a commitment for various reasons forcing closure due to the lack of help. Presently, operations and schedule has <u>dropped</u> from 6-days a week down to Saturdays and Sundays from Noon to 5 p.m. until September 15th. You should call prior going to see if operating.

112. Berkshire Museum - Pittsfield

Berkshire Museum of art, natural history and ancient civilization. Pittsfield.

Location: 39 South St, Pittsfield, MA 01201 (Berkshire County)
Destination GPS: N42° 26' 50.51" W73° 15' 14.17" (South Street)
Contact: berkshiremuseum.org (413)443-7171 info@berkshiremuseum.org

Information: In 1903, Berkshire Museum founder Zenas Crane, inspired by such institutions as the American Museum for Natural Science, the Smithsonian, and the Metropolitan Museum of Art, decided to blend the best attributes of these establishments in a new museum for the people of Western Massachusetts. Thanks in large part to Crane's efforts, the broad and varied collections of Berkshire Museum include objects from virtually every continent, from important fine art and sculpture to natural science specimens or ancient artifacts. A natural-history & art museum with frequent temporary exhibitions including an art-house cinema-foreign films, a sizable group of paintings from the Hudson River School, relics of ancient history and natural science: fossil collections, a 143-pound meteorite, an Egyptian mummy, shards of Babylonian cuneiform tablets, representations of Berkshire ecosystems including local mammals, birds, reptiles, fish, insects, plants, and minerals. Fee for admission, free for members or child 0 to17 years or special events.

Directions: In Lee, Interstate I-90, Exit-10, Turn right off the exit ramp onto Route-20, north for 11.0 miles, through Lee, Lenox, (Route-7 joins Route-20 as a divided highway in Lenox.) In Pittsfield, the museum is 0.1-mile north, pass where Route-20 turns left to N.Y and Route-7 goes north, on the right, just past the Colonial Theater.

113. Chesterwood - Stockbridge

Daniel Chester French's Studio "Chesterwood" Stockbridge, MA

Location: 4 Williamsville Road. Stockbridge 01262 (Berkshire County)
Parking GPS: N42° 17' 6.24" W73° 21' 4.97" (Williamsville Road)
Destination GPS: N42° 17' 5.41" W73° 21' 8.46" (Cottage)
Destination GPS: N42° 17' 6.18" W73° 21' 10.36" (Studio)
Contact: www.chesterwood.org   chesterwood@nthp.org   (413) 298-3579

Information: Chesterwood was the 1896 summer estate and studio of American sculptor Daniel Chester French (DCF) is located at 4 Williamsville Road in Stockbridge, Massachusetts. Most of French's originally 150-acre estate is now owned by the National Trust for Historic Preservation, which operates the property as a museum and sculpture garden.

His most noted contributions are the Lincoln Memorial and the Concord Minute Man Statue. The engraved inscription on the pedestal of French's "Concord Minuteman" is from Emerson's "A Concord Hymn." Emerson, a Concord resident, penned the immortal words "Shot heard around the world." However, it was at the battle green in Lexington where the first shots of the Revolution were first fired. Emerson's historical revisionism has been a source of friendly banter between residents of Lexington and Concord for over 100-years.

Large studio doors open out onto a railway allowing works–in-process to roll out into the sunlight for examination for specific time of day or sun angle.

The heir to Chesterwood was Daniel Chester French's only child, Margaret French Cresson. Once only a summer retreat, Margaret made Chesterwood her full time home in the 1940s and devoted her life to her father's artistic legacy by collecting his work and opening his studio to the public.

In 1978, Chesterwood established its first contemporary outdoor sculpture show which has brought over 600 artists to Chesterwood over 41 years. Chesterwood's residence, studio, gardens, galleries, and woodland walks have been open to the public for guided tours, educational workshops and lectures, and special events for the past 50 years.

Directions: In Lee, Interstate I-90, Exit-10, turn left onto Route-20 east and then immediately right onto Route-102 west. Continue going west on Route-102 for 4.2-miles until Route-7 junctions just east of Stockbridge center, continue straight through town west on, Main Street, Route-7/102, the Red Lion Inn is on the corner where Route-7 turns left and heads south for Great Barrington.

Stay straight on Route-102 west for 0.4-mile, where Route-102 bears right and heads north 1.4-mile until it junctions with Route-183 (at Flashing light.) Turn left onto Route-183/Glendale Road and heading south for 1.0-mile. Shortly pass the Norman Rockwell Museum on the right, turn onto Mohawk Lake Road and head westerly for 0.1-mile, turn left onto Willow Street, 0.2-mile it turns into Williamsville Road with another 0.2-mile you will arrive to the grounds of Chesterwood with the main parking lot on you right. Parking in the field across the street is sometimes used during large events or on busy days.

114. Clark Art Museum - Williamstown

Reflecting Pool-Clark Art Museum-Williamstown, MA

Location: 225 South Street. Williamstown 01267 (Berkshire County)
Parking GPS: N42° 42' 33.37" W73° 12' 51.18" (South Street)
Destination GPS: N42° 42' 29.05" W73° 12' 52.92" (Main Gallery Entry)
Contact: http://www.clarkart.edu (413)458-2303

Information: The Robert Sterling and Francine Clark Art Institute, commonly referred to as *the Clark*, is an art museum and research institution located in Williamstown, Massachusetts. The Clark Art established in 1950 by Sterling and Francine Clark and later opened the public 1955. Since its conception, the Institute has had a dual mission as both a museum and a center for research and higher education.

Robert Sterling and Francine Clark well-known collectors of Old Masters and 19th century paintings, together they created a remarkable private collection of paintings, silver, sculpture, porcelain, drawings and prints from the fourteenth to the early twentieth century. With a considerable fortune inherited from his grandfather (a principal in the Singer Sewing Machine Company) he began amassing a private art collection. Francine joined him in collecting works of art after their marriage in 1919.

Over a period of forty-five years the Clark's collecting led them from well-known masters to lesser-known artists. From works of the fourteenth and fifteenth centuries particularly Italian, Dutch, and Flemish painters, Barbizon and Impressionist Schools. Especially many works by some of their favorite artists—John Singer Sargent, Winslow Homer, Edgar Degas, and Pierre-Auguste Renoir.

Initial construction began in 1952 of the prominent white marble Museum building which opened to the public May 17, 1955 only housed 2 viewing galleries. Later in 1973, the red granite *Manton Research Center* adding additional galleries, a research library, office space, and auditorium.

A long-term vision master plan of the Clark was initiated in the late 1990's, with the first addition being in 2008 with the addition of *Lunder Center at Stone Hill*, designed with 2 small galleries, a large regional conservation center, and a location where the Berkshire Hills and landscape environment provides a haven to ponder. The Lunder Center is seasonal with public access from April 15 through November 15.

In 2014, The Museum Building was reconceived with the addition of more than 2,200 square feet of gallery space and the construction of the *Clark Center* as a new entry with 7,500-square feet of gallery space, dining and retail shops, a new greatly enlarged parking area and the creation of a large three-tiered reflecting pool.

Worthy of note, that the Williams College Museum of Art WCMA) along with the Massachusetts Museum of Contemporary Art (MassMoCA) and the Robert Sterling and Francine Clark form a triad of distinguished art museums in the Berkshires all within 5 miles or less of each other. When purchase together, discounted one-day adult admission to both the Clark and MASS MoCA is available, admission is free at the Williams College Museum of Art. Both the Clark and Mass MOCA admission is always free for members, children under 18, and students with a valid ID. Residents of the Berkshire's may be free for special events or community days.

Taking a tour will completely enlighten your museum experience.

Directions: **From the North:** In Bennington, VT take Route-7 south into Williamstown. At the intersection of Routes 7 and 2, turn right. Proceed all the way around a small rotary past Turn right onto South Street. The Clark is on the right about one-half mile down South Street.

From the East take Interstate, I-90 to Exit 10 (Lee). Turn right off the exit ramp onto Route-20 west toward Lee/Pittsfield. Follow Route-20 west to Route-7 north into Williamstown. As you enter town, Route-7 proceeds around a small rotary. From the rotary, turn right onto South Street. The Clark is on the right about one-half mile down South Street.

From the West take Interstate I-87 north to Exit-7 (Route 7 east). Follow Route-7 east to Route-278. Turn right onto Route-278. Follow Route-278 to Route-2 east. Take Route-2 east to Williamstown. As you enter town, Route-2 proceeds around a small rotary, turn right onto South Street, one-half mile down South Street, The Clark is on the right.

"The Thinkers."

115. Edith Wharton's - The Mount

Edith Wharton's "The Mount" & Gardens - Lenox, MA

Location: 2 Plunkett Street. Lenox 01240 (Berkshire County)
Parking GPS: N42° 20' 4.49" W73° 16' 53.66" (Plunkett Street-Entry)
Destination GPS: N42° 19' 50.93" W73° 16' 55.27" (Estate & Gardens)
Contact: www.edithwharton.org (413) 551-5111 infor@edithwharton.org

Information: The Mount is a turn-of-the-century "home", designed and built by Edith Wharton in 1902; the property was declared a National Historic Landmark in 1971. Situated on 113-acres, with a 35-room mansion, its grounds, well landscaped gardens, fountains and with unrestricted access along with a view of Laurel Lake, Edith will write some of her greatest works at her estate.

In 1897, she published her first book, *The Decoration of* Houses a non-fiction on architecture. In 40-years, she wrote 40-books including; *The House of Mirth* (1905) and *Ethan Frome* (1911) and *The Age of Innocence (1921).* She was the first woman awarded the Pulitzer Prize for Fiction for her highly esteemed novel *The Age of Innocence.* In addition, she received honorary Doctorate of Letters from Yale University and a full membership in the American Academy of Arts and Letters.

Edith Newbold Jones, born January 24, 1862, grew up in a rich, socially prominent family from the in New York City and Newport, aristocracy. Edith's overbearing mother strongly disapproved of her storytelling and writing. Edith was home schooled and immersed in a society noted for its manners, taste, snobbishness, and long list of social do's and don'ts.

Edith Wharton's Library at The Mount – Lenox, MA

Edith was proficient in French, German and Italian languages and had a passion for her father's library reading literature by Jonathan Swift, Daniel Defoe, William Shakespeare, John Milton, Victor Hugo and the poetry of John Keats, and Percy Bysshe Shelley.

Not until Henry Wadsworth Longfellow recommended that Edith's poems be published in the Atlantic Monthly magazine would her parents only then recognized her talent.

On April 29, 1885, Edith married Edward R. "Teddy" Wharton, a Bostonian with a large inheritance, but they were intellectually and sexually incompatible. The Wharton's lived a companionable and expensive lifestyle with world travels finally moving into their Lenox home in 1902.

As Edith's reputation and writing abilities became frequently published and as she spent time with literary personalities, Teddy found himself in the background. They sold *The Mount* in 1911, they divorced in 1913. Edith Wharton moved permanently to France where she is buried in Versailles, France on August 11, 1937 at the age of 75.

The exquisite north garden as seen from the rear terrace of The Mount.

The Mount viewed from the north garden. Lenox, MA

The Mount is wonderful experience with its elegant gardens and Edith Wharton's lifestyle immersed into culture and the arts. During the summer season the grounds are shared with resident sculptors and are displayed throughout the estate landscape. Plays and performances by *Shakespeare and Company* e.g. *Midsummer's Night Dream* or *Romeo & Juliet* become magical when incorporated onto the terraces and into gardens of the estate. There are more events with year around workshops and studies in literature, music, and poetry.

The Mount viewed from the south garden. Lenox, MA

Directions: <u>In Lee,</u> Interstate I-90, Exit-10, Turn right off the exit ramp onto Route-20, north for 3.0-miles through Lee Center, pass Laurel Lake, turn left onto Plunkett Street, head west for 0.8-mile, entry will be on the left into a field parking lot. There is an Admission fee with structured rates for visitors, members, student, seniors, and occasional free grounds entry or during special events.

116. Field House -Williamstown

The Guest House at Field Farm - Williamstown, MA

Location: 554 Sloan Road Williamstown (Berkshire County)
Parking GPS: N42° 39' 56.09" W73° 15' 37.39" (Sloan Road)
Destination GPS: N42° 39' 58.43" W73° 15' 37.53" (Guest house)
Destination GPS: N42° 39' 54.78" W73°15' 34.24" (The Folly)
Destination GPS: N42° 40' 30.90" W73° 15' 14.40" (McMaster's Cave)
Contact: www.thetrustees.org (413) 458-3135 fieldfarm@thetrustees.org

Information: The Trustees of Reservations *Field House,* has 316-acres of manicured landscape and four miles of easy to moderate trails. Access to the grounds is year-round, sunrise to sunset and is enjoyable by foot, snowshoes, or cross-country skis. Experience awesome views of Mt Greylock Reservation and the surrounding woodlands or picturesque fields inhabited by small to large critters seeking remnants from previous season growth of corn or hay. Deer will readily bee seen during early evening and late morning. The wetlands are home to a beaver colony, turtles, snakes and salamanders, as well as a wide variety of marsh-nesting birds: red-winged blackbirds, hawks soar and circle above. A majestic Great Blue Heron patiently waits until a luckless fish or other reptile passes beneath.

Unique in architecture is the 1948 Bauhaus-inspired Guest House which is operated as a B&B. Very unique is *The Folly*, a three-bedroom, pinwheel-shaped, shingled guest cottage, designed in 1965 by noted modernist architect Ulrich Franzen. It overlooks the pond and still contains furnishings designed by Franzen. Both structures are museums from their times, *The Folly* hosts tours only.

The Guest House of Field Farm is designed by Edwin Goodell, Jr. for Lawrence, and Eleanor Bloedel, who both were collectors of modern art and furniture of the Bauhaus design. These along with Post-World War II inspired objects and furnishings adorn its interiors. Representations of Eileen Gray tables, George Nelson saucer pendant lamps, Noguchi coffee table, Kagan sofas, and a reproduction Eames chair will be found throughout house. The gardens also are host to thirteen sculptures, including works by Richard M. Miller and Herbert Ferber. The Guest House at Field Farm offers an authentic modern art experience in spectacular natural surroundings. *The Guesthouse is closed for from January 1 and re-opens April 2018. Contact the Trustees of the Reservations for information & reservations.*

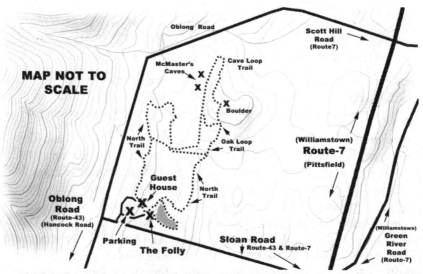

From the pond, north, counter-clockwise on North Trail and spur onto the Oak Loop trail, over the hill on the Cave Loop Trail, the caves do exist, but mainly for hard-core spelunking due to the small streams that flow and disappear into the muddy entry's and interiors.

Directions: In Williamstown Center Common, at the junction of Route-7 and Route-2, follow Route-7 & 2 south for 2.4-miles, Route-2 will bear right heading west up-hill towards NY. Continue south on Route-7 for 1.9-miles, at the bottom of a steep down-hill at the junction of Route-43 & Route-7, turn right onto Route-43 heading west and immediately turn right onto Sloan Road. Travel west on Sloan Road,1.0-mile to the entrance of Field Farm on right.

117. Herman Melville Home - Pittsfield

Herman Melville' "Arrowhead" Holmes Road - Pittsfield, MA

Location: 780 Holmes Road. Pittsfield (Berkshire County)
Parking GPS: N42° 24' 55.99" W73° 14' 58.98" (Homes Road)
Contact: www.mobydick.org (413) 442-1793 melville@berkshirehistory.org

Information: In 1819, Herman Melville was born in New York City, as a young man he had many struggles and life experiences searching for his niche in life, a store clerk, bank clerk, teacher, merchant marine (1839), signed on for a 3-year whaling voyage (1841) only to jump ship, eventually joining the U.S. Navy aboard the frigate *United States* and arriving back home in 1844. The writing of "Moby-Dick" began in New York, but predominantly was penned at Arrowhead after returning to Pittsfield, MA from 1850 to 1863. Its publication in 1851 is one of Melville's best-known novels in America literature. Other stories written at Arrowhead include: *Pierre*, *The Confidence-Man*, *Israel Potter*, a collection entitled *"The Piazza Tales,"* and such short stories as "I and My Chimney," "Benito Cereno," "Bartleby the Scrivener," and "The Paradise of Bachelors and the Tartarus of Maids."

Berkshire County Historical Society has owned the house and 45-acre property since 1975. Restoration along with a large collection of artifacts, manuscripts and many items of interest will be found here along with answers to this writer' character, relationships and lifestyle of the times.

Directions: In Lee, Interstate I-90, Exit-10. Follow Route-20 north towards Pittsfield for 8.5-miles; it will merge with Route-7 north in Lenox. Turn right onto Holmes Road at the traffic light. Arrowhead is 1.5 miles ahead on the left.

118. Jacob's Pillow - Becket

Inside/Out Stage-Jacob's Pillow - Becket, MA

Location: 358 George Carter Rd, Becket, MA 01223 (Berkshire County)
Parking GPS: N42° 15' 45.62" W73° 7' 0.98" (George Carter Road)
Contact: www.jacobspillow.org (413) 243-9919 info@jacobspillow.org

Dance performances at Jacob's Pillow take place on three stages. The *Ted Shawn Theatre* with a capacity of 620 reserved seats. The *Doris Duke Studio Theatre* built in 1990 and has 220 seats. The *Inside/Out Stage*, presents short performances free on Wednesdays, Thursdays and Fridays of established or emerging artists from all over the world to dance in the Berkshire.

Jacob's Pillow Dance Interactive is an online resource of video clips curated from the Archives in Becket. The archive features performances that have taken place at the festival from 1937 to present. This free resource allows the user to browse dance footage by artist, genre, and era. Jacob's Pillow like so many other Berkshire attractions, is a world class with notable professionals and upcoming students

Directions: Exit from Interstate I-90 at Exit-10 (Lee, Ma). Turn left at end of exit ramp onto Route-20 East. Continue to follow Route-20 (8.1-miles), at the top of the hill, turn left onto George Carter Road. Stay on George Carter Road 0.7-mile to entrance and parking. There are a few different parking locations depending on the program or attendance.

119. Jiminy Peak Mountain Resort – Hancock

Jiminy Peak Ski Slopes-Hancock, MA

Location: 37 Corey Road. Hancock 01237 (Berkshire County)
Parking GPS: N42° 33' 23.05" W73° 17' 27.24" (Base Parking)
Destination GPS: N42° 33' 19.56" W73° 17' 32.14" (Base Ski Lodge)
Destination GPS: N42° 33' 17.20" W73° 17' 28.93" (Slide-Coaster)
Contact: www.jiminypeak.com (413) 738-5500 www.jiminypeak.com

Information: Since its beginning in 1948, Jiminy Peak Ski Resort has blossomed into a prominent skiing destination offering 45-trails and nine lifts, snow making, night skiing with a multitude of chair-lift up grades along the way. In addition, continuing management changes brought in visions from real-estate development for vacation time shares and other seasonal recreation and sports venues e.g. the 2,890-foot Alpine Coaster (1977), the 3,660-feet of Mountain Coaster, Aerial Tree-Canopy course, an extensive lift-served Mountain Bike track, an exhilarating giant swing, a climbing wall, bungee-trampolines creating a year around recreation and sports resort for all ages. Seasonal dates and times for various activities can vary, safety equipment and responsibilities along with age or size requirements are enforced.

Directions: From Boston or Eastern Massachusetts: Interstate I-90 West to Exit-B3 (Berkshire Spur section). Route-22 north to Route-43, turn onto Route-43, travel east four miles to Brodie Mountain Road. Turn right, watch for Jiminy Peak 0.5-mile on your right side. **From the Albany:** Interstate I-90 east to Exit-8 (DeFreestville, just outside Albany.) Continue east on Route-43 for about 25-miles, after crossing Route-22 in Stephentown, head east for four miles, watch for JP sign at the corner of Brodie Mountain Road. Turn right, continue to travel 0.5-mile, watch for Jiminy Peak entry on your right-hand side.

120. MASS MOCA - North Adams

Museum of Contemporary Art-North Adams

Location: 87 Marshall Street North Adams, 01247 MA (Berkshire County)
Destination GPS: N42° 42' 3.08" W73° 6' 51.16"
Contact: info@massmoca.org (413)662-2111 https://massmoca.org
General admission or special event varies. Free admission-watch web site.

Information: MASS MoCA celebrated its opening in 1999. Presently, the 16 acres of grounds in North Adams encompasses a vast complex of 19th-century New England mill buildings. Courtyards and passageways along with red brick facades lend a distinct architectural ambiance to this historic industrial complex.

In 1860, the print works O. Arnold and Company established itself on a portion of the site and installed the latest equipment for printing cloth. Contracts to supply fabric for the Union Army ensured that the business prospered, and during the next four decades Arnold Print Works became the largest employer in North Adams. By the end of the 1890s, 25 of the 26 buildings in the present-day MASS MoCA complex had been constructed, and by 1905 Arnold Print Works employed some 3,200 people, as one of the leading producers of printed textiles in the world.

When Sprague Electric Company bought the site in 1942, the building exteriors remained intact, but the interiors were heavily modified to convert the former textile mill into an electronics manufacturing plant. Outfitted with state-of-the-art equipment, Sprague was a major research and development center for electrical and electronic components for military, aero-space and consumer electronic markets. At its height it employed 4,137 workers until the mid-1980's ceasing operation in 1985.

With 250,000 square feet of open and naturally lighted space has proven both inspiring and liberating to artists. This has allowed art to be embraced by both well-known and emerging artists by enabling them to focus on large-scale and immersive installations that otherwise would be impossible to present in conventional museums. In addition, performing arts including dance, musicians, rock or bluegrass festivals, outdoor films and avant-garde theater have been incorporated creating many opportunities for students, teenagers, teachers, adults, and families to experience new art forms.

Directions: From Greenfield: follow Route-2 West into North Adams. Approximately 3.5 miles past the hairpin turn, at the second set of lights on Route-2 (near the Super Big Y supermarket), turn on to Holden Street and take immediate left on to St. Anthony's Drive. Drive to the end of St. Anthony's Drive where it will intersect with Marshall Street, the MASS MOCA parking lot gate will be directly across from you at these traffic lights.

From Williamstown: from the junction of Route-7 & Route-2 at rotary/town green, follow Route-2 east 5.2 miles to the center of North Adams, where you will bear right onto an off-ramp marked "exit for downtown business district, Route-8." At the bottom of the exit ramp (at the traffic light), turn left on to Marshall Street. Drive 0.1 mile, under the overpass, and MASS MoCA parking lot gate will be directly on your left at the traffic lights.

121. Mt. Greylock Veterans Memorial Tower

Mt. Greylock Reservation Veterans Memorial Tower. Adams, MA

Location: Summit Mt. Greylock Reservation-DCR (Berkshire County)
Parking GPS: N42° 38' 16.09" W73° 10' 0.45"
Destination GPS: N42° 38' 13.85" W73° 9' 57.56" (Tower)
Destination GPS: N42° 40' 28.09" W73° 8' 29.81" (Notch Road Gate)
Destination GPS: N42° 33' 12.52" W73° 12' 47.33" (Rockwell Road Gate)
Contact: Mt. Greylock Visitor Center 30 Rockwell Rd, Lanesborough, MA 01237 mount.greylock@state.ma.us (413) 499-4262 Fee or Pass parking at summit. DCR Interpreter programs or events at the summit or Visitors Center

Information: Mt Greylock Veterans War Memorial Tower sits on highest point in Massachusetts; its tower adds 93-feet to the mountain's elevation of 3,491-feet for a total of 3,584-feet. Completed in 1932 and dedicated in 1933, the 93-foot tower is built using massive granite blocks from Quincy. Opened seasonally, the tower has a center spiral stairway to reach the top observation level which has awesome views. The Beacon is lit nightly with some exceptions and can be seen some 70-miles away on a clear night. The tower is a destination for many, driving up the Notch Road or Rockwell Road, hiking up trails or biking to the summit, although the paved road is only opened May until October. Its ~8-miles to the summit from either north or south gates.

Directions: Route-7 north through Lanesborough center, for 1.4-mile, turn onto north Main Street, follow for 0.75 and bear right onto Mt. Greylock Road, 0.5-mile bear left onto Rockwell Road, uphill 0.5-mile to Lanesborough Visitor's Center. (Trail maps or information.)

122. Naumkeag Estate - Stockbridge

Naumkeag - Stockbridge, MA

Location: 5 Prospect Hill Road, Stockbridge 01262 (Berkshire County)
Parking GPS: N42° 17' 23.59" W73° 19' 1.63" (Naumkeag Parking-rear)
Destination GPS: N42° 17' 25.10" W73° 18' 58.15" (Chinese Garden)
Destination GPS: N42° 17' 22.11" W73° 18' 57.84" (Afternoon Garden)
Destination GPS: N42° 17' 21.56" W73° 18' 59.45" (Blue Steps Garden)
Contact: www.thetrustees.org (413) 298-8138 naumkeag@thetrustees.org
Admission is free for members, except for special events having co-pays.

Information: Acquired in 1884 by Joseph and Caroline Choate who purchased 48-acres and built the 44-room, Gilded Age style cottage *Naumkeag,* a marvelous estate and acclaimed for its gardens. With spacious views, Naumkeag is the Native American name for Salem, Massachusetts, where Joseph Choate was born. Graduating from Harvard Law School, he moved to New York City becoming a premier courtroom lawyer, presenting cases in front of the Supreme Court. In 1899, Choate was appointed by President McKinley to be the Ambassador to the United Kingdom. Caroline Choate was a trained artist interested in women's education, co-founding Barnard College.

Naumkeag's cottage is also filled with original furniture, ceramics, and artwork collected from America, Europe, and the Far East. In the 1880's the original design for the estate's landscape and terraced gardens was by architect Nathan Barrett.

Their daughter, Mabel Choate, inherited Naumkeag in 1929, and for the next 30 years worked with the prominent landscape architect Fletcher Steele to create the magnificent gardens seen today: The Blue Stairs, The Rose Garden, Chinese Garden, Afternoon Garden, Tree Terrace and the Evergreen Garden. Beginning in 2013 several years of major restoration to the cottage, gardens and landscape were renovated of repaired to reflect their elegant past.

Miss Mabel Choate in 1958 bequeathed Naumkeag in its entirety, including all of the household furnishings and fine art, to The Trustees of Reservations. Since the property's opening in 1959, it has become a popular destination for area residents and visitors to the southern Berkshires. Additional land in 1985 was given by J. Graham and Margaret Parsons. Any time spend at Naumkeag is never wasted.

Flecher Steele Stairway at Naumkeag. Stockbridge, MA

Directions: In Lee, at Interstate I-90, Exit-10, turn left onto Route-20 east and then immediately right onto Route-102 west. Continue going west on Route-102 for 4.2 miles until Route-7 junctions just east of Stockbridge center, continue straight through town west on, Main Street, Route-7/102, the Red Lion Inn is on the left corner until Route-7 turns left and heads south for Great Barrington. Turn right onto Pine Street up-hill travel 0.2-mile, bear Left onto Prospect Hill Road travel 0.5-mile, Naumkeag will be of the left or in special event parking could be redirected and shuttle bus.

<u>123.</u> Norman Rockwell Museum - <u>Stockbridge</u>

Norman Rockwell Gallery and Museum (Route-183) - Stockbridge, MA

Location: 9 Glendale Road/Route-183. Stockbridge 01262 (Berkshire County)
Parking GPS: N42° 17' 17.77" W73° 20' 14.72" (Glendale Road)
Destination GPS: N42° 17' 15.70" W73° 20' 8.97" (Gallery)
Contact: www.nrm.org   (413) 298-4100   Admission Fee-Free Parking

Information: Founded in 1969, this museum has the world's largest and most significant collection of Norman Rockwell drawings and paintings. Originally located on Main Street in Stockbridge, the museum moved to its current location opening to the public on April 3, 1993. In addition, to 574 original works of art by Rockwell, the museum also houses the Norman Rockwell Archives, a collection of over 100,000 various items, which include photographs, and various business documents. Rockwell humor and humility is seen within many paintings or illustrations, tours either self-guided or with guides expand will point out more of his witty character or subtle details.

Directions: In Lee, Interstate I-90, Exit-10, turn left onto Route-20 east and then immediately right onto Route-102 west. Continue going west on Route-102 for 4.2-miles until Route-7 junctions just east of Stockbridge center, continue straight through town west on, Main Street, Route-7/102, the Red Lion Inn is on the corner where Route-7 turns left and heads south for Great Barrington. You continue straight (west) on Route-102 (Main St). Shortly after going through town, you will veer to the right to stay on Route-102 west for approximately 1.8-miles. At the flashing light, make a left onto Route-183 South and the Museum entrance is 0.6-miles down on the left.

124. Notchview Reservation - Windsor

Notchview Reservation Touring Center – Windsor, MA

Location: Trustees of Reservation. Route-9, Windsor. (Berkshire County)
Destination GPS: N42° 30' 18.24" W73° 2' 15.64"
Destination GPS: N42° 30' 18.59" W73° 2' 13.11" (Lodge)
http://www.thetrustees.org   information@thetrustees.org   (978)921-1944
Crossing Country Skiing fees are in effect for members and non-members.
For winter ski condition: (413) 684-0148

Information: Lt. Colonel Arthur D. Budd bequeathed his Notch View Farm to The Trustees of Reservations in 1965. The 93-acre Smithers Woodland Preserve was added to the Reservation in 1993. Located in the town of Windsor, Notchview offers more than 3,000-acres of rolling woodland terrain with over twelve miles of groomed and tracked trails for skating or classical diagonal cross-country skiing for every level of skiing. The majority of the reservation is above 2,000-feet which results in snow on the trails for more than 80+ days each year. Judges Hill is the highest point at 2,297-feet and is the steepest or most challenging of the trails. All trails are well-marked and have maps showing your location at many of the trail junctions.

Directions: From the junction of Route-8 and Route-9 in Dalton, travel east on Route-9 for 7.0-miles, turn left into the large parking area. From the Look Park traffic circle in Northampton, follow Route-9 west for 26-miles turning right into the parking area in Windsor.

125. Railroad History - Hoosac Tunnel

Norfolk-Southern exits Eastern Portal of the Hoosac Tunnel - Florida, MA

Location: River Road R&R Crossing. Florida (Berkshire County)
Parking GPS: N42° 40' 28.02" W72° 59' 44.32" (Deerfield River)
Destination GPS: N42° 40' 30.60" W72° 59' 49.51"(View Point)
Wow Factor: 8 **Accessibility:** Roadside, short walk 0.1 mile

History: On January 8, 1851, ground was broken in North Adams which would become known as the western portal of this 4.75-mile long and ambitious project; the *Hoosac Railroad Tunnel*. The tunnel was the answer to a more southern and western railway which was successful during the 1840's climbing over the Berkshire Mountains from Springfield to Pittsfield over Keystone Arch bridges engineered by Major George Washington Whistler. A fear of those times was that the northern towns and mills would wither away and would not prosper without a railroad westward gateway to move their wares west.

Initially planned to cost $2,000,000, a great expense in its day and with high skepticism, the project would flounder early. In 1852, at the eastern portal in Florida, a $25,000 engineering contraption was promised to bore a 24-foot-wide tunnel through the mountain in 1556 days. The machine seized up after 12-feet and remained embedded in the mountain, this test bore can still be found nearby.

In the spring of 1856, problems with the tunneling techniques became apparent; Hermann Haupt a respected railroad engineer from the Pennsylvania R&R was hired. By May 1857, the eastern portal had dug a scant 80-foot into the mountain. On the western portal a watery slurry of "porridge stone" was encountered and would require installing 6 to 8 layers of brick to support the tunnel walls. At the eastern portal, layers of hard rock required hand drilling using "Star Drills" to create the 2-foot-deep blasting shafts which were filled and tamped with black powder explosive, a slow dangerous technique. By 1861, political opposition along with the Civil War slowed construction significantly and eventually prompted Haupt's departure to support the Union while leaving the western portal only 600-feet deep and the eastern portal 2400-feet deep.

On July 1, 1863 a Thomas Doane became chief engineer and began initializing changes. The central shaft was begun; this was to provide two additional headings to help speed up tunnel construction and eventually provide ventilation for the billows of smoke created by the engine's fireboxes. Hand drilling was replaced by pneumatic drills that operated on compressed air provided by a compressor building on Deerfield River. The entire project was resurveyed including the installation of (6) stone alignment towers which would provide unprecedented accuracy for all points of digging east, west and center. In Addition, the use of an experimental explosive trinitroglycerin, a predecessor to nitroglycerin was introduced, along with new and safer electric detonator caps.

Bricked walls within the Hoosac Tunnel-Western Portal. North Adams, MA

In August 1867, Doane left amidst ongoing political harassment over the tunnel's cost, low progress in tunneling activities along with accidents that caused injury or death. Industrial accidents would

resulted in death or where the worker sustained serious injury would not be a stranger here. Compiled records from the commencement of the tunneling to its finished completion place the total number of deaths or casualties at ~252 from falling rock, machinery, explosions and falls. The most notable event was at the central shaft a.k.a. "The Bloody Pit" took place in October 1867 when an explosion along with fire took the lives of 13 men, destroyed all the scaffolding and buildings. Operations here would not resume here for over a year.

On January 7, 1869, Walter Shanley received the contract for the tunnel's construction and completion. With enhanced strategies, increased manpower, usage of nitroglycerin, the pace of tunnel advancement on both ends improved. On December 12, 1872, the eastern tunnel met the center shaft, on Thanksgiving Day November 26, 1873 only 16 feet of heading November 27, 1873; the remainder of the tunnel was opened to the west portal tunnel. Grading and track laying would continue for the remainder of 1874, on February 9, 1875 the first train passed through the tunnel with the Hoosac Tunnel being officially opened July 1, 1876.

On February 9, 1875 the first train passed through the tunnel (carrying a few flatbeds and a boxcar filled with people), on April 5th the first freight train passed, finally on October 13th the first passenger train passed / officially opened the tunnel July 1, 1876.

On February 11, 1887 the Fitchburg RR purchased The Hoosac Tunnel for $5-Million and 50,000-shares worth $20 each. The Fitchburg RR decided that lighting the tunnel would be safer and more pleasing, so they installed 1300 lights 38.5-feet apart. Continuous water leaks shorted out the lights frequently, so they were removed in 1889. The smoke in the tunnel was so bad that a 16-foot fan was installed at the top of the Central Shaft. The base of the Central Shaft was widened and a brick arching was installed with duct openings at track level offset by about 60-feet on each side. A room in the center of the tunnel known as "The Hoosac Hotel" was hollowed out for the track walker as well. 85-90 trains passed through daily.

Rear end collisions happened as a result of the blackness and smoke. Some collisions proved to be fatal. Ventilation was so poor, that train crews had to lie on the floor to find breathable air. Decreased oxygen within the tunnel made boiler fires die down to the point that the crews had to stick broom sticks out and against the wall to determine if they were still moving.

Directions Eastern Portal: On Route-2 (Mohawk Trail) from the Elk Statue located on the Whitcomb Hill summit in Florida, travel east towards Charlemont for 0.4-mile turning left onto Whitcomb Hill Road. Following downhill 2.5-miles, (it will be steep with several sharp curves) reaching its bottom, turn left onto River Road. Head west, on River Road 0.8-mile, just before the railroad crossing on your right is a "fisherman's" parking area, across on the left is another parking area which is railroad property. While the railroad property is used by many, you can be asked to leave or questioned about your purpose by authorities, The Hoosac Tunnel portal is 0.1-miles west away from the Deerfield River. If the railroad crossing bell begins to clang you will have either a train coming from the east and crossing the river's trestle or from out of the tunnel very shortly.

Directions Western Portal: From Main Street in North Adams, at the junction Eagle and Ashland Street (Route-8A south) follow Ashland Street south for 1.3-miles where it will merge in Church Street that comes in from the left. From this point, another 0.3-mile on the left a small, dirt/gravel service road for the western portal will be seen. Often it will be gated and sometimes not. If you pass West Shaft Road on the left or the large cemetery on the right you passed it. Walking or driving, it will be 0.15-mile to a parking area with an access point onto the railroad track. The western portal is an additional 0.2-mile down the track. Reminder you will be on railroad property. To be honest, I have not been to the western portal for many years due to the legal or safety concerns, especially after being given a lenient and stern warning.

There is a variety of people who are drawn to this tunnel and range from train buffs, some in intellectual pursuit of its historical significance, with others seeking the paranormal experiences of haunted locations. **It is important to note that many "No Trespassing "signs are posted at both ends of the tunnel's portals. It is illegal to enter the tunnel or walk on the railroad tracks without permission.** Since, September 11, 2001 security on either portal has increased, with that said; I have visited the tunnel's east and west portal with access being the easiest at the east portal off River Road in Florida, Massachusetts.

In February 2020, a recent tunnel collapse brought an increased in security especially on the western North Adams portal. Both ends of the tunnel are patrolled with over-night security guards in place and it is expected to continue for some time from what the rumors and propaganda say about the future tunnel renovations or maintenance.

125a. Hoosac Tunnel Alignment Towers

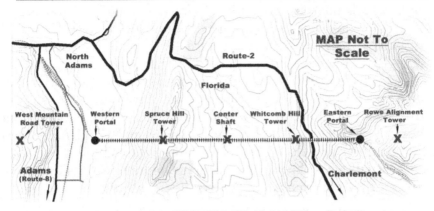

Eastern Portal: N42° 40' 30.60" W72° 59' 49.51"(View Point)
Rowe Alignment Tower: N42° 40' 30.50" W72° 58' 56.20"
Whitcomb Hill Alignment Tower: N42° 40' 31.00" W73° 1' 14.90"
Center Shaft: N42° 40' 31.15" W73° 2' 45.15" (Center Shaft Road)
Spruce Hill Alignment Tower: N42° 40'31.26" W73° 4' 5.81"
West Mountain Road Tower: N42° 40' 31.90" W73° 7' 24.40"
Western Portal: N42° 40' 31.42" W73° 5' 29.89"

Information: Beginning in1866, the alignment towers installed by the civil engineer Thomas Doane and were instrumental in allowing the tunnel's simultaneous digging at opposite ends and at different points along its 5-mile span to maintain a straight line. The towers played an essential role ensuring that the Central Shaft would align with the main tunnel 1028-feet below, thereby allowing two additional paths of digging towards the east and west portals from the inside. After reaching the proper depth, the central shaft digging began with one heading east and the other westerly. The western direction was closer at 12,244-feet (2.31-mile) while the eastern tunneling was further at 12,837-feet (2.44-mile.) All of the mechanics of surveying were repetitive at all the towers and into the tunnel shafts. Transit scopes, vertical red & white sighting rods and wired plumb bobs that were meticulous positioned, checked, and rechecked. The system worked with a misalignment of only a 9/16-inch over 4.75-miles.

125b. Rowe Neck Alignment Tower

Rowe Alignment Tower Site – (4) rods only parts left.

Tunnel Road parking: N42° 40' 26.90" W72° 57' 52.30" (upper)
Tunnel Road parking: N42° 40' 20.80" W72° 58' 14.30" (lower)
Hoosac Tunnel Trail: N42° 40' 26.10" W72° 58' 51.00" (Turn-off)
Rowe Alignment Tower: N42° 40' 30.50" W72° 58' 56.20" (Site)

Information: Out of the (6) original towers only four sites remain. The alignment towers at the east and west portals were removed after tunnel construction was completed, but (4) of the towers sites or what is left of them still remain 153-years later in the Berkshire hills. The first and most eastern alignment tower was built on the western side on Rowe's Neck just below its summit on a small rock crag. From this vantage point the surveyor could see the alignment tower down at the east portal and the top of Whitcomb Summit where the next tower was built. There is not much to see other than (4) metal rods which suggests a wooden structure only, no masonry or stone wall remnants exist here. However, there is a great view and along with the above graphic does allow for the visualization of the alignment process.

Directions: Access here to the most eastern Hoosac Tunnel Alignment site, the Rowe site, is a 3.8-mile round trip hike on the Hoosac Tunnel Loop Trail which is part of the Bear Swamp hiking trail. Be aware that there is no actual trail for the last 0.1-mile, no signs or blazes to the towers actual site, usage of GPS coordinates will assist in locating a turn-off point and off trail bushwhacking will also be required.

The approach to the Hoosac Tunnel Trail is via Tunnel Road a dirt road that usually is in good condition for it accesses portions of the upper reservoir for the Bear Swamp hydro-electric facility. However,

I would not think it is fully plowed during winter and that certain times in the spring could be rather muddy.

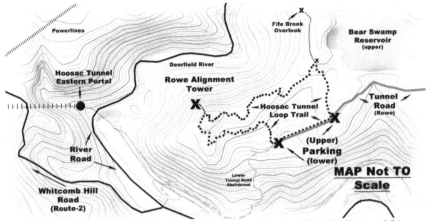

Hoosac Tunnel Loop Trail approach from Tunnel Road. Rowe, MA

From the junction of Route-8A and Route-2 (Mohawk Trail) in Charlemont drive west on Route-2 for 1.5-miles, (on the right, just before the bridge that crosses the Deerfield River), turn right onto Zoar Road. Follow Zoar Road for 2.5-miles, turn right onto Rowe Road, head north for 2.0-miles. Turn left onto Brittingham Hill Road, drive uphill 1.0-mile where it will junction with Tunnel Road. Turn left onto Tunnel Road heading west. Drive 0.3-mile where Tunnel Road will bear right and become a dirt road, Petrie Road with continue straight. Driving 0.6-mile, stay straight passing a dirt gated road on the right. Another 0.5-mile, turn right staying on Tunnel Road (Steele Brook Road goes straight), continue west for another 0.5-mile and passing the levee of Bear Swamp. In another 0.4-mile the upper parking lot and a kiosk of the Hoosac Tunnel Loop Trail is on the left. The trailhead for the trail is across from the kiosk. Another 0.3-mile further is the lower parking area, the trailhead here bears right like a logging road and the blue blazes along with a Paw Print logo of the Bear Swamp Trail are evident. Tunnel Road does continue west becoming very difficult to navigate, to the point that the steepness and terrain become perilous or unsafe being navigable by ATV or foot only.

Going clock-wise on the Hoosac Tunnel Trail from the lower parking area is the shortest approach to the summit which is about 1.1-mile. The entire trail itself originally was well marked, but blue blazes are fading and the trail itself does not appear to be overly used. Careful attention and looking forward for the next blaze or Bear Paw marker is sometimes a necessity to stay on trail. The option to seek out the alignment tower site requires bushwhacking down the western slope and having a handheld GPS being essential to find the site, otherwise much exertion will be spend beating the brush for the exact location. Returning back to the trail and continuing along the ridge crest east, the trail meanders along stone outcrops and sometimes it is better to step off mossy and slippery looking rock spines the trail crosses, for an accident here will suck.

125c. Whitcomb Hill Alignment Tower

Whitcomb Hill Alignment Tower Remnant – Florida, MA

Whitcomb Hill Parking: N42° 40' 37.96" W73° 0' 58.76"(Route-2-upper)
Whitcomb Hill Parking: N42° 40' 28.45" W73° 0' 54.03"(Route-2-lower)
Whitcomb Hill 4x4 Road: N42° 41' 15.73" W73° 1' 18.51
Whitcomb Hill Alignment Tower: N42° 40' 31.00" W73° 1' 14.90"

Information: From the Rowe Tower heading west, the next alignment tower is the Whitcomb Hill site. There are actually remnants of this alignment tower walls which are still up-right. Considering the harsh New England winters and the tendency of vandalism in remote places, anything still standing is a tribute to the steadfastness in the construction being 153+ years old. The building was masonry, with (4) walls of equal length with centered windows and a door. The roof was slanted and made of wood. The return of the forested woodlands prevents any view or sightline in either direction toward the Rowe or Spruce Hill alignment tower.

Directions: There are (2) approaches to this alignment tower. The first is from the summit of Whitcomb Hill on a narrow 4x4 dirt road. The road is relatively flat and after 1.1-mile will directly pass the tower site and continue out to a power line nearby. The other approach is by the power lines just mentioned and hiking up from where they cross Route-2 below.

Parking at the Elk Statue near the summit on Route-2, walk west 100-yards and cross over Route-2. (This area was at one time very popular spot for tourists on the Mohawk Trail with drive-in cabins and an observation tower.) There is a "Whitcomb Summit" sign on the corner of the very obvious roadway up into the woods. It is a passable roadway with the proper vehicle, but parking and turn around locations are minimal. Hiking on the roadway, the tower site is just off on the right. There are no signs or makings on the road.

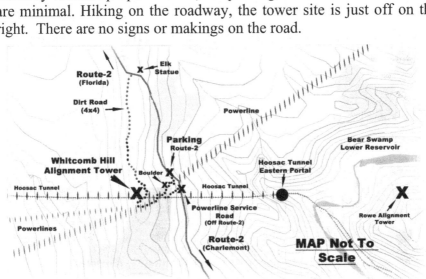

Two Approaches for the Whitcomb Hill Alignment Tower. Florida, MA

The power line approach will require some uphill hiking, but is half the distance to the alignment tower site compared to the 4x4 dirt road. Start from the Elk Statue on Whitcomb Hill summit, follow Route-2 east for 0.8-mile, just prior to where the power line crosses Route-2 there is break-down lane wide enough to park safely. Of concern here is getting up and onto the power line itself. A scramble up the steep embankment and a short walk through the woodlands east will bring you onto the power line and its service road. In addition, from this vantage point you will pass by a large boulder.

Another parking area 0.2 past the power line is where a recent access road has been constructed. This road parallels the power line entering onto it 0.2-miles above Route-2. Either parking area the hike to the alignment tower site is a ~0.5-mile. Hike up the power line until reaching the brink of the ridge, off on the right is the same 4x4 dirt road that begins at the Whitcomb Hill summit, walk north 0.1-mile and the tower will be off on the left slightly in the woods.

"Alignment Boulder" large erratic on the way to Whitcomb Hill Tower

The large erratic boulder is on the lower portion of the power line. Only labeled as "Alignment Boulder" has no association with the construction of the Hoosac Tunnel, in fact it is much older ☺

HOOSAC TUNNEL.

First proposed (for Canal),	1819.	Rock excavated, tons,	2,000,000.
Chartered,	1848.	Height, feet,	20.
Commenced,	1851.	Width, feet,	24.
Headings met Nov. 27th,	1874.	Water disch., East End, gal. per min.,	100.
Completed,	1875.	Water disch., West End, gal. per min.,	600.
Total length, feet,	25,031.	Men employed,	800 to 900
East End to Central Shaft, feet,	12,837.	Miles from Boston,	136.
Central Shaft to West Shaft, feet,	9,694.	First train through, Feb. 9th,	1875.
West Shaft to West End, feet,	2,500.	First Freight, Apr. 5th,	1875.
Depth Central Shaft, feet,	1,028.	First Passenger, Oct. 13th,	1875.
Depth West Shaft, feet,	318.	Above tide at East Portal,	966.
Size Central Shaft, feet,	15 x 27.	Total length of Brick Arching,	7,573.
Size West Shaft, feet,	10 x 14.	No. of Bricks used in Arching,	20,000,000.
Height Eastern Summit, feet,	1,429.	Cost,	$14,000,000.
Height Western Summit, feet,	1,718.	Lives Lost,	195.
Grade per mile,	26-40.	Contractors, F. & W. Shanley, Montreal	
Error in line at points of meeting, 9-16 in.		Chief Civil Engineer, Benj. D. Frost.	
Rock—Mica Slate, Mica Schist and Milky Quartz.		Explosive—Tri-nitro glycerine.	
		One lb. Glycerine equal to 13 of Powder.	

125d. Spruce Hill - Alignment Tower

Interesting note that the locations of the Whitcomb Hill Tower, Center Shaft and Spruce Hill Tower are directly above and in line with the Hoosac Tunnel 1,028-feet below. The Spruce Hill tower site is nothing more than a pile of stones and is accessible by the Hoosac Trail or the Busby Trail with a map found in Chapter #78. While not directly upon the Hoosac Trail its GPS (N42° 40'31.26" W73° 4' 5.81") a short distance east of the Hoosac Trail as the trail crosses an old utility line.

125e. West Mountain Alignment Tower

West Mountain Road Alignment Tower Remnant - 1866 North Adams, MA

Parking GPS: N42° 40' 25.69" W73° 8' 4.49" (West Mountain Road)
West Mountain Road Tower GPS: N42° 40' 31.90" W73° 7' 24.40"

Information: The most western alignment tower is located on the lowest northern slopes of Ragged Mountain, but not part of the Mt. Greylock Reservation. Very easy access with parking on the lower end of West Mountain Road just off Reservoir Road. The road is presently 4X4 vehicle only and is rather torn up due to recent logging activity that has also created spur roads that can cause confusion. Hiking east 0.7-miles up to just about to where the road begins to curve around and south towards Adams. Up on the right, 75-feet above the road, on the hillside bluff, the tower will be seen.

Very much like the Whitcomb Hill tower site, the remnants of (4) 12x12-feet stone masonry walls each side having a center cut where either a door or window would be located still stand. In addition, the forest regrowth also screens any view of where the western portal is located or the eastern Spruce Hill Alignment Tower site.

Directions: From the western end of Main Street in the center of North Adams, follow Route-8 south, immediately passing over the bridge, turn right onto Furnace Bypass Road (Heritage Park exit) uphill 0.1-mile, turn left at top onto Furnace Street. Travel 100-yards bearing right onto Reservoir Road which will climb uphill steeply, follow this road for 2.0-miles, just before the road curves sharply right and in view of the large Notch Reservoir Dam, West Mountain Road will be on the left. A short drive into the log landing parking area. From here, head east up the main dirt road. As mentioned, a lot of logging activity has created a muddy matrix of roads and paths.

Getting above this and finding the main road gets somewhat clearer, the main road often seemed to have a under lying of field stone that creates a road bed. There is a place 0.2 mile up where the road forks, bear to the right. Another 0.5 miles, the right side becomes a steeper ridge line, this is where you will see the tower walls 75-feet above the road way. A couple of ATV trails lead up to it or around its vicinity.

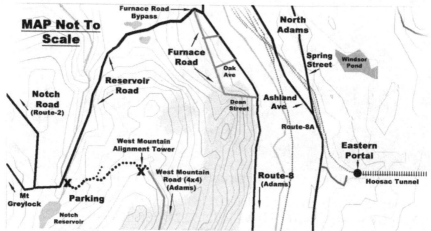

West Mountain Road Alignment Tower. North Adams, MA

On February 9, 1875 the first train passed through the tunnel (carrying a few flatbeds and a boxcar filled with people), on April 5th the first freight train passed, finally on October 13th the first passenger train passed / officially opened the tunnel July 1, 1876
On February 11, 1887 the Fitchburg RR purchased The Hoosac Tunnel for $5-Million and 50,000-shares worth $20 each. The Fitchburg RR decided that lighting the tunnel would be safer and more pleasing, so they installed 1300-lights 38.5-feet apart. Continuous water leaks shorted out the lights frequently, so they were removed in 1889. The smoke in the tunnel was so bad that a 16-foot fan was installed at the top of the Central Shaft. The base of the Central Shaft was widened and a brick arching was installed with duct openings at track level offset by about 60 feet on each side. A room in the center of the tunnel known as "The Hoosac Hotel" was hollowed out for the track-walker as well. Rear end collisions happened as a result of the blackness and smoke; some collisions proved to be fatal. Ventilation was so poor that train crews had to lie on the floor to find breathable air. Boiler fires would die down to the point that the crews had to stick broom sticks out and against the wall to determine if they were still moving. Despite these conditions 85-90 trains passed through daily.

126. Santarella – Gingerbread House

Santarella a.k.a "The Gingerbread House" - Tyringham, MA

Location: 75 Main Road. Tyringham 01264 (Berkshire County)
Parking GPS: N42° 15' 16.59" W73° 12' 52.29" (Studio-Parking)
Lexington Minuteman Statue GPS: N42° 26' 56.19" W71° 13' 48.41"
Concord Minuteman Statue GPS: N42° 28' 8.07" W71° 21' 4.68"
Rodger Conant Statue GPS: N42° 31' 24.40" W70° 53' 27.11" (Salem)
Contact: http://santarella.us denise@santarella (413) 243-0840

Information: Sir Henry Hudson Kitson, the English sculptor who is known for his Massachusetts statues of the Lexington Minuteman, the Plymouth Rock Maiden and Rodger Conant (the founding Father of Salem, MA,) In 1920, he began transforming a Tyringham barn into a sculpturing studio with a most striking design, it has appearance of a dwelling out of the Grimm Brothers Fairy Tales.

Of Kitson's studio, most impressive is its 80-ton asphalt shingled roof. Originally, Kitson had envisioned a replica of a thatched roof similar to the traditional thatched-roofs in his native Britain. Without a supply or local source of thatching material, its creation required asphalt tiles to be hand-cut into a wave-like shape and then laid in thick layers of different-colors. The whole project took three workers twelve years to complete. The studio and gardens became Kitson's primary focus for the last 25-years of his life; it was completed in 1937 and is a great work of art in itself.

Interestingly, the Boston's locations between Daniel Chester French's *Concord Minute Man* and Henry Hudson Kitson *Lexington Minute Man* is 6.5-miles. The distance between their Berkshire studio's *Chesterwood* in Stockbridge and *Santarella* in Tyringham is only 7.3 miles.

Lexington Minute Man - Lexington (left)   Rodger Conant - Salem (right)

The *Lexington Minuteman* statue was created by Henry Hudson Kitson and commemorates the stand of colonists against the British on April 19, 1775. It seems to be accepted that Captain Parker was said to have stated *"Stand your ground. Don't fire unless fired upon, but if they mean to have a war, let it begin here"* The statue sits at the intersection of Bedford Street and Massachusetts Avenue, on the southeast corner of Lexington Battle Green. It was at these sites that the opening shots of the Battles of Lexington and Concord were fired on April 19, 1775, starting the American Revolutionary War.

Rodger Conant was a founding father of Salem, MA and in surrounding townships as administrator for the Massachusetts Bay Company. In his cape, he's is an imposing figure located on North Washington Square, right in front of the Salem Witch Museum on the south western end of Salem Common

Directions: In Lee, at the junction of Interstate I-90 Exit-10, follow Route-20 east, an immediate right onto Route-102, and west for 0.10-mile and quickly turn left at the lights onto Tyringham Road. Go 3.3-miles, Santarella will be on your left. It is private property, with tours of the studio and gardens, conferences or weddings by arrangement. A roadside look-see visit is usually fine.

127. Hancock Shaker Village

Shaker Village "Village of Peace" Pittsfield, MA

Location: West Housatonic Street /Route-20. Pittsfield (Berkshire County)
Parking GPS: N42° 25' 49.26" W73° 20' 25.81" (Shaker Village parking)
Contact: hancockshakervillage.org   info@hancockshakervillage.org
(413)443-0188   Fee for admission, workshops and special events.

Information: Of the original 19 Shaker Villages establish in New York, New England, Kentucky, Ohio and Indiana this is their third community by the Shakers in 1790 and lived here for 179 years until 1960. Today, Hancock Shaker Village is a living history museum with 18 original historic buildings, the farm and gardens, animals, handicrafts like weaving, spinning, blacksmithing or hiking trails on 750 acres. Shaker religious expression took the form of singing and ecstatic dance, which is why they were called the "Shakers" or "Shaking Quakers." Religious and cultural tenets that the Shakers embraced; celibacy, equality, pacifism, community, sustainability, land stewardship, innovation, craftsmanship and simplicity. The village is handicapped accessible and has modern amenities. For more information and history: Google or contact Shaker Village above.

Directions: In Lee, from the junction of Interstate I-90, Exit-10 and Route-20, head north on Route-20 towards Pittsfield for 11 miles.
Turn left onto West Housatonic Street and continue on Route-20 west for 4.8 miles, (towards N.Y.) The Shakers Village's entrance is off Route-20 west on the left, 0.5-mile past where Route-41 junctions with Route-20.

128. Tanglewood - Lenox

Tanglewood Music Shed and Lawn seating. Lenox, MA

Location: 297 West Street/Route-183. Lenox 01240 (Berkshire County)
Parking GPS: N42° 21' 8.85" W73° 18' 42.13" (Main Entry, Route-183)
Parking GPS: N42° 20' 53.16" W73° 18' 42.06" (West Hawthorne Entry)
Destination GPS: N42° 20' 56.22" W73° 18' 37.51" (Koussevitzky Shed)
Destination GPS: N42° 20' 50.23" W73° 18' 22.49" (Seiji Ozawa Hall)
Contact: www.bso.org customerservice@bso.org 888-266-1200
Tanglewood Information: 413-637-5180

Tanglewood Box Office in Lenox: **Monday to Friday;** 10am-6pm or Intermission **Saturday;** 9am- 6pm or Intermission **Sunday;** 10am-6pm or Intermission For most **Ozawa Hall**; concerts the Box Office opens 3-hours in advance. The Tanglewood Box Office closes at the end of intermission, or 30 minutes after the start of a performance if there is no intermission. After the Box Office closes, any remaining will-call tickets will be moved to the Main Gate for late pick-up. The Main Gate is located at 297 West Street. You may not enter the grounds without a ticket. Tickets cannot be purchased after the box office closes.

BSO.org is the only official online source for purchasing tickets to performances and events at Symphony Hall and Tanglewood. If you do not see BSO.org listed in your web browser's address bar when viewing the performance schedule and purchasing tickets, please close your browser and visit www.BSO.or **Order tickets online**; at tanglewood.org, 24 hours a day. There is a $6.50 per order handling fee for tickets ordered by mail; a $6.50 fee per ticket for orders by phone or online. Call **Symphony Charge:** Mon-Fri 10-5PM and Sat 12:30-4:30PM at 617-266-1200 or 888-266-1200

129. The Bidwell House - Monterey

Bidwell House 1750 – Monterey, MA

Location: 100 Art School Road, Monterey 01245 (Berkshire County)
Parking GPS: N42° 12' 30.00" W73° 13' 5.10" (Art School Road)
Contact: www.bidwellhousemuseum.org   bidwellhouse@gmail.com
(413)528-6888   Fee for house tour, grounds and gardens are open year-round for hiking, snow shoeing or cross-country skiing, free of charge.

Information: Built circa 1750's for the first minister of Township No. 1, the Reverend Adonijah Bidwell, The Bidwell House is a gracious two-story post-and-beam Georgian saltbox. Rev. Bidwell arrived in 1750 to be the first minister of this frontier region, which eventually became the towns of Monterey and Tyringham. Bidwell built an imposing residence, with six large, paneled rooms, four fireplaces, two beehive ovens, and three closets situated on 192 acres of fields.

His 1784 death inventory, tells of a well-furnished house for the time and location. He owned a significant collection of pewter, three high chests, six beds, chests and tables, a large library, and an amazing 48 chairs! As women often brought furniture as part of their dowry, this large furniture collection might have been a result of numerous wives. The high rate of mortality for women meant that more than one wife was common and indeed this was the case for Rev. Bidwell, three to be exact! Once the house was completed and he was settled into his position, Rev. Bidwell married his first wife, Theodosia Colton, in 1752. Theodosia died childless of an unknown cause in 1759. One year later Rev. Bidwell married Theodosia's first cousin, Jemima Devotion, the daughter of a prominent Connecticut minister. Jemima lived for ten short years as Mrs. Bidwell, bearing all of his children, two boys and two girls, before she died. Having young children to raise, Rev. Bidwell lost no time in marrying his third and final wife, Ruth Kent, in 1772. Not all women died young. Ruth lived to be a healthy 85, Rev. Bidwell's death occurred in 1784

The Bidwell House and property remained in the Bidwell family and was handed down from father to son to grandson, each generation adding to the architecture of the house. Rev. Bidwell farmed the property from 1750 to 1784. His eldest son, Adonijah Bidwell Jr., developed the farm into a large and prosperous dairy farm, expanding the land holdings and building a compound of barns and out-buildings. His tenure was 1784-1836. The grandson, John Devotion Bidwell, continued to farm and also added a tanning yard.

In 1853 the house and property were sold out of the family. Three generations of the Carrington family farmed the property until 1911, when it was sold to a logging company. In 1913 it was purchased by Raymond P. Ensign, who established the Berkshire Summer School of the Arts on the property. In 1960, it was purchased by Jack Hargis and David Brush, two fashion designers from New York City. They bought the farm and the surrounding 196-acres for the sum of $30,000 and proceeded to spend the next 25 years restoring the house. Added to the National Register of Historic Places in 1982, the house became a museum in 1990. It is open for tours from Thursday through Monday between Memorial Day and Columbus Day, as well as for special events.

Traditional crafts and trades demonstrated at The Bidwell House craft fairs. Period clad re-enactors blacksmiths, masonry, carpentry adds to the event

Directions: In Lee, Exit-10 off Interstate I-90, from the exit ramp turn left/east onto Route-20, immediately turn right onto Route-102, travel west for 0.10-mile, at the lights, turn left onto Tyringham Road which will become Main Road. Travel south for 5.7-miles, straight through the Center Tyringham and turning right onto Monterey Road, head west for 2.3-miles. Turn right onto Art School Road, heading west for 1.0-mile until the end.

130. Ventfort Hall - Lenox

Dining room-Ventfort Hall - Lenox, MA

Location: 104 Walker Street. Lenox (Berkshire County)
Parking GPS: N42° 21' 11.24" W73° 16' 48.57"
Contact: 104 Walker St, Lenox, MA 01240-2725
https://gildedage.org/ (413) 637-3206 info@gildedage.org

Information: Ventfort Hall built in 1893, created by George and Sarah Morgan as their summer home in Lenox and is an imposing mansion that typifies the "Gilded Age" when many prominent financiers and industrialists constructed their ornate summer homes in Lenox and the surrounding area. Ventfort Hall was completed in 1893 and is one of the many "Cottages" built in Lenox and Stockbridge during this period. Originally situated on 26 acres, with many landscaped gardens, it presently occupies 11.7 acres.

The house is designed with 28 rooms listing 15 bedrooms, 13 bathrooms, a total of 17 fireplaces; other rooms include an elegant paneled library, a dining room, a billiard room, bowling alley, a staircase with opulent wood paneling and a three-story great hall. Innovated for its time with all the latest modern amenities including, gas and electric light fixtures, an elevator, burglar alarms and central heating. In addition, the property contained several outbuildings, including six greenhouses, two gatehouses and a carriage house.

After the deaths of both Sarah and George Morgan, the house was rented for several years to the widow, Margaret Vanderbilt, whose husband, Alfred Gwynne Vanderbilt, who had died on the Lusitania. In 1925, W. Roscoe and Mary Minturn Bonsal purchased the house, they sold Ventfort hall in 1945. After a series of owners where it was once used as a dormitory for Tanglewood students, a summer hotel, the Fokine Ballet Summer Camp and housing for a religious community. In the mid-1980s the property was sold to a nursing home developer who wanted to demolish the building. In response to this, a local preservation group, The Ventfort Hall Association (VHA), was formed in 1994. On June 13, 1997, with the help of many private donations and loans, and with a five-year loan from the National Trust for Historic Preservation, VHA purchased the property.

Listed on the National Register of Historic Places, Ventfort Hall is now the home of *The Museum of the Gilded Age.* As one of the few surviving mansions that are open to the public, it continues as a work-in-progress with its restoration or operation costs supported through admission fees, lectures, exhibits, theatrical performances, weddings and other events. Presently, the first floor along with the grounds is completely open to the public along with many of the rooms on the second floor.

Directions: From Interstate I-90, Exit-10 in Lee, follow Route-20 north for 4.0-miles, through Lee Center, pass Laurel Lake, shortly after where Route-7 joins Route-20 and becomes a divided highway, at the next set of light, Walker Street (Route-183) crosses. Turn left heading west onto Route-183/Walker Street towards Lenox center. Ventfort Hall is located approximately 0.5-mile set-back on the left.

Ventfort Hall - Lenox, MA

131. Williams College Museum of Art

Williams College Museum of Art-Williamstown, MA

Location: 15 Lawrence Hall Dr #2 Williamstown 01267 (Berkshire County)
Destination GPS: N42° 42' 40.19" W73° 12' 9.95" (Lawrence Hall)
Contact: (413)597-2429

Information: The Williams College Museum of Art is a progressive college art museum in Williamstown, Massachusetts. Situated on the Williams College campus it is very near to the Sterling and Francine Clark Art Museum, close by is Massachusetts Museum of Contemporary Art in North Adams and really not the far to the Bennington Museum in Vermont. While the WCMA has free admission, a special ticket package deal is in place for the other museums admissions. Limited parking is available at the front of the museum on Lawrence Hall Drive. Visitors can also park on Spring Street and walk to the main entrance (no stairs) or the use the back entrance (stairs).

While the WCMA is small, it definitely has galleries that are in constant change within contemporary art collections, photography, Indian painting and student display. Should the display not in a category you fancy, soon or something new will be shown quickly.

Directions: In Williamstown, at the common/traffic circle where Route-7 turns north towards Bennington, VT and Route-2 (Mohawk Trail) continues east towards North Adams, follow Route-2 east for 0.3-mile. On the right, Lawrence Hall Drive with a 1-way traffic entry allows 2-hours free parking. The museum entry is at the back right.

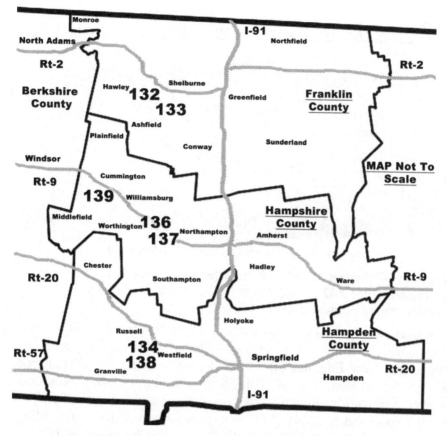

Western Massachusetts Points of Interest

132. Berkshire East Mountain Resort. (Charlemont)
133. Bridge of Flowers. (Shelburne Falls)
134. Grandmother's Garden. Chauncey Allen Park. (Westfield)
135. Mill River Historic Sites. (Plainfield)
136. Smith College Botanical Garden. (Northampton)
137. Smith College Museum of Art. (Northampton)
138. Stanley Park. (Westfield)
139. William Cullen Bryant Homestead. (Cummington)

132. Berkshire East Mountain Resort - Charlemont

Berkshire East Mountain Resort - Charlemont, MA

Location: 66 Thunder Mountain Road Charlemont (Franklin County)
Destination GPS: N42° 37' 22.71" W72° 52' 40.10" (Main Lot)
Contact: www.berkshireeast.com (413) 339-6618

Information: Berkshire East Resort is a four-season resort in Western Massachusetts; it has grown into one of the premier adventure sports scenes that New England offers. A host of activities is offered from Skiing, Snow Boarding or Tubing in the winter, to a Mountain Coaster, a downhill Mountain Bike track along with an unrivalled Tree Canopy rope and multiple Zip Lines or a superb white water rafting tour in the summer on the Deerfield River. The ski area has 45 trails and five lifts and is close to Berkshire County and the Pioneer Valley.

Mount Institute is a 1,538-feet peak with about 200-acres which is shared by Hawley and Charlemont town boundaries. Beginning as a skiing destination in the mid-1950's by Arthur Parker who installed a small ski rope-tow. Its first season was a struggle and closed quickly. In 1961, its first double-chair-lift was installed with another double-chair-lift installed in 1962. In late 1965, new ownership with long term investment, a new vision and a name change to *Berkshire East Resort* began its expansion and has not stopped since. In 2011, the ski area added a 56,900-kWh wind turbine making the ski slope 100% powered by onsite renewable energy.

Directions: Located off Route-2 (Mohawk Trail) in Charlemont, half-way between North Adams (14.5-miles from Hairpin-Turn) and Greenfield (17.5-miles from Route-91 rotary.) In Charlamont, turn onto Route-8A, over the Deerfield River Bridge; stop at railroad crossing and turn left onto West Hawley Road, down 0.2-mile onto Thunder Mountain Road.

133. Bridge of Flowers - Shelburne Falls

Bridge of Flowers (from west end) - Shelburne Falls, MA

Location: 22 Water Street. Shelburne Falls (Franklin County)
Destination GPS: N42° 36' 15.96" W72° 44' 22.27" (East end)
Destination GPS: N42° 36' 13.78" W72° 44' 28.44" (West end)
Contact: www.bridgeofflowersmass.org bridgeofflowersmass@gmail.com
The Bridge of Flowers. P.O. Box 335 Shelburne Falls, MA 01370

Information: The original 18-foot-wide, concrete trolley bridge was constructed in 1908 by the Shelburne Falls and Colrain Railway. In 1927, the trolley went bankrupt. The bridge which spans across the Deerfield River from Shelburne Falls over to Buckland and would be very costly to demolish or complicated as it also carried a water main. In 1927, The Shelburne Falls Fire District purchased the bridge for $1,250.

  Historically, Antoinette Burnham (Mrs. Walter E. Burnham) is credited as the first to have the idea of transforming the "eyesore" of the old trolley bridge into a bridge of beauty. The Bridge of Flowers Committee was initiated by the Shelburne Falls Area Women's Club in 1929 and has since transformed the 400-foot concrete bridge into a structure of flowers, shrubs, vines, trees and a variety of plants. Its gardeners, plus the many volunteer members work hard to keep this iconic bridge blooming, they are very dedicated constantly caring, up-grading or maintaining the gardens year around and have become known as the "Blossom Brigade."

"The Bridge of Flowers." An exquisite experience and destination.

In 1975, a deterioration concern of the bridge was identified. An engineering study cited the condition of the structure and repairs would cost an estimated $580,000. In 1981, The Women's Club conducted the Bridge of Flowers Preservation campaign for the purpose of raising funds, working with the Towns of Buckland, Shelburne and the Shelburne Falls Fire District. Success was achieved through grants and contributions from over 500 individual, business, or organizational efforts. The bridge's restoration began May 2, 1983. Interesting is, during the restoration time every plant, tree and shrub was removed from the Bridge and was cared for in individual's private gardens. When the bridge was completed, every shrub and flower was returned

Access to the bridge is free! Your donation will be appreciated and essential for this worthy and beautiful Bridge of Flowers to continue.

Directions: In Greenfield, from Interstate I-91 take Exit-43 and from the rotary follow Route-2 west (Mohawk Trail) for 8.5-miles. Watch for signs for Route-2A (South Maple Street to Bridge Street) into the village of Shelburne Falls. (Approximately 0.4-mile on your left, past the Massachusetts State Police Barracks which will also be on the left.)

During the summer parking can be difficult. Shelburne Falls is a popular destination for the restaurants, shopping; Salmon Falls with its colorful rock and pot-holes along with the *Shelburne Falls Trolley Museum* is another unique and interesting long-time attraction.

www.sftm.org   413-625-9443   trolley@sftm.org

134. Grandmother's Garden - Westfield

Grandmother's Garden-Westfield, MA

Location: Smith Avenue. Westfield (Hampden County)
Parking GPS: N42° 7' 27.07" W72° 45' 39.00"
Contact: www.wmmga.org (413) 562-2022 info@wmmga.org
"Friends of Grandmother's' Garden" 32 Elm St, Westfield, MA 01085

Information: In the City of Westfield Massachusetts, is the municipally owned Chauncey Allen Park. In the 1920's, Albert Steiger, a local businessman, inherited a ten-acre parcel from his father-in-law. At the time it was not much more than a sand-pit. In 1930, after filling the sandpit and seeding the property, he presented the park to the town of Westfield. The most significant feature of the park is an award-winning garden *Grand Mothers' Garden* constructed by volunteer efforts under the direction of Elizabeth Bush Fowler in 1934. The highlight of the garden was Grandmothers' Day, which continued for over 40 years , honors were given to the youngest and oldest grandmothers and one grandmother was crowned "Queen."

After her pasting in 1954, the garden's lack of maintenance for many years became over-grown, invaded by weeds and deteriorated. In 1994, the formation of the "Friends of Grandmother's' Garden" (F.O.G.G.), is a non-profit organization with many members and volunteers dedicated to the mission of the garden.

In 1995, a 75-year lease was granted by the City of Westfield to the Friends of Grandmothers' Garden who accepted responsibility for its maintenance and for the preservation of the garden and park.

Over the past 16-years, F.O.G.G., through its Board of Directors and many members and volunteers, has guided the restoration of the garden. The garden is again a place of pride for the city and serves not only as a link to the past, but as an educational center for school and youth groups. FOGG schedules several events during the year, such as garden tours, artist days and a restored Grandmothers' Day.

Directions: East or west, on Interstate I-90, get off at Exit-41 Westfield. Turn right on to Routes-10 and Route-202 south. Continue on Routes-10 and Route-202, heading south (*Elm Street)* for 2 miles, reaching the center of Westfield's town common and traffic circle. Note: Route-10, Route-202 & Route-20, all interchange here; going the Grandmother's Garden, from off the traffic-circle, turn west onto Court Street, head west 0.5-mile, turn right onto High Street, down to the end, turn left onto King Street. Heading west on King Street, ~ 0.1-mile, turn right onto Smith Avenue, drive 0.1-mile, on the right is Grandmother's Garden parking lot (Across the street from the Westfield Vocational High School.)

135. Mill River Historic Sites – Plainfield

Incredible craftsmanship went into the selecting, shaping and laying the stone.

Location: River Road. Plainfield (Hampden County)
Parking GPS: N42° 29' 51.30" W72° 54' 57.62" (River Road Sites)
Saw-Grist Mills GPS: N42° 29' 50.12" W72° 54' 56.00" (River Road Sites)
Wilcott Mill GPS: N42° 30' 7.26" W72° 54' 56.79" (South Union St.)
Contact: Plainfield Historical Society 525 W Main Street Plainfield, MA www.plainfieldmahistory.org (413) 562-2022 info@plainfieldmahistory.org

Information: After the America Revolution, the post-war culture created many new industries for economic growth and sustainability. Industrialization of grist mills, saw mills or for that matter almost any type of mill were clustered along New England's rivers and streams which provided the water power needed to process, manufacture and to increase production.

Amazingly, almost like ghosts, historic foundations are clustered along and on the Mill River in Plainfield, MA. These sites provide insight into the 1800's and the reliance in flowing water. Water pouring over or under a water-wheel or channeled through turbines allowed the transformation of circular motion via drive shafts, rudimentary wooden gears, cogs or belts, and other designs that could grin corn into flour, sawmills for lumber, tanning hides etc. Ponder the increased reliance on water, streams were diverted or channeled to direct or control the amount and water flow or its direction. Dams were built to help maintain an uninterrupted water supply during low or seasonal droughts.

Mills clustered directly on New England Rivers indicate their usage for power.

These industrial ruins are not a playground and literally provide the only insight of what and how our earlier forefather's persevered by innovating or designing machinery and components from the materials they had on hand. These foundations and earthen embankments have stood for many years, walking a top, removing or disrupting anything could cause irreparable damage or collapse.

The Wilcutt mill was operational before ceasing operations in 1927. It is located upon private property, while viewing is acceptable, do not enter the building.

The Plainfield Historical Society has over-seen the property discussed here. They have created a self-guided tour and provided informational kiosks on site. Visit: **https://plainfieldmahistory.org/mills-on-mill-river/** to download a PDF tour and map of the area. Access by appointment to these sites and locations along with additional information may be obtained by calling, e-mailing to or visiting their web site.

The Plainfield Historical Society.

(413) 634-8099   (413) 634-2128

www.plainfieldmahistory.org   info@plainfieldmahistory.org

Take note that while Plainfield was a major industrial center, it took place over 100 years ago. Plainfield populace slowly dwindled with many residents heading west or towards larger cities seeking new opportunities.

Directions: From the Plainfield Town Hall cross Route-116 and take South Union Street for 1.0-mile, merge left onto River Road and park at the intersection of River Road and Lincoln St. There is room for 2 cars if you squeeze them in. There is also room for 2 cars at the intersection of West Hill and River Roads.

River Road is a seasonal road only and not well maintained. South Union Street as with many back roads are dirt and gravel, blocked by snow in the winter and mud in the spring or fall.

136. Smith College Botanical Garden

Lyman Conservatory-Smith College Botanical Garden-Northampton, MA

Location: 18 College Lane. Northampton 01063 (Hampshire County)
Destination GPS: N42° 19' 7.66" W72° 38' 25.28"
Contact: www.smith.edu (413) 585-2740 garden@smith.edu

Information: The public is invited to explore the campus arboretum and specialty gardens. Open daily year-round, except Thanksgiving Day and winter class Break: (December 22, through January 1.) Regular hours are 8:30 AM to 4:00 PM daily. Admission: Donation $2.00 suggested. Personal photography only, no tripods, other rules at front desk, read them.

There are two visitor parking spaces and one handicapped space in front of the Lyman Plant House. There is no parking on College Lane. On-street parking is allowed on Elm Street (Route-9). The Smith College parking garage on West St. has visitor spots and there is metered parking on Green Street and a long-term lot behind the Forbes Library on West St. Campus lots are permit only except on weekends and after 5 pm weekdays

Directions: In western downtown Northampton, at the intersection of Route-66, Route-10 and Route-9 (Main Street), take Route-9 west. Bear right to stay with Route-9 (Elm Street) towards Pittsfield. Travel west, 0.3 mile turning left onto College Lane, The Lyman Conservatory and garden are 0.1-on the left. Parking is an issue, read above for guidance.

137. Smith College Museum of Art

Smith College Museum of Art. (Route-9) Northampton, MA

Location: 20 Elm Street Ave. Northampton, MA 01063 (Hampshire County)
Destination GPS: N42° 19' 7.55" W72° 38' 10.18" (Museum entry)
Contact: (413)585.2760   artmuseum@smith.edu
Admission is free: to all Five College employees and family, Youth (18 and under), College Students, Free passes may be obtained from Forbes Library (20 West Street) and Lilly Library (19 Meadow Street) Every 2nd Friday the museum open and free to all from 4 p.m. to 8 p.m. All others are required to pay a small fee for entry. Tuesday through Saturday 10–4, Thursday 10–8, Sunday 12–4 Closed Mondays and major holidays.

Information: The Smith College Museum of Art has embraced that educational experiences through works of art are powerful elements of a liberal arts education by consolidating aesthetic judgment, human history and social culture all contributing to an education with expanded purpose and prominence. This commitment allows growth in all aspects; classic painting, contemporary media, and examination of sculpture in traditional or ground breaking materials.

A visit will be impressive and certainly stimulating with surprises on every floor, including the restrooms which are embellished by artist-inspired interiors. The museum has no direct parking, street parking is regulated with stipulation of times and locations, metered parking enforced 8am to 6 pm, Monday through Saturday.

Experience classic or contemporary Art. A to Z Interactive thought board.-

Directions: <u>From above Northampton</u>, follow Interstate I-91 south and take Exit-26. From the bottom of the off-ramp, proceed straight south on Route-5 (King Street). Continue on King Street for 1.4-miles, at the junction of Route-9 (Main Street), turn right onto Route-9 and continue west. Travel through downtown Northampton for 0.4-mile, Main Street becomes Massachusetts Avenue, bearing right staying on Route-9 which becomes Elm Street. The museum is on the left across from Bedford Terrace as you leave the downtown area.

<u>From below Northampton</u>, follow Interstate I-91 north and take Exit-25. From bottom of the off-ramp, continue around the traffic circle, taking the 3rd right, heading west into Northampton. Continue 1.1-miles, as you pass under the train bridge and enter downtown Northampton the road becomes Main Street. Travel 0.4-miles west; continue west and bearing right, stay on Route-9 which becomes Elm Street. The museum is on the left across from Bedford Terrace as you leave the downtown area.

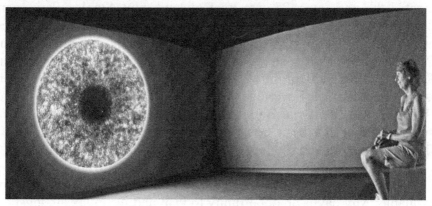

138. Stanley Park - Westfield

Carillon Bell Tower-Rose & Flower Garden-Stanley Park. Westfield, MA

Location: 400 Western Avenue. Westfield (Hampden County)
Destination GPS: N42° 7' 31.67" W72° 46' 59.77" (Western Ave Entry)
Destination GPS: N42° 7' 14.28" W72° 46' 57.91" (Kensington Ave Entry)
Contact: www.stanleypark.org   (413)568-9312   No entry or parking fees.
Pavilions rentals or events require reservations and permits. (413) 568-9312
x100

Information: Stanley Park located in Westfield, is a non-profit privately owned park including an arboretum and botanical garden. It is open to the public daily without charge from May to November and although the park is closed to vehicles during the winter, people can still enter the park for x-country skiing or snowshoeing.

Named for its benefactor Frank Stanley Beveridge, who in 1949 created the park on a 25-acre tract of land, now Stanley Park spans nearly 300-acres of trails, woods, picnic areas, recreational facilities, and gardens. These include hundreds of Rose bushes, Annual and Perennial Flower beds, an Asian Garden, an Arboretum, Herb Garden, Rhododendron Garden, the Wildflower and Woodland Garden. There is the Frank Stanley Beveridge Wildlife Sanctuary, the Carillon Tower (World Peace Memorial Bell Tower), a Duck Pond filled with geese, swan, duck or maybe a Great Blue Heron, all with a backdrop of flowering azaleas and rhododendron.

Sunny days and summer nights will provide many enjoyable times visiting Stanley Park. Often special events such as concerts may be available. Any day is an opportunity to visit and just relax amongst the flowers, fountains with family or oneself.

In 1948, Black Squirrels from Michigan were given to Frank Stanley, the squirrels found their new environment suitable becoming permanent residents of Westfield. Black squirrels are numerous in the park and are to be found adapting elsewhere in Hampden, Berkshire County and the Pioneer Valley.

Donations are always accepted, it just depends what they ask for.

Directions: East or west, on Interstate I-90, get off at Exit-41 Westfield. Turn right on to Routes-10 and Route-202 south. Continue on Routes-10 and Route-202, heading south (*Elm Street)* for 2-miles, reaching the center of Westfield's town common and traffic circle. Note, that Route-10, Route-202 & Route-20, all interchange here; to go to Stanley Park, turn west onto Court Street, head west 0.8-mile and merge onto Western Avenue. Head west on Western Avenue for 0.2-mile, off on the left, down *Granville Road* 0.75-mile to on your right to Kensington Avenue for the rear-entry to Stanley Park or continue straight on Western Avenue for an additional 0.8-mile, to the main entry (Gillett Road) will be on the left for Stanley Park.

139. William Cullen Bryant Homestead

William Cullen Bryant Home - Cummington, MA

Location: 207 Bryant Road Cummington 01026 (Hampshire County)
Parking GPS: N42° 28' 13.71" W72° 56' 6.45" (Homestead)
Parking GPS: N42° 28' 11.79" W72° 55' 54.21" (Rivulet Trailhead)
Contact: www.thetrustees.org (413) 532-1631 bryanthomestead@thetrustees.org

Information: The William Cullen Bryant Homestead a National Historic Landmark is the boyhood home of one of America's foremost 19th-century poets, editor and publisher of the New York Evening Post for 50 years and a conservationist that inspired Frederic Law Olmsted and Charles Eliot, founders of the Trustees of Reservations.

Born November 3, 1794, William Cullen Bryant astonished the literary world with the publication of his first major poem at age 13. Later in 1817, his most famous poem "Thanatopsis," was published while he practiced law in Great Barrington MA.

The *Rivulet*, is a small stream which inspired and is immortalized by Bryant's 1823 poem of the same name is located on the property, is largely unchanged for more than 150-years with enormous specimens of Hemlock, Pine, Cherry and Maple Sugar trees. The *Rivulet Trail* is a 1.0-mile loop though old growth forest, the trailhead is on the right off the West Cummington Road 0.1-mile from the 5-corner junction on Route-112. The trailhead kiosk has the poem and a map of the trail.

In 1834 Bryant embarked on the first of many lengthy trips, traveling widely in the U.S. and taking seven trips abroad. Many of his exotic travel mementos are now at the Homestead.

Famous as a publisher and editor, Bryant's public life involved him on many fronts as a politician and conservationist, leading to the creation of New York City's Central Park. Artists of the Hudson River School considered Bryant their muse. At his death in 1878, Bryant was an iconic figure. His fame was so widespread that the centennial of his birth in 1894 drew thousands of people to the Homestead to celebrate his life and accomplishments.

Enormous old growth 300-year-old Hemlocks are on the *Rivulet Trail*. Very few old-growth forests exist in New England. This small area contains trees greater than 200-years of age, and provides a wonderful sample of undisturbed forests.

Today, the house is restored to its original appearance as seen in 1870. Of the 478-acres originally associated with the homestead, 195-acres are preserved. The property is a National Historic Landmark been owned by The Trustees of Reservations since 1927 when Minna Godwin Goddard bequeathed original acreage along with an endowment. Additional land was purchased in 1981 with funds given by Mrs. Winthrop M. Crane III.

The grounds are open daily year-around, 2.5-miles of footpaths and carriage roads allow easy to moderate hiking. Dogs are allowed and must be always kept on a leash. Mountain biking is not allowed, all motorized vehicles are prohibited. Photography is not permitted inside the house. The house and all facilities are seasonal with house tours being open weekends or during special programs only.

Directions: At the junction of Route-8 and Route-9 in Dalton, follow Route-9 east for 15.75-miles until in Cummington, at the intersection where Route-112 junctions with Route-9, turn right and follow uphill, Route-112 south for 1.5-miles, reaching the five-corner intersection, the Homestead is straight ahead on Upper Bryant Road in 0.2-mile.

From the traffic circle at the intersection of Route-9, Bridge Street, North Main Street and entry to Look Park, head west on Route-9 towards Cummington for 17-miles. Where Route-112 junctions with Route-9, turn left and follow uphill, Route-112 south for 1.5 mile, reaching the five-corner intersection, the Homestead is straight ahead on Upper Bryant Road in 0.2 mile.

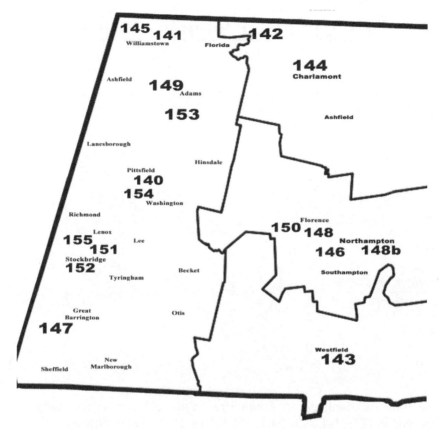

Western Massachusetts Statues & Memorials

140. Civil War Soldier Park Square. (Pittsfield)
141. Civil War Soldier Williams College. Williamstown
142. Elk Whitcomb Summit. (Florida)
143. General William Shepard. Augustus Lukeman: (Westfield)
144. Hail to the Sunrise. (Charlemont)
145. Haystack Prayer Monument. Williamstown
146. Lanning Fountain - Smith College. (Northampton)
147. Newsboy. (Great Barrington)
148. Pregnant Women II. Lou Stubs: (Florence)
149. President McKinley. Augustus Lukeman: (Adams)
150. Sojourner Truth. (Florence)
151. Spirit of Life-Daniel Chester French. (Stockbridge)
152. Spitting Cat Dog Fight. (Stockbridge)
153. Strafford Hill Memorial 1927. (Cheshire)
154. WWI Memorial Veterans Park. Augustus Lukeman: (Pittsfield)
155. Young Faun with Heron. Nuamkeag: (Stockbridge)

140. Civil War Soldier - Pittsfield

Civil War Memorial- Pittsfield, MA

Location: Park Square-East, South Street, Pittsfield (Berkshire County)
Destination GPS: N42° 26' 54.15" W73° 15' 13.29" (Park Square)

Information: The statue was erected in 1872 in Park Square, the six-foot tall Sergeant Color Bearer, stands atop a 15-foot granite pillar is not any particular soldier as it honors the 108 men from Pittsfield who died during the Civil War. The statue was created by Launt Thompson a sculptor from New York on September 24, 1872. It is reported to be casted in bronze from Civil War cannon barrels. Two bronze plaques on the pillar's base lists the 108 Pittsfield men who died in the Civil War from 1861-1865, including four from the all African-American 54th Massachusetts Regiment. "For the dead a tribute, for the living a memory, for posterity an emblem of loyalty to the flag of their country." In addition, the Massachusetts coat-of-arms is also cast in bronze on its base.

There had been little if any maintenance on this monument for the last 141 years and the elements had taken their toll. On September 21, 2013 after completion of major restoration work, the Memorial was rededicated in honor of Pittsfield's Veteran's.

<u>141.</u> Civil War Soldier - Williamstown

Civil War Memorial (In front of Griffin Hall) Williams College, MA

Location: 820 Main Street/Route-2   Williamstown (Berkshire County)
Destination GPS: N42° 42' 43.34" W73° 12' 6.38" (Civil War Statue)

Information: Commissioned by the Society of Alumni of Williams College in 1863 to commemorate Williams College students who died in the Civil War and is reportedly among the first Monuments to commemorate the Civil War dead. Dedicated on July 28, 1868

The cloaked, mustached, Union Army soldier is at rest with what appears to be an 1861 Springfield Musket grasped at the muzzle by his hands. The figure was sculpted by James Goodwin Batterson, designed by Joseph R. Richards and was cast at the Ames Mfg. Co. Foundry of Chicopee, MA. In 1926, lighting struck the monument destroying its original base. A new octagonal granite base was designed by Cram and Ferguson, and the Civil War Soldier was reinstalled by the Sawyer Construction Co.

The statue stands on a small grassy knoll in front of Griffin Hall and is set back 75-feet from Route-2, facing south across from the Hopkins Observatory on the Williams College Campus.

142. Elk Whitcomb Summit - Florida

Elk Statue- Whitcomb Summit-Florida, MA

Location: Mohawk Trail/Route-2 Florida (Berkshire County)
Destination GPS: N42° 41' 16.02" W73° 1' 13.50" (Elk Statue-Roadside)

Information: The Elk on the Trail Monument was erected on Whitcomb Summit by the Benevolent and Protective Order of Elks in 1923 by the Greenfield Elk's Club. The statue stands in memory of those members who lost their lives in World War I. The memorial was dedicated on June 17, 1923, it was estimated that 10,000 people, in some 3,000-vehicles, attended the dedication at the top of Whitcomb summit which is the highest elevation on the Mohawk Trail-Route-2

Having a full rack of antlers, the posture of the Elk majestically holds his head high as if a true monarch of the mountains. This iconic 8-foot-high bronze statue of an Elk stands on a 3-foot-high rough cut granite base and presently behind a 4-foot-high fenced in area. Designed by Eli Harvey, the Elk was cast at the Gorham Mfg. Company of Providence, RI. A bronze plaque which is inscribed:

THE ELK ON THE TRAIL
IN MEMORY OF THE BROTHERS OF THE
MASSACHUSETTS ELKS ASSOCIATION
WHO DIED IN THE WORLD WAR
ERECTED BY THE ASSOCIATION
17TH JUNE 1923.

Of note is a vault nearby with the label; Mass Elks Association – William J Hopkins III – President - Time Capsule – Open June 2023

143. General William Shepard-Westfield

General William Shepard-Westfield, MA

Location: Broad Street (Route-10/202) Westfield (Hampden County)
Destination GPS: N42° 7' 11.07" W72° 44' 55.72" (South of Center)

Information: The bronze statue of Major General William Shepard was created by sculptor Augustus Lukeman in 1918 and dedicated on September 3, 1919 it stands at the intersection of Elm, Court, and Broad Streets in the center of Westfield. The statue stands 8-feet-high and is placed upon a 7-foot granite pedestal. The statue stands with his back to the city green because it was thought that Westfield would expand in the other direction, it didn't. During the Revolutionary War, he became the highest-ranking member of the Continental Army from western Massachusetts. He was wounded while protecting General George Washington's retreat from Long Island from which he recovered and ultimately participated in twenty-two battles. In 1787, he led the Federal forces protecting the Springfield Armory from attack during Shay's Rebellion.

In the 1940's it was noted the statue had not oxidized; it was learned that the copper was very low because it was made during War World I when copper was extremely scarce. In 1951, an acid wash was applied to the bronze becoming the green patina seen today.

144. Hail to the Sunrise - Charlemont

"Hail to the Sunrise" Mohawk Park - Route-2. Charlemont, MA

Location: Mohawk Trail/Route-2 Charlemont (Franklin County)
Destination GPS: N42° 38' 23.03" W72° 54' 47.89" (Statue)

Information: Located on the famous Mohawk Trail, facing east overlooking the Deerfield River. The addition of the "Mohawk Indian" was sponsored by the Improved Order of the Red Men and their women's auxiliary, the Allied Councils of Pocahontas of the Old Deerfield conference. Unveiling ceremonies were held on October 1, 1932 it is a monument to the Five Indian Nations of the Mohawk Trail. *Hail to the Sunrise* depicts a Mohawk Indian beckoning with uplifted arms in supplication to the Great Spirit the new-born day of hope and peace for America.

Sculpture is by Joseph P. Polia, 1932, the eight-foot statue is a 900-pound bronze casting and stands up on a nine-ton boulder that overlooks a wishing well fountain which is adorned with many inscribed stones from various tribes and councils from across the United States. **"Hail to the Sunrise—In Memory of the Mohawk Indian. The Mohawks of the Five Nations began to settle in New York State in 1590 and for 90 great suns they fought the New England tribes. The New York Mohawks that traveled this trail were friendly to the white settlers."**

145. Haystack Prayer Monument-Williamstown

Haystack Prayer Monument - Williamstown, MA

Location: Mission Park Drive Williams College, (Berkshire County)
Parking GPS: N42° 42' 53.59" W73° 12' 9.67" (Limited Parking)
Destination GPS: N42° 42' 55.76" W73° 12' 11.75" (Haystack Memorial)

Information: In a grove of trees near the Hoosic River, in what was then known as Sloan's Meadow, five Williams College students Samuel Mills, James Richards, Francis LeBaron Robbins, Harvey Loomis, and Byram Green, met in the summer of 1806. Their prayer meeting was interrupted by a thunderstorm, the students took shelter under a haystack until the sky cleared and continued to debate the theology of missionary service. The Haystack Prayer Meeting is viewed by many scholars as a fateful event for the development of American Protestant missions in the subsequent decades and century. Within four years of that gathering, some of its members established the American Board of Commissioners for Foreign Missions. In 1867, to honor the men involved in the Haystack prayer meeting, a marble monument topped with a sphere representing the world, was erected in Mission Park in Williamstown. In 1906, a centennial gathering took place in Mission Park at Williams College in celebration of the earlier prayer meeting. In the summer of 2006, it celebrated its 200th anniversary since the Haystack meeting. At that time, over 5,000 missionaries have served to establish ministries, hospitals and schools in many countries.

146. Lanning Fountain – Smith College

Mary Manning-Smith College Botanical Garden. Northampton, MA

Location: 18 College Lane. Northampton (Hampshire County)
Destination GPS: N42° 19' 5.34" W72° 38' 21.93" (Statue)

Information: Mary Tomlinson Lanning was in her second year at Smith College in 1910 when she became ill and died. A member of the Smith class of 1912, she went home to Hastings, Nebraska, for her sophomore-year Christmas break, took ill on New Year's Day and died 15 days later of complications from typhoid fever. The fountain, a gift from the Lanning family, was erected at Smith College in 1911. The fountain is inscribed: "In Memory of a Beautiful Life" and lists Mary Lanning's name, birth and death dates, along with school and class affiliations

The inscription on the fountain's base has made it easy to error that she is portrayed in the bronze sculpture. The American Art Bronze Foundry of Chicago cast the figure of the girl after a model by American sculptor Nellie Verne Walker (1874–1973) who modeled this life-sized statue after *Marguerite*, an 1886 statuette by French sculptor Jean Gautherin.

<u>147.</u> Newsboy Fountain - Great Barrington

Newsboy Fountain - Great Barrington, MA

Location: Maple Avenue/Route-23 Great Barrington (Berkshire County)
Destination GPS: N42° 11' 2.25" W73° 22' 12.57" (Statue-Fountain)

Information: In October 10, 1895, Col. William L. Brown the part-owner of the original New York Daily News newspaper funded this monument to what he considered to be the unsung heroes of the newspaper industry, the anonymous newsboy. The monument was sculpted by David Richards (1829-1897) and cast by Maurice J. Power, founder. A 5-foot-high bronze figure of a newsboy stands on top of a 10-foot-high polished granite base. The main shaft is of polished Quincy granite, and the remainder of Dolomite granite. Having once served as a watering trough for horses, dogs and cats from its various fountain heads that are embedded in the base. Drinking water once poured out of the heads of a lion (for horses), a dog, a cat and a devil's head (for people) into individual basins.

   The statue located within a small triangular park at the intersection of Newsboy Lane/Silver Street/Maple Ave (Route-23) is well over 100-years old, road salt, acid rain and nature's elements have taken their toll. The statue was evaluated and repaired in 1995, corrosion control and repairs to make the fountain operational resumed in 2003. At that time the fountain's pump was restored with an automatic shut-off.

148. Pregnant Women II - Northampton

"Pregnant Woman II" Sculptor Lu Stubbs - Florence, MA

Location: 30 Locust Street (Route-9) Northampton (Hampshire County)
Parking GPS: N42° 19' 49.33" W72° 39' 8.59" (Cooley-Dickinson Hospital)
Destination GPS: N42° 19' 47.71" W72° 39' 10.13" (Pregnant Women II)
Destination GPS: N42° 19' 8.31" W72° 37' 51.46" (Happy Frog)

Information: A noteworthy contemporary sculptor and educator is Northampton's local artist Lu Stubbs. Her exceptional sculptures have a very graceful and have pleasing form. Two of her sculptures are within Northampton, a larger-than-life bronze statue *Pregnant Woman II* she donated to the Cooley-Dickinson Hospital and the *Happy Frog* on the corner of Main Street and Center Street in downtown Northampton was designed to help feed the hungry.

Information: Born in New York City in 1925, Lu made good of her growth years by establishing a family, developing her natural talent of painting and sculpture. Graduating from the School of the Boston Museum of Fine Art, her hands-on-approach in the foundry process along with casting provided her skills and a mastery of materials, specifically in bronze.

In 1978, her daughter Sue was expecting her first child and Lu made an exceptional larger-than-life, 8-foot sculpture of her in the last stages of her pregnancy. The stance, posture and its inner dimension becomes most intriguing as if draped externally in a veil of material clinging and shaped by her tale-tale stage of pregnancy. Donated to the hospital in 2001, it is located on a small cement patio just south of the Main Entry of the hospital. In addition, what pleases Lu especially is that the mother-to-be looks up at the Childbirth Center of the hospital, where her other daughter, Mahi, was a nurse. This is a wonderful statue to see.

"The Happy Frog"   Sculpture by Lu Stubbs 2008. Northampton, MA

Location: Center Street/Main Street Northampton (Hampshire County)
Destination GPS: N42° 19' 8.31" W72° 37' 51.46" (*The Happy Frog*)

Information: In downtown Northampton, a whimsical or fun-loving figure of a frog lays sprawled a top a concrete base in front of the First Churches of Northampton. Installed since 2008, this is *The Happy Frog* and invites pedestrians to feed him with donations to help feed the hungry, a plaque reads; *Feed the Frog – Feed the Hungry* where all donations are received by Friends of Hampshire Homeless who sponsor free meals for the hungry each week.

Another prominent statue by Lu Stubbs is a bronze life-size statue of a Revolutionary War heroine, who dressed as a man in order to fight against the British. This captivating statue is situated in front of the Sharon Public Library (11 North Main Street) and was dedicated on Nov 11, 1989. The statue seems to possess a greater amount of detail, with the powder horn, musket, a soldier's coat along with a bag.

Deborah Sampson by Sculptor Lu Stubbs,
N42° 7' 27.13" W71° 10' 42.12"
Sharon Public Library

149. President McKinley - Adams

President McKinley-Adams, MA

Location: Maple Street/Park Street Adams (Berkshire County)
Destination GPS: N42° 37' 26.94" W73° 7' 11.86" (McKinley Square)

Information: In front of the Adams Public Library on Park Street and Maple Street, is a larger-than-life statue of President William McKinley created in 1903 by Augustus Lukeman. During his presidency from 1897 to 1901, the 25th President of the United States visited Adams on three occasions amidst much fanfare and celebration. His policies supported tariffs which were favorable to the cotton industry in the U.S. and which helped make the Berkshire Cotton Mfg. Co. mill complex in Adams one of the largest in the country, hence his popularity in Adams. During his second visit in 1897, McKinley laid the cornerstone for the library that he stands in front of now.

In Buffalo, New York, on September 6, 1901, the President while at the Pan American Exposition was shot; he succumbed to his wounds on September 14, 1901. In tribute to President McKinley's kinship to Adams, on October 10, 1903 there was an unveiling ceremony of the McKinley statue at McKinley Square. It is almost impossible not to see him while passing through Adams on Route-8.

150. Sojourner Truth - Florence

Sojourner Truth Memorial Park - Florence, MA

Location: 121 Pine Street. Florence (Hampshire County)
Destination GPS: N42° 19' 55.37" W72° 40' 29.02" (Statue)
Contact: sojournertruthmemorial.org   sojournertruthmemorial@gmail.com

Information: Sojourner Truth was born an enslaved person in 1797 near Kingston, New York. Her given name was Isabella Baumfree. She labored for four masters and beginning in 1815 had five children. In 1827, she ran away with her youngest infant Sophia. Seeking refuge with an abolitionist family, the Van Wageners, who bought her freedom for twenty dollars and helped Truth successfully sued for the return of her five-year-old-son Peter, who was illegally sold into slavery in Alabama.

Moving to New York City in 1828, she worked for a minister and by the early 1830's participated in many religious revivals becoming a charismatic speaker. She declared that the Spirit called upon her to preach the truth and renamed herself Sojourner Truth.

Sojourner Truth became a nationally known advocate for justice and equality making innumerable speeches against slavery or for women's rights.   By 1843, eventually she made her way to Florence, Massachusetts.   In time, Truth met many of the country's important abolitionists: William Lloyd Garrison, Wendell Phillips, Frederick

Douglass, and David Ruggles. These leaders, along with Samuel L. Hill, Elisha Hammond, George W. Benson, Austin Ross, and J.P. Williston, helped establish Florence as a center of anti-slavery. She met women's rights activists, Elizabeth Cady Stanton and Susan B. Anthony

During the time she lived in Florence and afterward, Truth made a living as a public speaker, successfully brought cases to court, marched and performed sit-ins for reform causes, petitioned Congress, met with presidents, and tried to vote in the 1872 election. She also broadened the definition of "reformer" beyond the white, educated, middle-class women who primarily made up the women's movement.

Truth left Florence in 1857 and eventually moved to Harmonia Community, Michigan, and then to Battle Creek, Michigan, where she died in 1883.

The idea for a memorial statue that would honor Sojourner Truth began 1993. On April 1, 2001, sculptor Thomas Jay Warren was selected to create the statue. The life-size statue stands upon a low granite pedestal, set in a central terrace surrounded by a lush garden. The statue was unveiled on Sunday, October 6, 2002; informational plaques about Sojourner Truth can be found within the park.

Directions: From the traffic circle at the intersection of Route-9, Bridge Street, North Main Street and entry to Look Park, head toward Florence on Route-9/ North Main Street. Head southeasterly for 0.6-miles turning right onto Park Street. Head south for 0.3-mile, on your left, the site for the Sojourner Truth statue is a small park at the corner of Pine and Park Streets in Florence.

151. Spirit of Life - Stockbridge

"Spirit of Life" Daniel Chester French – Stockbridge, MA

Location: St Paul's Episcopal Church 29 Main Street Stockbridge, MA 01262 (Berkshire County) (413) 298-4913 stpaulsstockbridge@gmail.com
Destination GPS: N42° 16' 57.04" W73° 18' 42.92" (Statue)

Information: Daniel Chester French (1850 –1931) one of the most prolific and acclaimed American sculptors is well known for the *Minute Man* statue in Concord, Massachusetts which was unveiled April 19, 1875, on the centennial of the Battle of Lexington and Concord. He is best known for the statue of Abraham Lincoln (1920) in the iconic Lincoln Memorial in Washington, D.C. With a career spanning six decades of public monuments and statues, finding a local statue is precious "The Spirit of Life" gifted by Daniel Chester French, resides at St. Paul's Episcopal Church located on Main Street (Route-7) and Pine Street (Route-102), is located across the street from the Red Lion Inn in Stockbridge, MA. Daniel Chester French was at the time considered America's foremost sculptor of public monuments including: A larger-than-life *The Spirit of Life* dedicated in 1915 resides in Congress Park, Saratoga Springs, N.Y. Reportedly six smaller casts were made between 1923 to 1931. However, here at St. Paul's Episcopal Church, in its foyer upon a pedestal, is one signed and dated "D.C. French 1919" and inscribed "In Sweet Remembrance of Daniel Chester French and Mary His Wife. 1949"

The Konkapot Watering Fountain 1899, Town Common. Lee, MA

Konkapot Indian Chief Watering Fountain is another monument recently restored and brought back into operation in July 2019. While it may not be as intensely exquisite as other memorials and statues, it indicates French's willingness to assist in the development of small-town memorials. Heading east on Route-102 for 4.6 mile into Lee, MA; where it junctions with Route-20 and Exit-10 of Interstate I-90. Travel north of Route-20 for 0.7-mile into the center of town. Located in a small park on the South end of Main Street.

Daniel Chester French
125 West Eleventh Street
New York

March 7, 1898

My dear Mr. Rogers:

I send you today by express a roll of drawings, as suggestions for your fountain made by Mr. *Mackintosh* , and a box containing a little model in *PlASTER* .

It is a great advantage in a drinking trough for horses that it should be high enough to avoid the *neceesity* of *Unchecking(?)* *them* and we have therefore made the model with the trough four feet high or more. according as you call the the scale of the model 1½" or 1" to the foot, it is barely worth while to put much ornament on the trough as it is likely to get defaced by the poles and shaft of *vehicles* (hitches?) It is *intended* that the spouts on front or back should be of bronze I think I remembering your objecting to a head spitting water, and it is not a very agreeable idea if one stopes to think about it, but it has been done *since* (and before) this year out(?) and one gets *substituted.* *hardened* to anything!! If you don't approve something else can be *_____)*

I do not know whether either of the designs is at all what you want. If not, do not hesitate to say so and to discard them. I am anxious to know how much the one *represented* by the *model* would cost cut in Lee marble.

Yours very truly,

Daniel C. French

152. Spitting Cat & Dog Fight Fountain

Dog and Cat Fighting Fountain - Stockbridge, MA

Location: Main Street/South Street. Stockbridge (Berkshire County)
Destination GPS: N42° 16' 55.47" W73° 18' 44.49" (Dog & Cat Fountain)

Information: The cat and dog fountain is a Stockbridge landmark, located at the intersection of Route-7 and Route-102 and adjacent to the Red Lion Inn. The original marble fountain that was installed in 1862, but due to wear and erosion the statue was replaced with a cast stone copy created by Otello Guarducci in 1976.

The life size sculpture of a cat and a dog sits on a 5-foot-high ornate base in the center of a 12-foot diameter basin. Facing each other, the cat is arching its back as it hisses, spraying water into the face of the dog. The startled dog reacts by leaning back in astonishment on its hind legs with its tail curved forward onto its back.

The Laurel Hill Association tends to the fountain which is situated on a small traffic island surrounded with hedges and planted flowers in front of a large spruce tree. The fountain is open to view and operational only during the summer months, being crated up within a protective wooden enclosure during the fall or winter months. It is whimsical and a delight to see this unusual fountain in operation.

153. Strafford Hill Monument - Cheshire

Stafford Hill Memorial Tower-Cheshire, MA

Location: Strafford Hill Road. Cheshire (Berkshire County)
Parking GPS: N42° 34' 26.16" W73° 6' 47.94" (Stafford Hill Road-Turn)
Destination GPS: N42° 34' 28.21" W73° 6' 55.60" (Monument)

Information: Built in 1927, The Sons of the American Revolution erected the Stafford Hill Memorial to honor Colonel Joab Stafford who formed the "Silver Greys" a Cheshire militia company that fought in the Battle of Bennington in August 1777 during the Revolutionary War. Colonel Stafford and Captain Samuel Low trained their companies comprised of Berkshire County volunteers on the level fields atop Stafford Hill. The field stone tower is a replica of the Newport Tower in Newport Rhode Island. Joab Stafford was a native of Newport, Rhode Island, who was sent to the area to survey the land that was then known as New Providence and later incorporated as Cheshire. The structure, 25-feet (7.6 m) in diameter and in height, the lower level of the memorial consists of eight arches, with the interior being finished in concrete. Above the south arch a marble plaque is set in the stone; it bears the legend "1777, Erected in Memory of the Pioneers and Patriots of New Providence, 1927." The memorial and its surrounding land are owned and maintained by the town of Cheshire.

154. WWI Veterans Memorial - Pittsfield

Previous patina (L) Restored -2010 (R) Veterans Park. Pittsfield, MA

Location: Veterans Way/South Street (Rt-7.) Pittsfield (Berkshire County)
Parking GPS: N42° 26' 29.81" W73°15' 20.78" (Veterans Way-Turn)
Destination GPS: N42° 26' 26.16" W73° 15' 21.74" (Statue)

Information: In 1923, the City of Pittsfield established a memorial in tribute to all the Veterans who fought in WWI. Henry Augustus Lukeman (1871-1935) an American sculptor was commissioned to create this historical monument which was casted in 1925 at the Roman Bronze Works, New York. On July 8, 1926, this memorial was dedicated in tribute to Pittsfield's sons and daughters who served in WWI. The memorial continues to stand as a symbolic shine for all Veterans who serve in the past, present and future.

The large intricate bronze sculpture contains four uniformed figures standing in front of a granite wall and standing atop a granite base. Each figure represents members of the United States Marines, Army, Air Corps, Navy and Athena the Goddess of War is centered above them is holding a laurel branch symbolizing their victory. The rectangular base is flanked on each side with low rectangular wall extension and bearing bronze plaques that commemorate the wars following World War I.

Veterans & Family's gather at Veteran's Park. November 11, 2016

<u>An inscription at the base of the memorial reads</u>

1917-1918
A TRIBUTE TO THE LOYALTY
AND SACRIFICE OF HER SONS
AND DAUGHTERS WHO GLORIOUSLY
DEFENDED THE LIBERTIES WON
BY THEIR FATHERS
ERECTED BY THE CITY OF PITTSFIELD 1926

The memorial statue was dedicated 84 years ago on July 8, 1923, It had suffered over time from corrosion and exposure to the various harsh elements of New England weather. By 2009, the external statue's bronze surface was rusty or tarnished, scratched with graffiti and parts of the statue itself were broken or missing. Needed repairs also included stabilizing and repairing the internal iron framework of the statue. The task was determined that the cost for the all-inclusive restoration would be $80,000. The funds were raised, the statue's surface was cleaned, treated, polished, the graffiti removed and its many cracked or seams repaired. In addition, repairs were needed to the base structure stonework; the pedestal would require cleaning, pointing and caulking.

The broken or missing pieces, the laurel leafs, a bayonet and a rifle strap were re-created by sculptor David LaRocca, who spent many months sculpting and fitting the pieces before they were sent to the foundry. The results are sensational; with intricate details surfacing from the statue's faded and discolored bronze, the inherent details and intricacies of each figure's Branch of Service are clearly represented by their accessories and uniforms. After the extensive restoration, ceremonies on Memorial Day May 31, 2010 re-dedicated the statue in Veterans Park.

155. Young Faun with Heron - Stockbridge

"Young Faun with Heron" Naumkeag-Stockbridge, MA

Location: 5 Prospect Hill Road, Stockbridge (Berkshire County)
Destination Parking GPS: N42° 17' 23.59" W73°19' 1.63" (Naumkeag)
Trustees of the Reservations: Fee for entry to gardens and grounds.

Information: "Young Faun with Heron" located in the *Afternoon Garden* at Naumkeag in Stockbridge, MA, is a large bronze statue designed by architect Stanford White for Ambassador and Mrs. Joseph H. Choate and was created by Sculptor Frederick William MacMonnies (1863–1937.) In 1880, MacMonnies notably began an apprenticeship under sculptor Augustus Saint-Gaudens. In 1884 MacMonnies traveled to Paris to study sculpture at the École des Beaux-Arts. The classic pagan motif of a taunting faun, identified by its wreath of leaves, is wrestling with a heron and firmly grasps the its neck and restrains one of its legs. The heron protests by clenching its talons and opening its beak, emitting a cry. This sculpture was produced for Naumkeag in 1889 and was cast in 1890. MacMonnies was one of the earliest American sculptors to augment his fees from major commissions by offering reduced-size reproductions, such as this statue to many museums. (E.g. Metropolitan Museum, Orlando Museum of Art, Princeton University, Phoenix Art Museum and the Mead Museum-Amherst College have this statue in a smaller size.)

Last - But Not Least

156. Split Rock – Lanesborough

Split Rock. A short distance from the Appalachian Trail. Lanesborough, MA

Location: Mass Wildlife Management. Lanesborough (Berkshire County)
Parking GPS: N42° 28' 54.19" W73° 10' 41.64" (Gulf Road, Dalton End)
Destination GPS: N42° 29' 14.00" W73° 10' 47.50" (AT-Trail Boulder)
Destination GPS: N42° 29' 26.01" W73° 10' 42.20" (AT Point-A west)
Destination GPS: N42° 29' 16.70" W73° 10' 45.28" (AT Point-B return)
Destination GPS: N42° 29' 26.10" W73° 10' 53.67" (Split Rock)
Wow Factor: 10 **Accessibility:** Moderate some bushwhacking 1.8-mile RT

Information: The *Split Rock* is easily accessible by heading north on the Appalachian Trail from where the AT crosses Gulf Road in Dalton. Unique to this split rock is the large slab of rock that rests on the top and over a long wide crack creating an awesome tunnel. Entry on either end is easy with walking through being very roomy and tall.

From the AT trailhead on Gulf Road head north. Starting can be confusing for the trail has been relocated some and now parallels the road for a small distance west, then turns north and slightly uphill. After a 0.5-mile, a large boulder (AT-Boulder) will be encountered, continue ~0.2-mile above the boulder to where you will turn left, off the AT trail (Point A) and bushwhack west towards the *Split Rock* for another ~0.2-mile. This approach from Point A allows one to easily transverse the slope at the same elevation as *Split Rock* and with less of a struggle than bushwhacking uphill through brush and the "whips."

Split Rock has a Hi-Low positioning on the hillside. The lower entry to the tunnel is on its eastern side and the upper entry off the higher ridgeline and top. Returning is easier to head downhill southerly for 0.1-mile and then bearing easterly for another ~ 0.1-mile until you junction with the AT trail. Turn downhill on the AT south and back pass the AT Boulder to the parking area.

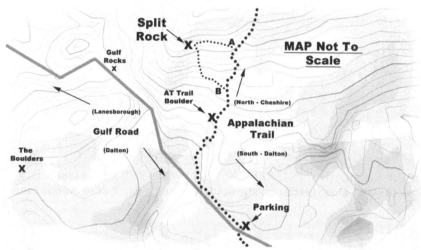

Directions: In Pittsfield, from the center of Coltsville, follow Route-8 south and Route-9 east (Dalton Avenue) stay straight at all four traffic lights for 1.5-miles. Turn left onto Park Avenue and proceed north for 0.5-mile. Turn left onto Gulf Road and proceed west for 0.1-mile to the AT parking area which is before where the road changes to gravel.

Being long and roomy the interior passageway is easily access on both ends.

157. Wolf Rock – Southampton

Wolf Hill Boulder (top) (N42° 13' 7.81" W72° 46' 9.55") is a uniquely large 18 to 20-foot stand-alone glacial erratic nestled among a patch of mountain laurel.

An extremely large field stone rock foundation indicates perhaps a very large farm house with an additional very large three-wall stone foundation past the house presumably a barn. (N42° 13' 22.70" W72° 46' 7.70") Many stone walls scattered along the road side that leads eventually to the Tighe-Carmody Reservoir. While this is a watershed property for the reservoir, no postings were readily seen. Several hikers and mountain bikers were met along the way. No Directions provided. Public access status unknown.

158. English Grass Cave – Montgomery

English Grass Cave is a small obscure talus cave

Historically, *English Grass Cave* is where English Loyalist's or British soldiers hid during or shortly after the Revolutionary War. Other talus shelter caves are often characterized as locations where scallywags such as counterfeiters or as a robber's den held up. These mountains of rubble are also home too many critters from bats, snakes or other small mammals and rodents. This location is overseen by the Massachusetts Wildlife Management, with increased awareness in recent years; the area is listed as a sensitive habitat where human presence unknowing can bring bacteria or viruses into an environment. (E.g. White Nose Syndrome for Bats.) Access is steep and difficult with no trails. In addition, a large tract of abutting private property isolates its location and as an environmentally sensitive area, no directions are provided. N42° 11' 24.50" W72° 49' 48.00"

159. Little Egypt Mine –Adams

An old mine dug horizontally follows a vein of (molybdenite) lead ore.

Full of water and partially collapsed, the *Little Egypt Lead Mine* is also known as the *Gates Mine*. Venturing into here will be wet and very muddy, not my cup of tea. Who knows what will be found at the end of this tunnel; Old Coot from Mt Greylock, Injun Joe or a very trapped and angered critter? There are various stories or lore on how the moniker *Little Egypt* occurred. Ranging from two fishermen complaining about the heat... hot just like in Egypt; to the large piles of sawdust that lumber mills once produced being shaped like triangular cones…reminiscent to the pyramids of Egypt.

So, if you think your job is tough, try digging and tunneling in a small confined space. Certainly, there will be no gold or riches, any riches here are long gone, only a curious hand dug venture with someone who was really hoping to be get rich. This mine is listed on www.mindat.org.

FYI: Variations of the name molybdaena and molybdenite were used for lead ores by Dioscorides (50-70 CE), Pliny the Elder (79 CE), and Agricola (1556), but the modern use of molybdenite did not begin until Johan Gottschalk Wallerius wrote about molybdenite in Mineralogia, eller Mineralriket published in 1747. There was still a multiplicity of minerals receiving the same name, but modern molybdenite and graphite were the most common minerals given this name. The element molybdenum was discovered by Carl Wilhelm Scheele in 1778 and he provided molybdenite to Peter Jacob Hjelm who was able to isolate molybdenum in 1781. Scheele showed that molybdenite, in the modern sense, was soluble in acid, while graphite was not. From the Greek μόλυβδος meaning "lead", but a name having a new usage unlike that of former times.   N42° 36' 19.60" W73° 4' 22.40" No directions provided.

About the Author.

Christy Butler is a visual artist with an Associate Degree in Liberal Studies-Majoring in Design and a Bachelor of Arts in Business Administration majoring in Marketing and Management. Other related studies include Mass Communications, Filmmaking and Photography. After being published in variety of Literary and Specialty Magazines, along with other Audio-Visual endeavors, Butler, a Vietnam Veteran, created and directed a grant-funded and web-based archive of veteran's personal photos from their military experiences: **www.shoeboxphotos.net**. This was followed by a series of New England State Waterfall posters created with Jan Butler: **www.berkshirephotos.com**.

Author Christy Butler exploring the nooks and crannies all over New England. a.k.a *The Hike Master*

Collaborations with author Russell Dunn began with the publication of *Berkshire Region Waterfall Guide* and later *Connecticut Waterfalls*: *A Guide*. Our exploring and hiking guide book list continues to grow.

Rockachusetts: An Explorer's Guide to Amazing Boulders of Massachusetts. **www.rockachusetts.com**

Erratic Wandering: An Explorer's Hiking Guide to Astonishing Boulders in Maine, New Hampshire and Vermont. **www.erraticwandering.com**

Berkshire Destinations: An Explorer's Guide to Waterfalls, Boulders, Vistas and Points of Interest of the Berkshire Hills and Western Massachusetts. **www.berkshired-destinations.com**

Connecticut Destinations: An Explorer's Hiking Guide to Waterfalls, Boulders, Vistas and Points of Interest from the many historical and natural locations from across the state of Connecticut.
www.connecticutdestinations.com

New Hampshire Destinations: An Explorer's Guide to Waterfalls, Boulders, Vistas and Points of Interest from the nooks & crannies of the White Mountains and throughout New Hampshire.
www.new hampshiredestinations.com

Acknowledgements

As with any undertaking *Berkshire Destinations* would not be in existence if not for the assistance and suggestions from acquaintances, friends, hikers, volunteers along with the staff or members of the many land trusts organizations conserving and saving hundreds of acres for future enjoyment.

A special acknowledgement to the *Berkshire Natural Resource Council*-BNRC for their never-ending effort to protect and provide access to so many special land acquisitions which otherwise would be lost. The *MassWildlife Western Division,* along with the *Department of Conservation and Recreation*-DCR for over-seeing, protecting or maintaining miles of trails and thousands of acres. *Berkshire Environmental Action Team*-BEAT for educating and protecting our very special natural environments of the Berkshires or Western Massachusetts. The Trustees of Reservations for saving, preserving and renovating the very special historical or cultural landmarks that provides visitors and residents with exceptional lifestyle experiences.

Individual friendships that influenced, assisted or shared the experiences include: Barbara and Russell Dunn, Jim Boyle, Rob Thurston, Mike Whalen, Alec Gillman, Eric Socha, Justin Graeff, Mike Majchrowski, Deb Willette, Captain Mike Ripa, Jim Virgilio, Dave Pierce (*chesterrailwaystation.net* Elizabeth Massa & Karen Sikes-McTaggart (*westernmasshilltownhikers.com*),) along with Bess Dillman (*berkshirehiker.com*) plus, Patti Chraplak for her refinement and improvement of this book. Plus, always improving with insight provided by Tom Hoffman. T.Y.

My lovely and patient wife Jan Butler who once again followed me everywhere knowingly that I will bring her back. Many thanks to all who assisted or never hindered my progress! Happy Trails and Good Karma to all!

Comments or corrections: chrisjan@berkshirephotos.com
May 2024

Made in the USA
Middletown, DE
31 May 2024